AF167507

Lecture Notes of the Institute for Computer Sciences, Social Informatics and Telecommunications Engineering 617

The LNICST series publishes ICST's conferences, symposia and workshops.

LNICST reports state-of-the-art results in areas related to the scope of the Institute. The type of material published includes

- Proceedings (published in time for the respective event)
- Other edited monographs (such as project reports or invited volumes)

LNICST topics span the following areas:

- General Computer Science
- E-Economy
- E-Medicine
- Knowledge Management
- Multimedia
- Operations, Management and Policy
- Social Informatics
- Systems

Xiaohua Feng · Patrick Siarry · Liangxiu Han ·
Longzhi Yang
Editors

Cloud Computing

12th EAI International Conference, CloudComp 2024
Luton, UK, September 9–10, 2024
Proceedings

 Springer

Editors
Xiaohua Feng 🆔
University of Bedfordshire
Bedfordshire, UK

Patrick Siarry 🆔
Paris-Est Créteil University
Paris, France

Liangxiu Han 🆔
Manchester Metropolitan University
Manchester, UK

Longzhi Yang 🆔
University of Northumbria
Newcastle, UK

ISSN 1867-8211　　　　　　　ISSN 1867-822X (electronic)
Lecture Notes of the Institute for Computer Sciences, Social Informatics
and Telecommunications Engineering
ISBN 978-3-031-92516-0　　　ISBN 978-3-031-92517-7 (eBook)
https://doi.org/10.1007/978-3-031-92517-7

This Springer imprint is published by the registered company Springer Nature Switzerland AG
The registered company address is: Gewerbestrasse 11, 6330 Cham, Switzerland

If disposing of this product, please recycle the paper.

Preface

We are delighted to introduce the proceedings of the 13th edition of the European Alliance for Innovation (EAI) International Conference on Cloud Computing (CloudComp 2024). This conference brought together researchers, developers and professionals around the world who are making good use of and developing Cloud-Edge Computing technology for the world. The theme of CloudComp 2024 was Inspiring and Leading Future Cloud-Edge Computing Technologies globally.

The technical program of CloudComp 2024 consisted of 16 full papers, including one invited Keynote speech, in oral presentation at the main conference track. The conference tracks were: Track 1–Standard Cloud-Edge Computing and Communications Technology, and Applications; Track 2–Late Submissions; Track 3-Later Submissions and PhD student Cloud Applications. Aside from the high-quality technical paper presentations, the technical program also featured one keynote speech. The keynote speaker was Wenbing Zhao from Cleveland State University, USA. The invited talk addressed Blockchain technology and employment of cloud technology in future applications.

Coordination with the conference committee was excellent; we sincerely appreciate their constant support and the guidance we received from the European Alliance for Innovation. It was also a pleasure to work with such an excellent organizing committee team for their hard work in organizing and supporting the conference. In particular, the Technical Program Committee, led by our TPC Co-Chairs, completed the peer-review process of technical papers and made a high-quality technical program. We are also grateful to Conference Manager Natasha Onofrei and her colleagues for their support and to all the authors who submitted their papers to the CloudComp 2024 conference.

We strongly believe that CloudComp 2024 provided a good forum for all researchers, developers and professionals to discuss all science and technology aspects that are relevant to Cloud technology. We also expect that future CloudComp conferences will be as successful and stimulating, as indicated by the contributions presented in this volume.

Xiaohua Feng
Patrick Siarry
Longzhi Yang
Liangxiu Han

Organization

Steering Committee

Xiaohua Feng   University of Bedfordshire, UK
Xinheng Henry Wang   Xi'an Jiaotong-Liverpool University

Organizing Committee

General Chair

Xiaohua Feng   University of Bedfordshire, UK

General Co-chairs

Longzhi Yang   University of Northumbria, UK
Yuping Zhao   Peking University, China
Patrick Siarry   Paris-East Créteil University, France

TPC Chair and Co-chairs

Liangxiu Han   Manchester Metropolitan University, UK
Claudio Savaglio   University of Calabria, Italy
Raffaele Gravina   University of Calabria, Italy

Sponsorship and Exhibit Chairs

Giancarlo Fortino   University of Calabria, Italy
Emma Short   London Metropolitan University, UK

Local Chairs

Asad Ullah   University of Bedfordshire, UK
Sehrish Sher Khan   University of Bedfordshire, UK

Workshops Chair

Pan Wang	Nanjing University of Posts & Telecommunications, China

Publicity and Social Media Chair

Vladimir Dyo	Royal Holloway, University of London, UK

Publications Chair

Patrick Siarry	Paris-East Créteil University, France

Web Chair

Harry Yu	University of Derby, UK

Posters and PhD Track Chairs

Pan Wang	Nanjing University of Posts & Telecommunications, China
Md. Biswas	University of Bedfordshire, UK
Lukasz Migacz	University of Bedfordshire, UK

Panels Chair

R. Gravina	University of Calabria, Italy

Demos Chairs

Jonathan Hitchcock	University of Bedfordshire, UK
Khalid Hussein	University of Bedfordshire, UK
Mohamed Diab Idris	University of Bedfordshire, UK

Tutorials Chairs

Vincenzo Piuri	University of Milan, Italy
Wenbing Zhao	Cleveland State University, USA
Samson Akintoye	Manchester Metropolitan University, UK

Technical Program Committee

Patrick Siarry	Paris-East Créteil University, France
Harry Yu	University of Derby, UK
Stefania Tomasiello	University of Tartu, Estonia
Claudio Savaglio	University of Calabria, Italy
Oscar Lin	Athabasca University, Canada
Wenbing Zhao	Cleveland State University, USA
Emma Short	London Metropolitan University, UK
Jonathan Hitchcock	University of Bedfordshire, UK
Ali Emrouznejad	University of Surrey, UK
Vladimir Dyo	Royal Holloway, University of London, UK
Pan Wang	Nanjing University of Posts & Telecommunications, China
Samson Akintoye	Manchester Metropolitan University, UK
Mohamed Diab Idris Mohamed	University of Bedfordshire, UK
Asad Ullah	University of Bedfordshire, UK
Sehrish Sher Khan	University of Bedfordshire, UK
Xiang Fei	Coventry University, UK
Marc Conrad	University of Bedfordshire, UK
Jayasekhar Konduru	Google Ltd., USA
Vincenzo Piuri	University of Milan, Italy

Contents

Emerging Applications /The Cloud-Edging Integration Applications

The Cloud-Edging Computing

Admission Control and Scheduling of Offloaded Tasks Over Mobile Edge Servers

Muhammad Omer Farooq[1,2] and Thomas Kunz[2(✉)]

[1] Department of Computer Science, Munster Technological University, Cork, Ireland
[2] Department of Systems and Computer Engineering, Carleton University, Ottawa, Canada
tkunz@sce.carleton.ca

Abstract. Mobile Edge Computing (MEC) brings resourceful mobile edge servers to a network's edge. The latest wireless communication technologies provide high bandwidth. The combination of state-of-the-art communication technologies and MEC enables a multitude of real-time communication and computing use cases, such as connected cars, augmented reality, etc.. Offloaded tasks most often belong to real-time applications, hence a mobile edge server needs to complete execution of such tasks within defined latency requirements. To satisfy these latency requirements, admission control and scheduling algorithms are presented here. The admission control algorithm ascertains that only those tasks' offloading requests are admitted for execution on a mobile server whose latency requirements can be satisfied, and that the admission of a new task does not result in missing execution latency deadlines of already offloaded tasks. The admission control algorithm also allocates a time-slice (per unit-time) for offloaded tasks corresponding to each core on which tasks execute. Afterwards, our scheduling algorithm schedules offloaded tasks on cores selected by the admission control algorithm, and it ascertains that each task's execution latency requirements are satisfied. We show how the proposed admission control and scheduling algorithms outperform existing algorithms.

Keyword: Mobile Edge Computing, Task Offloading, Admission Control, Scheduling

1 Introduction

Advances in hardware design and communication technologies are enabling many socially and economically beneficial computing and communication use cases, such as connected cars, augmented reality, real-time interactive gaming, smart cities, etc. Mostly, such use cases not only demand high bandwidth for communication, but also real-time data processing. In most cases, devices involved in the mentioned use cases are resource-limited, for example, available computing resources and power (most devices are battery operated). Hence, these

X. Feng et al. (Eds.): CloudComp 2024, LNICST 617, pp. 3–21, 2026.
https://doi.org/10.1007/978-3-031-92517-7_1

device limitations argue for a powerful communication and computing infrastructure that supports emerging bandwidth and computing resource-intensive applications. Until recently, cloud computing was the popular solution to enable devices to support such use cases in the face of device limitations. However, cloud computing has its limitations. Specifically, the time incurred to transfer data to centralised cloud servers for processing, and then returning the processed data back to a device may not be tolerable for most real-time use cases.

Mobile Edge Computing (MEC) [1] is a new computing paradigm that provides support for real-time communication and computing use cases for relatively resource-constraint computing and communication devices. MEC is different from cloud computing: in MEC, resourceful computing servers are installed at a network's edge, hence processing of data that requires real-time treatment can be done at the edge to reduce latency, rather than relaying the data to the centralised cloud servers. Existing communication technologies support relatively high bandwidth, and a mobile edge server is invariably equipped with powerful computing resources, therefore in MEC a mobile device, a wireless sensor, an IoT device, etc. can offload their computationally expensive and real-time tasks to a mobile edge server [2,3]. However, communication bandwidth and instruction processing abilities of mobile edge servers are finite, hence care must be taken while offloading real-time computational tasks on the servers as overburdening a server with offloaded tasks can easily result in missing tasks' execution latency requirements. This would defeat the primary motivation for offloading tasks on the mobile edge server(s).

Here, an admission control algorithm is presented to ensure that a mobile edge server only accepts those task offloading requests whose execution latency requirements can be satisfied by the server. The admission control algorithm takes into account tasks' execution latency requirements. Then, based on the current status and computational capabilities of an edge server, such as number of admitted offloaded tasks and their latency deadlines, number of cores in the server, and a core's instruction processing requirement, the algorithm decides to accept or reject a new task offloading request. Moreover, if the admission control algorithm decides to accept a task's offloading request, it selects cores over which the task will execute along with a scheduling time-slice for each selected core of the server. We also present an offloaded tasks' preemptive scheduling algorithm that takes this information and schedules the admitted offloaded tasks over different cores of the server as per the calculated time-slice for each admitted task.

The remainder of this paper is organised as follows: Related work is presented in Sect. 2. The proposed admission control algorithm, combining computational resource allocation and scheduling of tasks over a mobile edge server is presented in Sect. 3. Simulation results are presented in Sect. 4, and conclusions are given in Sect. 5.

2   Related Work

2.1   Schedule for Offloading Tasks

A latency-oblivious distributed task scheduling framework for MEC is presented in [4]. In this work, scheduling refers to creating a schedule for offloading tasks over an edge server by a mobile device. The presented framework aims to enhance MEC throughput and quality of service. The foundation of the framework is based on the assumption that it is very hard to predict a task's execution latency. Thus, the framework uses mathematical modeling to predict the task's total latency. Based on the predicted latency, a schedule for tasks' offloading is constructed. Joint task admission control and resource allocation algorithms for MEC are presented in [5]. The objective is to maximize the value of a utility function and fairness in a network. Based on available computational resources at a mobile edge server, the admission control algorithm decides about a task's admission. The algorithm assumes that there is only one edge server in a MEC environment. The estimate of available computational resources does not take into account the amount of computational resources required at the edge server to execute the presented algorithms, hence the algorithm overestimates the available computational resources, i.e., free CPU cycles. In [6], a task scheduling mechanism is presented for offloading tasks on an edge server. The mechanism constructs an offloading schedule that is interference-free and consumes minimum energy. A genetic algorithm and conflict graph-based scheduling of offloaded tasks is presented in [7]. A task is partitioned into multiple sub-tasks. The goal of the scheduling algorithm is to assign a task's sub-tasks to different available mobile edge servers, considering servers' data transmission rate, error probability, and computational capabilities. The presented algorithm considers assigning sub-tasks to available servers considering sequential and parallel execution of sub-tasks. The algorithm assumes that there is only one computational core inside an edge server, moreover it is assumed that during execution the edge server does not use multi-tasking, hence scheduled task will never be preempted. In general, the scheduling algorithms in this category do not consider scheduling tasks' over an edge server's CPU in a manner that all tasks' computation resource allocations and/or latency requirements are satisfied.

2.2   Offloaded Tasks' CPU Scheduling in MEC

Joint channel and CPU frequency allocation for offloaded tasks in MEC is presented in [8]. Along with channel resource reservation, the method also reserves CPU cycles for each offloaded task. Heuristic-based task scheduling over mobile edge server is presented in [9]. Tasks are assigned to an edge server based on the current load on the server. Afterwards, a core in a multi-core edge server is selected to execute a task. If a single core cannot satisfy the requirements of the task, the task is partitioned into multiple sub-tasks and they execute over a server's multiple cores. The presented method assumes that once a task is scheduled it cannot be preempted. In [10], offloaded task scheduling algorithm based on the "age of task" metric is presented. The algorithm assumes a single mobile user with N applications executing on the mobile device, and each application can generate K tasks. There is single edge server in a network. Once a task is scheduled over the edge server, it runs to completion and the algorithm assumes that the edge server only has one computation core. An edge server's operational environment is controlled by an operating system (OS), and contemporary OSs use preemptive multi-tasking, therefore the assumption that once a task is scheduled it will not be preempted is not a realistic assumption in most/typical settings. Moreover, with an ever increasing demand of offloading computational tasks on edge servers, the single core edge server assumption may also be quite limiting.

2.3   Offloaded Tasks' CPU Scheduling in Vehicular Networks with Edge Computing

An imitation-learning-based online task scheduling algorithm for vehicular edge computing scenarios is presented in [11]. The algorithm aims to satisfy a task's delay constraint with minimum energy consumption. Road side units (RSUs) assist in making tasks' offloading decisions. Based on a task's latency requirement, a RSU may decide to offload a task on a vehicle providing edge computing facility or to a cloud server. Similarly, a hybrid intelligent algorithm for scheduling offloaded tasks over an edge server in vehicular edge computing environments is presented in [12]. The algorithm considers multiple edge servers in the environment, and for each server it determines the execution order of offloaded tasks. However, the algorithm assumes that once a task is scheduled it does not get preempted, and there is only one core inside the edge server. In [13], a heuristic-based energy-efficient offloaded tasks scheduling algorithm for MEC-enabled Internet of Vehicles (IoV) scenarios is presented. While scheduling, the presented algorithm aims to minimize RSUs' energy consumption and satisfy delay requirements of offloaded tasks. First, the algorithm constructs a set of RSUs that can satisfy the delay requirement of an offloaded task. In case there are multiple RSUs in the set, the one that can execute the task and report results back with minimum energy consumption is selected for the execution of the offloaded task. The presented scheduling algorithm is non-preemptive, and it considers that the edge server consists of a single computing core. The downside of the presented algorithms is that they mostly consider a single core edge computing platform, and do not take into account the preemptive task scheduling nature of state-of-the-art OSs. Hence, the presented algorithm cannot be easily integrated with exists OSs and multi-core computing platforms.

Given the popularity of MEC and anticipating computational load on mobile edge servers, researchers have focused on proposing energy-efficient multi-core architectures for the edge servers. Hence, multi-core architectures for mobile edge servers are becoming a reality. In [14,15], energy-efficient multi-core architectures for mobile edge server are proposed.

Overall, existing work does not consider that a typical OS uses preemptive scheduling algorithms, hence a scheduling algorithm that aims to satisfy latency requirement of an offloaded task should come with a preemption support. Second, it is not uncommon that contemporary edge servers come with multiple cores, hence an offloaded tasks scheduling over edge server and admission control algorithm should be combined with multi-core scheduling. Here, we present algorithms that address both of these shortcomings in the related work.

3   Admission Control with Computation Resource Allocation and Scheduling of Offloaded Tasks

3.1   System Model

A mobile edge computing environment consists of M mobile devices, X mobile servers each with N_i computing cores ($i \in X$), an edge gateway/controller, and a radio access network as shown in Fig. 1. The controller controls the edge computing environment and provides access to the Internet. Each edge server can execute a number of offloaded tasks. A mobile device can offload computationally expensive task onto any of the available edge servers. Here, we assume that each offloaded task has an associated soft delay requirement. In general, the following steps are required to offload and execute a task over an edge server: (i) transmit the executable corresponding to the offloaded task to the edge server, (ii) execute the offloaded task on the server, and (iii) report the results back to the mobile device. In light of the above, Eq. 1 captures the total delay associated with an offloaded task. In the equation, Tol_{delay}, $Trans_{delay}$, $Exec_{delay}$, and Res_{delay} represent total, executable file transmission, execution, and results report back delay time units respectively.

$$Tot_{delay} = Trans_{delay} + Exec_{delay} + Res_{delay} \tag{1}$$

A mobile device/edge computing controller can estimate $Trans_{delay}$ and Res_{delay} in different ways, for example, by monitoring the wireless channel. Such a method can estimate $Trans_{delay}$ and Res_{delay} by considering different factors, such as channel bandwidth, data traffic load, channel error rate, and protocol functionalities. Data packet collisions can impact CSMA/CA back-off period and similarly can also impact the TCP contention window, hence for a good estimate network protocol functionalities need to be considered. Here, the assumption is that a mobile device/edge computing controller has access to such a method, and it can estimate reasonably accurately both $Trans_{delay}$ and Res_{delay}. The design and details of such a method is beyond the scope of the work presented here. The focus here is to present an algorithm that decides whether a particular task's execution delay requirements can be satisfied by any of the available edge servers, assign computational resources to the task, and schedule tasks over an edge server in a manner that satisfies the task's per unit time resource requirements. Note, the amount of time the task has to wait at the server is ignored. The reason is that here we are presenting a preemptive scheduling algorithm, and the resource allocation algorithm takes care of the waiting time.

$$Tot_i^{delay} \approx Trans_i^{delay} + Exec_i^{delay} + Res_i^{delay} \tag{2}$$

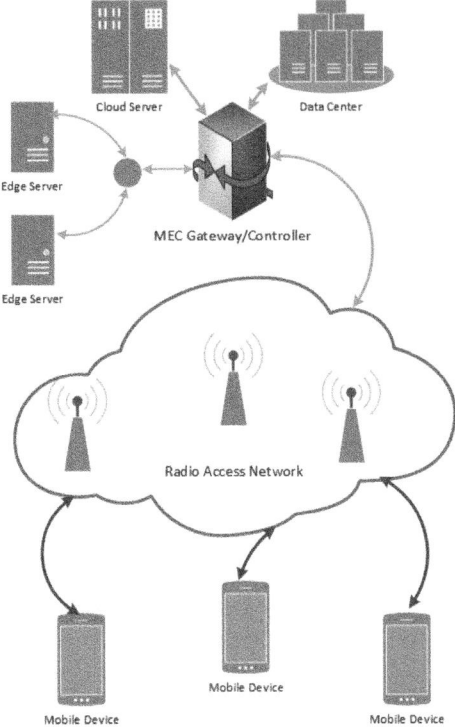

Fig. 1. Mobile Edge Computing Setup

As per Eq. 2, a mobile device's i^{th} task has a total soft delay requirement of Tot_i^{delay} time units. Therefore, ideally the task's offloading process, execution, and reporting of results have to complete within Tot_i^{delay} time units. Assuming that a mobile node/controller can reasonably accurately estimate $Trans_i^{delay}$ and Res_i^{delay}, an edge server needs to complete execution of the task within the time budget calculated through Eq. 3.

$$Exec_i^{delay} \lessapprox Tot_i^{delay} - Trans_i^{delay} - Res_i^{delay} \qquad (3)$$

A CPU executes machine instructions. $Exec_i^{delay}$ time units along with the number of machine instructions in an offloaded task can be used to determine the number of instructions that should execute on per unit time basis. If there are Z machine instructions in an offloaded task then the per unit time instruction execution requirement is $\left(\frac{Z}{Exec_i^{delay}}\right)$ instructions.

3.2 Assumptions and Features

The following are assumptions pertaining to the methods presented here:

- An edge computing server consists of multiple cores.
- Cores inside an edge server can be heterogeneous, i.e., the cores may differ in the following aspects: processing power and configured cache. However, the cores inside the edge server are based on the same instruction set architecture. The cache is not shared among different cores of the edge server.
- There is a uniform probability for each core in an edge server to access random access memory (RAM) connected over the system bus. Moreover, cores come with storage buffers, hence write latency is not impacted by stalls in the instruction pipeline. Moreover, there is a data pre-fetch unit to read data ahead of time from the system RAM. The pre-fetch unit greatly eliminates the latency associated with reading data from the system RAM, hence the instruction pipeline stalls due to reading from the system RAM are greatly reduced as well.
- Nodes offload computationally expensive tasks onto an edge server, therefore offloaded tasks do not need to access secondary storage devices.
- A mechanism is available that can generate an executable for offloaded tasks that can execute over an edge server.
- If there are multiple edge servers in a system, a task can only be offloaded onto a single server, i.e., the task's execution cannot be split in a manner that a portion of it executes over one server, and the other portions execute over other servers.
- Inside an edge server, at different time instances, an offloaded task can get scheduled over any available core from the set of cores whose CPU cycles are allocated to the task.
- A core inside an edge serve is reserved to schedule offloaded tasks over other cores inside the edge server.
- A core inside an edge server is reserved to execute algorithms presented here.
- The context switching time, i.e., the time required to take a core from a scheduled task and schedule another task on the same core is negligible.

The following are salient features of the presented methods:

- Inside an edge server, offloaded tasks are scheduled based on their per unit time machine instruction processing requirement.
- The system only accepts a new offloaded task if the new task acceptance does not result in negatively impacting the instruction processing requirements of existing offloaded tasks on the edge server, and the new task's processing requirement can also be satisfied.
- Considering an offloaded task's per unit time instruction processing requirements, it determines a set of cores inside an edge server that can execute the offloaded task. Afterwards, the task only executes over the cores in the set.
- The method ensures that at any given time a task does not simultaneously execute on more than one core, i.e., at any time instance multiple cores inside an edge server cannot execute the same offloaded task.

3.3   Interaction Among MEC Entities

Fig. 2 shows the interactions among different MEC entities to execute the functionality pertaining to the methods presented here. A mobile edge device sends an offloading request to the controller with the number of instructions that need to execute per unit time. An offloaded process may consists of a total X number of instructions, but based on inputs and/or other conditions the total number of instructions that needs to execute from start to termination of the process is variable and can be higher or lower than X. To obtain the number of instructions that need to execute on an edge server per unit time, the candidate offloading task comes with meta data, i.e., the average number of instructions that execute from the start to the termination of the task. Using this information, along with the latency requirement of the task, the number of instructions that the edge server needs to execute is obtained. The controller authenticates the request, and forwards the request to all edge servers being controlled by the controller. Upon reception of the request, each server executes the admission control and computation resource allocation algorithm (details presented in subsequent sections). After successful execution of the algorithm, the server can either accept or reject the task's offloading request, and informs the controller about its decision. Figure 2 shows that in this case all servers can accept the request. In such a scenario, the controller can use performance metrics such as channel condition, server error rate, etc. to select a server. In the diagram, the controller selects $server_1$, and it informs $server_1$ accordingly. Hence, $server_1$ marks its computational resource allocation for the request as final. In the same manner, the controller informs $server_X$ to delete the computational resource allocation that it made for the request. Upon reception of this message $server_X$ deletes the reservation. The controller informs the mobile device that its request has been accepted, therefore the device transmits its executable to the controller. Subsequently, the controller forwards the executable to $server_1$. Afterwards, $server_1$ loads the executable in its memory to prepare it for execution. If no server can satisfy the request requirement, the request will be rejected and the device will be informed about the decision.

3.4   Admission Control Algorithm

With a task offload request, the requesting device informs the edge server about its per unit time machine instructions execution requirement ($inst\_req$), along with other related information, such as, $device\_id$. Upon reception of the request at an edge server, the server starts by constructing the list of cores ($core\_list$) that have spare CPU cycles per unit time. It is possible that a particular core is already executing other offloaded task(s), hence it is important that existing offloaded tasks are not negatively impacted by accepting the new request. For the stated reason the presented algorithm takes into account a core's spare CPU cycles. Afterwards, for each core it determines the number of machine instruction a core can execute per unit time using the following relation $\frac{spare\_cycles}{cycles\_per\_inst}$. $cycles\_per\_inst$ gives the number of cycles required to execute a

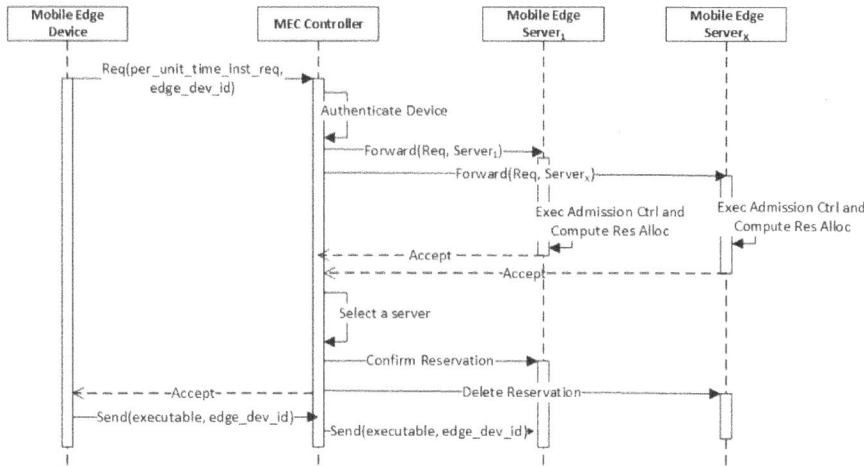

Fig. 2. Admission Control with CPU Resource Allocation - Interaction Among MEC Entities

single machine instruction over a core under consideration. Subsequently, the server sorts *core_list* in descending order, considering the number of instructions that each node can execute in its spare time per unit time. The server then selects the core at the head of the sorted *core_list*, and it accumulates the number of instructions that can be executed by the core. Next, it inserts the core in the list (*sel_core_list*) that was at the head of *core_list*, and removes the core from *core_list*. Finally, the server performs a check, i.e., whether the number of accumulated instructions is greater than or equal to *inst_req*? If the answer is yes, the server assigns core(s) in the *sel_core_list* to the offloaded task. Otherwise, the controller continues to traverse the *core_list* until it is fully examined or it had found enough cores that can satisfy the offloaded task's requirement. If *core_list* is fully examined, and the number of instructions requirement cannot be satisfied by the server, the server rejects the request. Algorithm 1 presents the admission control and resource allocation algorithm.

To further demonstrate the presented algorithm, consider the following example. The following assumptions are made: (*i*) An edge server has 3 cores that can execute offloaded tasks, (*ii*) each core is operating at $1\,GHz$ clock frequency, and (*iii*) the core architecture can execute one machine instruction per CPU cycle. Details of different task offloading requests received by an edge server are shown in Table 1. At time instance 0, the server receives a request that requires execution of 800 million instructions per second. At this time instance all cores have spare capacity, hence as per the presented algorithm $Task\_1$ is assigned to $core\_1$. $core\_1$ can satisfy the processing requirement of $Task\_1$ in 0.8s, hence the algorithm stores the information that $core\_1$ can assign the remaining 0.2s to another offloaded task, if need arises. At time instance 10, the server receives an offloading request for $Task\_2$. The task requires execution of 700 million

---

Algorithm 1: Admission Control and Resource Allocation Algorithm

---

1 **Input:** $inst\_req$, $client\_id$, srv_cores;
2 **Output:** sel_core_list;
3 $index = 0$, $list\_head = null$, $inst = 0$;
4 $is\_core\_set\_found = false$, $inst = 0$;
5 $task\_id = 0$;
6 $core\_list = obtain\_cores\_with\_spare\_capacity(srv\_cores)$;
7 **foreach** $Core\, c_i \in core\_list$ **do**
8     $c\_i.spare\_cycles = calc\_spare\_cycles(c\_i)$;
9     $c\_i.inst = \frac{c\_i.spare\_cycles}{cycles\_per\_inst}$;
10 **end**
11 $sort\_list\_wrt\_descending\_inst(core\_list)$;
12 **foreach** $Core\, c_i \in core\_list$ **do**
13     $list\_head = obtain\_list\_head(core\_list)$;
14     $inst = inst + list\_head.inst$;
15     $sel\_core\_list[index] = remove\_from\_list\_head(list\_head)$;
16     $c_i.spare\_cycles = c_i.inst = 0$;
17     $index = index + 1$;
18   **if** $inst \geq inst\_req$ **then**
19        $is\_core\_set\_found = true$;
20        $break$;
21   **end**
22 **end**
23 **if** $is\_core\_set\_found == true$ **then**
24     $sel\_core\_list[index - 1].inst = inst - inst\_req$;
25     $sel\_core\_list[index - 1].spare\_cycles =$
       $sel\_core\_list[index - 1].inst \times cycles\_per\_inst$;
26     $assign\_task\_to\_core(client\_id, task\_id, sel\_core\_list)$;
27 **end**
28 **else**
29     $clear\_list(selected\_core\_list())$;
30 **end**
31 $return\ selected\_core\_list$;

---

instructions per second. All three cores have spare capacity, hence the algorithm arranges them in descending order with respect to the number of instructions they can execute per second, resulting in $core\_list = [core\_2, core\_3, core\_1]$. As $core\_2$ can satisfy the instruction processing requirements of $Task\_2$, the algorithm assigns $Task\_2$ to $core\_2$. $core\_2$ can execute 1000 million instructions per second, hence if need arises it can allocate 300 million instructions to another offloaded task. At time instance 30, an offloading request for $Task\_3$ is received, and it requires execution of 500 million instruction per second. At this time instance the sorted $core\_list$ with respect to the number of instructions is $core\_list = [core\_3, core\_2, core\_1]$. As $core\_3$ can satisfy $Task\_3$'s requirement, therefore the algorithm assign it to $core\_3$. After this assignment, $core\_3$ can still assign 500 million instructions to another task. At time instance 40, an

Table 1. Offloading Requests' Details

Task Name	Request Arrival Time	Instruction Processing Requirement (Millions)
$Task\_1$	0	800
$Task\_2$	10	700
$Task\_3$	20	500
$Task\_4$	30	800

offloading request for $Task\_4$ is received, and it requires execution of 800 million instructions per second. The algorithm sorts the list of available cores that have spare CPU cycles, and the sorted list is $core\_list = [core\_3, core\_2, core\_1]$. In this case no core alone has enough spare capacity to satisfy the requirements of $Task\_4$, hence the algorithm tries to satisfy the task's requirements using multiple cores. The algorithm first selects $core\_3$ for the task, and records that it can assign 0.5s (500 million instructions) per second to the task. However, the task's requirement is 800 million instructions per second. Therefore, the algorithm continues its execution, and it finds that $core\_2$ can assign 0.3s (300 million instructions) to the tasks. Hence, collectively $core\_3$ and $core\_2$ can satisfy the requirement of $Task\_4$. In this assignment process, the algorithm also determines the scheduling time slice for each offloading task corresponding to the core(s) the tasks are offloaded to. Table 2 shows this final offloaded task allocation.

Table 2. Allocation of Offloaded Tasks and Time Slice

Core Name	Assigned Tasks	Minimum Time Slice
$core\_1$	$Task\_1$	$0.8s\,Task\_1$
$core\_2$	$Task\_2,\ Task\_4$	$0.7s\,Task\_2\ 0.3s\,Task\_4$
$core\_3$	$Task\_3,\ Task\_4$	$0.5s\,Task\_3\ 0.5s\,Task\_4$

3.5   Scheduling Offloaded Tasks

A separate core inside an edge server is reserved for the following tasks:

– Scheduling tasks on different available cores inside an edge server.
– Taking a core from a task whose time slice has expired.

To fulfill the requirements of the above listed functionalities, two algorithms are presented here. The first algorithm is used for scheduling tasks over the edge server, and the second algorithm is used to keep track of the remaining time slices of all scheduled tasks on different cores of the edge server. The second algorithm is triggered at each timer tick, and the timer tick's granularity is configurable.

Algorithm 2: Algorithm for Scheduling Offloaded Tasks

---

1 **Input:** *core_busy_lst*;
2 *index = 0, scheduled_tsk_lst = null*;
3 *core_lst = get_lst_of_cores()*;
4 *core = core_lst.head()*;
5 **while** *true* **do**
6 | **if** *core == null* **then**
7 | | *core = core_lst.head()*;
8 | **end**
9 | *obtain_lock(core_busy_lst)*;
10 | **if** *core_busy_lst[core.id].is_busy == true* **then**
11 | | *release_lock(core_busy_lst)*;
12 | | *continue*;
13 | **end**
14 | *release_lock(core_busy_lst)*;
15 | *tsk_lst = get_assigned_tsk(core.id)*;
16 | **while** *index < tsk_lst.len* **do**
17 | | *obtain_lock(tsk_lst)*;
18 | | **if** *tsk_lst[index].is_scheduled == false* **then**
19 | | | *obtain_lock(core_busy_lst)*;
20 | | | *core_busy_lst[core.id].is_busy = true*;
21 | | | *tsk_lst[index].is_scheduled = true*
    | | | *schedule(tsk_lst[index].tsk, core, timeslice) release_lock(tsk_lst)*;
22 | | | *release_lock(core_busy_lst)*;
23 | | | *index = 0*;
24 | | | *break*;
25 | | **end**
26 | | **else**
27 | | | *release_lock(tsk_lst)*;
28 | | | *index + +*;
29 | | **end**
30 | **end**
31 | *yield()*;
32 | *core = core_lst.next()*;
33 **end**

The algorithm for scheduling offloaded tasks executes continuously in a loop until it voluntarily yields itself or is interrupted by a timer tick. In each iteration of the loop, the algorithm obtains information about a core from a list of cores that can execute offloaded tasks. The algorithm examines whether the core is busy or not. If the core is not busy, the algorithm obtains the list of offloaded tasks that are assigned to the core. Afterwards, the core finds a task from the list that is not currently executing, and schedules it over the core. After each loop iteration, the scheduling process calls a *yield()* function so that another algorithm gets a chance to execute over the same core. During scheduling, the algorithm makes use of global data structure: *core_busy_list* and *task_list*. These data structures are shared between the scheduling algorithm and the algorithm that keeps track of scheduled tasks' remaining slice time. Hence, the algorithm uses *obtain_lock*(), and *release_lock*() functions to access or change values in shared data structures. Algorithm 2 presents the scheduling algorithm.

The algorithm that keeps track of the remaining time slice for each scheduled task over different edge server cores executes at each timer tick interrupt. The algorithm decrements the remaining time slice for each scheduled task equivalent to the time after which the timer tick interrupt is asserted. After decrementing the time slice for all scheduled tasks, the algorithm checks whether any task's time slice has reached 0. If that is the case, the algorithm schedules another function that marks the core that was executing the task as *not busy*, and the task as *not scheduled*. The scheduled function also stores the context of the currently executing task, and takes the core away from the task. The priority of this function is lower than the function that executes on the timer interrupt, and the function that executes Algorithm 2. Hence, the function only gets scheduled after the timer interrupt function exists and Algorithm 2 has called the *yield*() function.

4   Performance Evaluation

4.1   General Simulation-Based Study

Table 3. Simulation Setup

Parameter	Value
Number of Edge Server	1
Cores inside Server	3
Each core's frequency	$1\,GHz$
Machine instruction execution latency	1 cycle
Write buffer	Configured at each core-level
Pre-fetch unit	Configured at each core-level
Tightly coupled Data RAM	Configured at each core-level
Tightly coupled instruction RAM	Configured at each core-level

Performance evaluation was done through simulation-based studies. General simulation parameters are shown in Table 3. The number of task offloading requests is varied from 20 to 100, and their arrival time is randomly distributed in the range $[0 - 60]$ seconds. Similarly, the number of machine instructions execution requirement for each offloaded task is randomly distributed in the range $[4 \times 10^9 - 8 \times 10^9]$ instructions, and the latency requirement for each task is randomly distributed in the range $[10 - 20]$ seconds. The pre-fetch unit configured with each core can load data and instructions ahead of time to the tightly coupled data and instruction RAMs respectively. The access latency of tightly coupled RAMs is a single cycle. Moreover, access to the write buffer is also a single cycle, hence writing to system RAM (RAM external to a core) does not introduce stalls in the instruction pipeline. The simulator for the simulations presented here is written in Python.

The proposed scheduling and admission control method is compared against a method presented in [5]. The reason for evaluating the presented method against the method proposed in [5] is that it comes with an admission control and scheduling algorithm for offloaded tasks. Here, we refer to this method as $ACNPS$. We also compare the proposed method against round-robin hard-affinity-based offloading task scheduling over available cores in a mobile edge server. In hard-affinity-based scheduling, an offloaded task is assigned to a core in a mobile edge server (there is no admission control), and then different tasks assigned to the core are scheduled in a preemptive round-robin fashion. Similarly, in latter simulations, a comparison with soft-affinity round-robin scheduling is also shown. In soft-affinity round-robin scheduling, if a task is in a ready queue then it can be scheduled over any of the available cores. The time-slice for hard and soft-affinity-based round-robin scheduling is set to 100 ms. Hard-affinity and soft-affinity based preemptive round-robin scheduling are the most popular task/process scheduling algorithms used in contemporary OSs. Therefore, comparison of the presented method against these scheduling algorithms that do not include admission control reveals the benefit of an admission control algorithm. Furthermore, such a comparison also helps to present a cost-benefit analysis, i.e., is the admission control overhead justified?

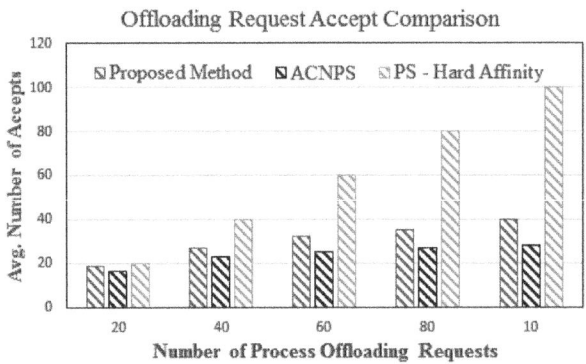

Fig. 3. Offloading Tasks - Admission Accepts Comparison

Figure 3 compares average offloading tasks admission request acceptance. Figure 3 demonstrates that the hard-affinity-based offloading task scheduling method accepts all offloading requests as it does not employ an admission control algorithm. As the number of task offloading requests increases, ACNPS and the proposed admission control and scheduling method reject task offloading requests. However, ACNPS rejects more requests compared to the proposed method. At different time instances, both methods reject a task offloading request because at the time when the offloading request arrives, ACNPS or/and the proposed method conclude that accepting the new request can result in not satisfying the task's latency requirement or that the latency requirements of already admitted tasks can be negatively impacted. In ACNPS, if a new task offloading request arrives at a mobile edge server, and all cores of the server are busy executing existing offloaded tasks, the edge server rejects the offloading request as it does not have a free core where it can schedule the new task. This is primarily because of the fact that ACNPS does not support preemptive task scheduling. The presented method accepts more offloading requests because it supports preemptive scheduling and hence can assign offloaded tasks to different cores based on tasks' latency requirements. Moreover, the presented method can assign a task to different cores at different time instances, and it also calculates the execution time slice for tasks corresponding to the cores that can execute tasks.

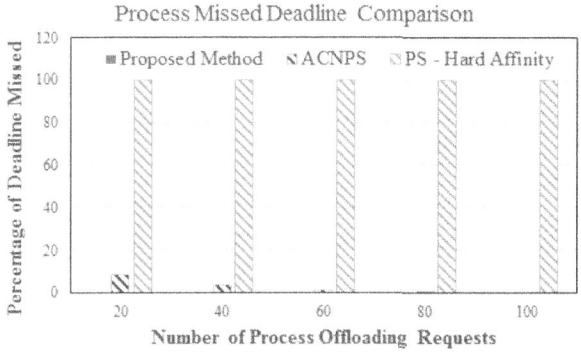

Fig. 4. Offloading Tasks - Missed Deadline Comparison

Figure 4 compares the number of tasks that missed their deadline. In all cases, hard-affinity-based round-robin scheduling method does not satisfy the latency requirement of any offloaded task. This offloaded task scheduling method does not come with an admission control mechanism, hence in this simulation-based study it demonstrated 100% missed deadline. Among ACNPS and the proposed method, the proposed method demonstrates better performance as it results in 0% offloaded task missed deadline. ACNPS does result in a small percentage of task that missed their latency deadline. For ACNPS, as the number of task offloading requests increases, the number of task missing their latency deadline decreases. Jointly considering Fig. 3 and Fig. 4 reveals that ACNPS not only rejects more offloading requests compared to the proposed method, but offloaded tasks also sometimes experience latency deadline misses. In summary, ACNPS (*i*) unnecessarily rejects offloading task admission request, (*ii*) experiences latency deadline misses due to its ignorance of the admission control process overhead, and (*iii*) tasks do not switch between different cores.

Table 4. Tasks' Details

Task ID	Instructions to Execute	Latency Deadline (seconds)	Arrival Time (seconds)
1	1×10^{10}	10	0
2	0.8×10^{10}	10	0
3	0.5×10^{10}	10	0
4	0.2×10^{10}	5	4
5	0.2×10^{10}	5	4

Table 5. Task Assignment

Core ID	Presented Method	ACNPS	PS - Hard Affinity
1	1	1	1, 4
2	2	2	2, 5
3	3, 4, 5	3	3

4.2   Targeted Simulation-Based Study

In a second simulation-based study, five offloading requests are considered. The tasks' details are given in Table 4. The first three requests arrive instantaneously at simulation time 0. The fourth and fifth offloading requests arrive instantaneously at simulation time 4. Table 5 shows the offloaded tasks assignment to the available cores. The table does not show the tasks assignment to the cores in case of the PS - soft affinity method. This is because depending upon a core's availability and if there is a task in ready queue (a queue that holds tasks that are ready to execute, however they are not yet scheduled) the same task can get scheduled on different cores at different time instances.

In this simulation-based study, we use task finish time and effectiveness as our performance metrics. The effectiveness is denoted by κ, and it is represented by Eq. 4. κ is designed in a way that it takes into account both types of wrong admission decisions: (*i*) offloading a task on a server whose admission can negatively impact latency requirements of already admitted tasks and/or the offloading task's own latency requirement can not be satisfied, and (*ii*) unnecessarily denying offloading a task, i.e., the task's admission does not negatively impact latency requirements of already offloaded tasks on a server, and the task's own latency requirements could have been satisfied.

$$\kappa = \frac{Number\,of\,correct\,admission\,decisions}{Total\,number\,of\,admission\,requests} \tag{4}$$

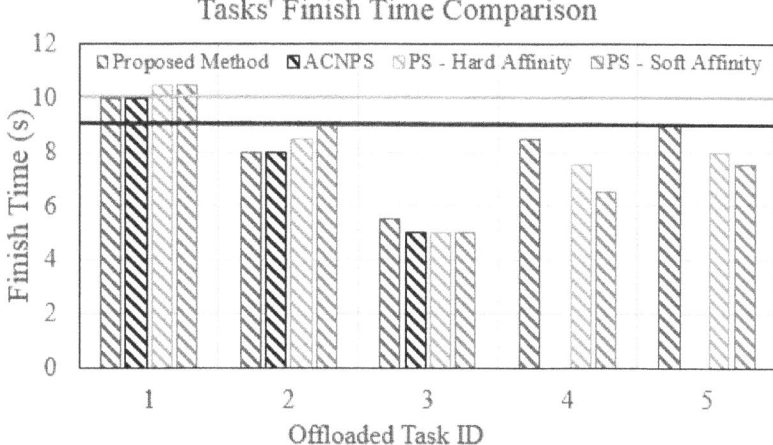

Fig. 5. Offloaded Tasks' Finish Time Comparison - Green horizontal line indicates deadline for tasks 1, 2, and 3. Blue horizontal line indicates deadline for tasks 4 and 5.

Figure 5 shows the offloaded tasks' finish time w.r.t. the methods evaluated here. The green horizontal line shows the latency deadline for task 1, task 2, and task 3. Similarly, the blue line shows the latency deadline for task 4 and task 5. Figure 5 demonstrates that only the proposed method satisfies the latency requirements of all offloaded tasks. PS - hard affinity and PS - soft affinity do not satisfy the latency requirement of task 1. ACNPS only admitted three tasks, and it satisfied the latency requirement of the admitted tasks. However, it has unnecessarily rejected two tasks, hence ACNPS does not use the available resources in an efficient manner. The following characteristics of the proposed method results in its superior performance: ability to consider instruction execution requirements of all offloaded tasks, ability to estimate spare capacity of each core inside an edge server, ability of assigning a task to multiple cores inside an edge server, ability to decide a task's time slice corresponding to each core the task is assigned to, and its task scheduling algorithms.

Figure 6 shows the effectiveness demonstrated by the evaluated methods. The proposed method outperforms the other evaluated methods as it demonstrates perfect effectiveness. On the contrary, ACNPS has demonstrated the lowest effectiveness because it has unnecessarily rejected offloading requests corresponding to task 4 and task 5. PS - hard affinity and PS - soft affinity have

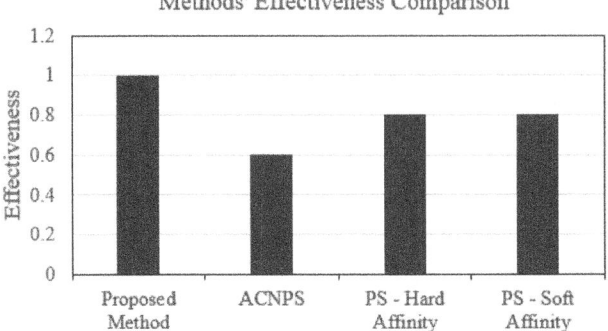

Fig. 6. Methods' Effectiveness Comparison

demonstrated the same level of effectiveness as both methods failed to satisfy the latency requirement of task 1. The presented simulation results demonstrate that the proposed method is capable of satisfying latency requirements of offloaded tasks, and at the same time it utilizes the available computational resources in an efficient manner compared to the other other evaluated methods.

5   Conclusions

Task offloading admission control along with preemptive scheduling of accepted offloaded tasks over a multi-core mobile edge server are presented. The admission control considers task offloading requests' execution latency requirement along with the remaining execution latency requirements of already admitted offloaded tasks over the mobile edge server. The presented method only accepts a new offloaded task if not only the latency requirement of the new task can be satisfied, but latency requirements of already offloaded tasks' are not impacted. During the admission control process, the presented method not only selects CPU cores on which the new task will be scheduled, but it also calculates the time-slice per unit time the task will execute on the selected cores, if admitted. Through simulation-based studies, the proposed method is compared against existing admission control and scheduling methods. Simulation results demonstrate the effectiveness of the proposed admission control and scheduling methods. As per the simulation results, the presented methods satisfy execution latency requirements of all admitted offloaded tasks, and also utilise the available computing resources in an effective manner as they do not unnecessarily reject task offloading requests.

References

1. Li, H., Ota, K., Dong, M.: ECCN: orchestration of edge-centric computing and content-centric networking in the 5G radio access network. IEEE Wirel. Commun. **25**(3), 88–93 (2018)

2. Wang, H., Peng, Z., Pei, Y.: Offloading schemes in mobile edge computing with an assisted mechanism. IEEE Access **8**, 50721–50732 (2020)
3. Xu, X., Zhang, X., Liu, X., Jiang, J., Qi, L., Bhuiyan, M.: Adaptive computation offloading with edge for 5G-envisioned internet of connected vehicles. IEEE Trans. Intell. Transp. Syst. **22**(8), 5213–5222 (2021)
4. Samanta, A., Chang, Z., Han, Z.: Latency-oblivious distributed task scheduling for mobile edge computing. In: IEEE Global Communications Conference (GLOBE-COM), pp. 1–7 (2018)
5. Huang, J., Lv, B., Wu, Y., Chen, Y., Shen, X.: Dynamic admission control and resource allocation for mobile edge computing enabled small cell network. IEEE Trans. Veh. Technol. **71**(2), 1964–1973 (2022)
6. Zhu, T., Shi, T., Li, J., Cai, Z., Zhou, X.: Task scheduling in deadline-aware mobile edge computing systems. IEEE Internet Things J. **6**(3), 4854–4866 (2019)
7. Al-Habob, A.A., Dobre, O.A., Armada, A.G., Muhaidat, S.: Task scheduling for mobile edge computing using genetic algorithm and conflict graphs. IEEE Trans. Veh. Technol. **69**(8), 8805–8819 (2020)
8. Yu, Y., Zhang, J., Letaief, K.B.: Joint subcarrier and CPU time allocation for mobile edge computing. In: IEEE Global Communications Conference (GLOBE-COM), pp. 1–6 (2016)
9. Lai, W.K., Shieh, C.-S., Chen, Y.-P.: Task scheduling with multicore edge computing in dense small cell networks. IEEE Access **9**, 141223–141232 (2021)
10. Song, X., Qin, X., Tao, Y., Liu, B., Zhang, P.: Age based task scheduling and computation offloading in mobile-edge computing systems. In: IEEE Wireless Communications and Networking Conference Workshop (WCNCW), pp. 1–6 (2019)
11. Wang, X., Ning, Z., Guo, S., Wang, L.: Imitation learning enabled task scheduling for online vehicular edge computing. IEEE Trans. Mob. Comput. **21**(2), 598–611 (2022)
12. Sun, J., Gu, Q., Zheng, T., Dong, P., Valera, A., Qin, Y.: Joint optimization of computation offloading and task scheduling in vehicular edge computing networks. IEEE Access **8**, 10466–10477 (2020)
13. Ning, Z., Huang, J., Wang, X., Rodrigues, J., Guo, L.: Mobile edge computing-enabled internet of vehicles: toward energy-efficient scheduling. IEEE Netw. **33**(5), 198–205 (2019)
14. Gamatie, A., Devic, G., Sassatelli, G., Bernabovi, S., Naudin, P., Chapman, M.: Towards energy-efficient heterogeneous multicore architectures for edge computing. IEEE Access **7**, 49474–49491 (2019)
15. Yoo, S.: Leveraging multicores for mobile edge computing. In: International Conference on Information Networking (ICOIN), pp. 869–874 (2018)

Integration of AI and Cloud Computing: Advantages and Challenges

Sehrish Sher Khan[(⊠)]

School of Computer Science and Technology, University of Bedfordshire, Luton, UK
sehrishsher.khan@beds.ac.uk

Abstract. Cloud technology has led to a major growth in business cooperation. Each of the procedures has been improved by the use of AI. An organisation can benefit from excellent data security and low maintenance costs with a cloud computing solution the success of cloud services techniques is significantly influenced by the application of artificial intelligence in particular industries. As a result, the combined effect of these two developments increases the prosperity of certain firms. Public clouds function better when smart devices and computer vision models are used. It has also shown how businesses may gain from integrating AI into public cloud plans in several ways.

This research provides insight into the advantages and challenges of combining artificial intelligence with cloud computing.

Keywords: Artificial Intelligence · Cloud Computing · Advantages · Integration · Challenges · Data Privacy · Data Security · Applications

1 Introduction

As technology advances, artificial intelligence (AI) and cloud computing have emerged as two of the most transformative developments in recent years. Individually, these technologies are revolutionizing the way businesses operate. However, combined, they can drive innovation, efficiency, and strategy to unprecedented levels [1]. Cloud computing refers to the use of multiple server machines interconnected through a digital network, functioning seamlessly as a unified system [2]. The "Cloud" represents a virtualized environment that includes networks, servers, applications, storage, and services, all easily accessible to users on demand with minimal administrative involvement. It provides resources and services without requiring users to have a deep understanding of the underlying systems, offering a wide array of applications and scalable services tailored to both individuals and businesses [3]. The various research areas have been identified due to the rapidly evolving Cloud Computing research areas to solve the research challenges and to maximize utilization of the available technologies and paradigms in an efficient manner [4] (Fig. 1).

The fast-developing subject of artificial intelligence (AI) has the potential to completely transform a wide range of aspects of our lives. Another quickly developing area

© ICST Institute for Computer Sciences, Social Informatics and Telecommunications Engineering 2026
Published by Springer Nature Switzerland AG 2026. All Rights Reserved
X. Feng et al. (Eds.): CloudComp 2024, LNICST 617, pp. 22–28, 2026.
https://doi.org/10.1007/978-3-031-92517-7_4

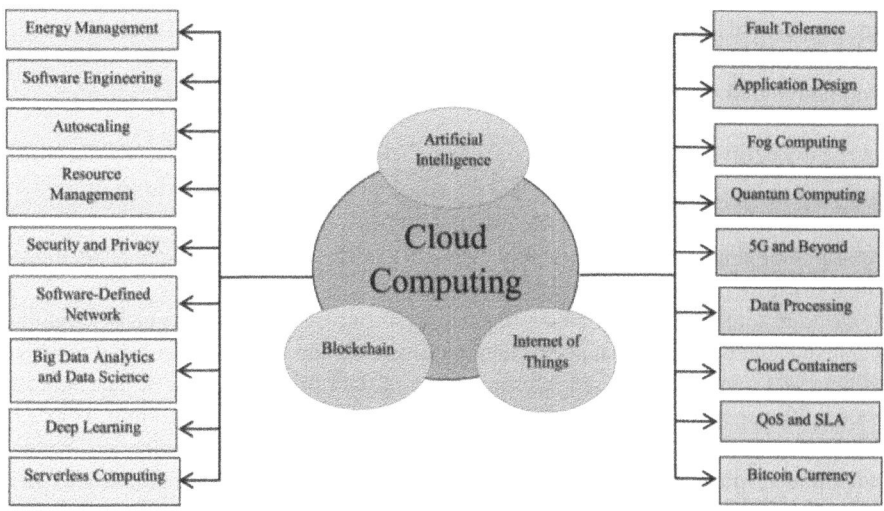

Fig. 1. Evolution of computing paradigms and technologies [4]

that will impact how we access and utilize computer resources is cloud computing. Cloud computing and artificial intelligence (AI) combined have the potential to produce novel and creative applications that address some of the most important issues facing humanity[5]. Since both AI and cloud computing rely heavily on automation, they have become inescapable. Simple processes are streamlined by AI, which boosts productivity and frees up IT people to work on more creative projects. Because it has the processing power, storage capacity, and scalability to manage the enormous volumes of data needed for AI algorithms, the cloud offers the perfect architecture for AI applications [6].

On the other hand, Artificial intelligence is a constellation of various technologies working together to enable machines to sense, comprehend, act, and learn with human-like intelligence. Technologies like machine learning and natural language processing are integral components of the AI landscape. Each is evolving along its path and, when combined with data, analytics, and automation, they can help businesses achieve their goals, whether it's improving customer service or optimizing the supply chain [5]. Artificial intelligence refers to a computer's distinct capability, even when remotely controlled, to efficiently carry out various crucial tasks. It relies on human intelligence for functions like speech recognition, decision-making, and visual perception. Today, AI is employed across several major industries, including healthcare management, financial process research, and social media monitoring [5].

In cloud computing, artificial intelligence (AI) converges to automate tasks including data management, security, analysis, and decision-making. Because AI can apply machine learning and generate unbiased interpretations of data-drive insights, it can enhance process efficiency and result in significant cost savings for the organisation. Utilizing AI software that is built on machine learning algorithms in cloud environments allows companies to provide users and consumers with integrated and user-friendly experiences. This paper provides a brief overview of the combination of artificial intelligence and cloud computing. This paper presents the future opportunities and challenges of combining AI with cloud computing.

1.1 Cloud Computing and AI

It's becoming increasingly obvious that the advancements of AI and cloud computing are complementary. Consequently, using AI in the cloud may improve its digital transformation, performance, and efficiency [1].

In cloud computing, artificial intelligence (AI) converges to automate tasks including data management, security, analysis, and decision-making. Since AI can apply machine learning and generate unbiased interpretations of data-driven insights, it can improve process efficiency and result in significant cost savings for the organization. Utilizing AI software that is built on machine learning algorithms in cloud environments enables companies to provide users and consumers with connected and user-friendly experiences. To increase the value of the current cloud computing settings, artificial intelligence (AI) technologies and software are integrated with cloud computing capacity[7]. Businesses become strategic, intelligent, and efficient as a result of this combination. Cloud-hosted data and apps save money for businesses overall while enabling them to be more responsive and adaptive. In the first quarter of 2020 compared to the first quarter of 2019, cloud computing investment climbed by 37% to $29 billion in the post-COVID future [8]. Thus, combining AI and cloud computing can improve operational efficiency and enable organisations connect with customers more effectively. The classic monolithic cloud application has given way to lightweight, loosely linked, and finely grained microservices thanks to the cloud native paradigm, which was inspired by cloud computing [9]. AI is thereby improving cloud computing in a number of ways. Cloud-based artificial intelligence is presently being successfully deployed with the Software as a Service (SaaS) paradigm [10].

Cloud AI services and applications are becoming increasingly prevalent in a variety of industries. Sentiment analysis and natural language processing (NLP) are two examples of such applications. To be able to extract sentiment and spot trends, AI algorithms can examine text data from a variety of sources, including support tickets, social media posts, and customer reviews. By performing this, companies can obtain important insights about the preferences, attitudes, and market trends of their customers and adjust their offerings accordingly [5]. Predictive analytics is another way in which AI is used in cloud computing. With the use of historical data and patterns, AI algorithms are able to forecast future events with high accuracy. This is very helpful for tasks like fraud detection, demand forecasting, and preventative maintenance. Through the use of AI-driven cloud solutions for predictive analytics, companies may reduce risks, maximise profits, and make data-driven decisions. Furthermore, chatbots and virtual assistants driven by AI are becoming increasingly common in customer care. These AI-powered programs are capable of handling client inquiries, offering prompt assistance, and even carrying out transactions. Businesses may increase customer happiness, improve response times, and offer immediate support by integrating chatbots with cloud platforms.

1.2   Applications of AI in Cloud Computing

Several applications in a range of industries have resulted from the integration of artificial intelligence and cloud computing. Let's examine a few typical use cases for artificial intelligence in the cloud:

Internet of Things (IoT): Data generated by AI platforms on IoT devices can be processed and stored by cloud architectures and services, which enable the Internet of Things. This makes it possible to do predictive maintenance, make smart choices in real-time using data from the Internet of Things, and analyse data in real time.

Chatbots: Chatbots are artificial intelligence (AI) programs that communicate with people using natural language processing. Chatbot data is stored and processed by cloud platforms, which then forward it to the relevant applications for additional handling. In the modern age of instant contentment, chatbots have emerged as a useful customer service tool.

AI as a Service (AIaaS): In recent years, public cloud providers have provided AI outsourcing services, which let businesses test and employ commercial AI products for a fraction of the price of developing AI internally. This approach minimises capital costs and lets companies test AI without sacrificing their core infrastructure.

Business Intelligence (BI): AI cloud computing accumulates market, target audience, and competition data, which is a major contribution to business intelligence. Data transfer and storage are made faster by the cloud, and AI uses predictive analytics models to generate insightful reports that help decision-makers make well-informed choices.

Cognitive Cloud Computing: AI models are used in cognitive computing to imitate and duplicate human thought processes under difficult situations. Businesses can use cognitive insights-as-a-service from platforms like IBM and Google in a variety of industries, including finance, retail, healthcare, and more.

1.3   Advantages of Integrating AI and Cloud Computing

Enhanced Security: Cloud service providers offer various kinds of security features that can aid in preventing unwanted access to AI applications. This can assist companies in compliance with data protection laws. In today's data-driven world, data is king, thus handling it better is imperative [6]. In a modern high-risk environment, banks and other financial institutions mostly depend on this technology to be secure and competitive. Cloud-based AI programs and tools that identify, update, catalogue, and offer customers real-time data insights. AI methods can also be used for identifying unusual system trends and detecting program's fraudulent activities [11].

Reduced Costs: Developing and implementing AI applications can be significantly less expensive with the use of cloud computing. This is to ensure that organizations can reduce their costs on hardware and software by taking advantage of the pay-as-you-go pricing model that cloud providers offer. Because companies can only pay for the resources they utilise due to cloud computing [6]. This saves an extensive amount of money in comparison to the usual infrastructure costs associated with constructing and operating large data centres [12].

Improved Adaptability: Businesses have the freedom to implement AI applications anywhere in the globe because of cloud computing. Businesses that need to implement AI applications in several places could find this useful [5].

Automation: Thanks to AI and the cloud, intelligent automation can now be adopted across an entire enterprise, eliminating the last remaining barriers [6, 13]. Cloud computing and artificial intelligence (AI) solutions can exceed the boundaries of efficient infrastructure management, minimising impact, and downtime, and assist enterprises in moving from semi-structured to unstructured documents through cognitive automation [14].

1.4 Challenges

When combining AI and cloud computing, there are several challenges to be resolved despite the numerous advantages. Some of the key challenges include:

Integration: Starting a smooth integration of two disparate technologies is never straightforward. Companies must first migrate all of their apps and technologies to the cloud in order to complete this integration [6, 13]. Businesses could experience such a drastic change before even considering cloud-based AI. As a result, the technological sync is too dependent on businesses that regularly put into practice substantial digital system changes [6].

Data privacy: Applications that are installed on cloud providers' platforms generate and retain data on those applications. It is possible to track users using this data or create specialized advertising campaigns.

When implementing AI apps on cloud platforms, businesses must consider the ramifications for data privacy [5].

Inadequate data: High-quality, large-scale datasets are perfect for AI applications. For AI to be beneficial, businesses must ensure that their data is both clean and accessible [6, 15].

Data Security Issues: The security of the data kept on their platforms is the responsibility of cloud providers. Sensitive data has, nevertheless, been lost in instances where cloud providers have been attacked. When storing data on cloud platforms, businesses must take precautions to safeguard it [5]. Businesses must be diligent in safeguarding their financial and sensitive data from adversaries who are likely to target them in order to prevent data breaches [16].

Compliance: Businesses have to comply with a number of laws pertaining to security, privacy, and data protection. These laws can differ from one country to another. Companies using cloud platforms to implement AI applications must be aware of the laws that are applicable to them [5].

2 Conclusion and Future Directions

As cloud computing advances throughout industries, the cloud market's revenue growth may slow down. Yet as big IT organisations increasingly use AI capabilities in the cloud, cloud computing is predicted to be revitalised by the AI surge. Generative AI on the cloud is the focus of initiatives such as Amazon's Bedrock cloud service. AI-generated text can effectively improve software for developers, showcasing AI's promise in cloud computing. This developing field has a lot of potential. We could expect to see more scalable, economical, versatile, and safe AI applications in the future. Consider the application of AI to address some of the most urgent global issues, including poverty, sickness, and climate change [5]. Businesses continue to advance due to the symbiotic link between AI and cloud computing, which is revolutionizing their operations and laying the groundwork for a more intelligent and connected future.

References

1. Pusztai, T., et al.: Slo script: a novel language for implementing complex cloud-native elasticity-driven slos. In: 2021 IEEE International Conference on Web Services (ICWS), pp. 21–31. IEEE (2021). https://ieeexplore.ieee.org/abstract/document/9590275/. Accessed 30 Jun 2024
2. Rehan, H.: Revolutionizing america's cloud computing the pivotal role of AI in driving innovation and security. J. Artif. Intell. Gen. Sci. JAIGS ISSN 3006–4023 **2**(1), 239–240 (2024)
3. Guzman, N.: Advancing NSFW detection in AI: training models to detect drawings, animations, and assess degrees of sexiness. J. Knowl. Learn. Sci. Technol. ISSN 2959-6386 Online **2**(2), 275–294 (2023)
4. Singh Gill, S., et al.: Transformative effects of IoT, Blockchain and Artificial Intelligence on cloud computing: evolution, vision, trends and open challenges, ArXiv E-Prints, p. arXiv-1911 (2019)
5. Mohamed, N., Rao, L.S., Sharma, M., Shukla, S.K.: In-depth review of integration of AI in cloud computing. In: 2023 3rd international conference on advance computing and innovative technologies in engineering (ICACITE), pp. 1431–1434. IEEE (2023). https://ieeexplore.ieee.org/abstract/document/10182738/. Accessed 30 Jun 2024
6. Gill, S.S., et al.: AI for next generation computing: Emerging trends and future directions. Internet Things **19**, 100514 (2022)
7. Abdelaziz, A., Elhoseny, M., Salama, A.S., Riad, A.M.: A machine learning model for improving healthcare services on cloud computing environment. Measurement **119**, 117–128 (2018)
8. Achar, S.: Cloud-based system design. Int. J. Res. Educ. Sci. Methods **7**(8), 23–30 (2019)
9. Zhong, Z., Xu, M., Rodriguez, M.A., Xu, C., Buyya, R.: Machine learning-based orchestration of containers: a taxonomy and future directions. ACM Comput. Surv. **54**(10s), 1–35 (2022). https://doi.org/10.1145/3510415
10. Pop, D.: Machine learning and cloud computing: survey of distributed and saas solutions (2016), arXiv: arXiv:1603.08767, http://arxiv.org/abs/1603.08767. Accessed 30 Jun 2024
11. Rajeswari, S., Ponnusamy, V.: AI-Based IoT analytics on the cloud for diabetic data management system. In: Integrating AI in IoT Analytics on the Cloud for Healthcare Applications, pp. 143–161. IGI Global (2022). https://www.igi-global.com/chapter/ai-based-iot-analytics-on-the-cloud-for-diabetic-data-management-system/295227. Accessed 30 Jun 2024
12. Robertson, J., Fossaceca, J.M., Bennett, K.W.: A cloud-based computing framework for artificial intelligence innovation in support of multidomain operations. IEEE Trans. Eng. Manag. **69**(6), 3913–3922 (2021)
13. Surya, L.: Streamlining cloud application with AI technology. Int. J. Innov. Eng. Res. Technol. IJIERT ISSN, pp. 2394–3696 (2018)

14. Marshall, T.E., Lambert, S.L.: Cloud-based intelligent accounting applications: accounting task automation using IBM watson cognitive computing. J. Emerg. Technol. Account. **15**(1), 199–215 (2018)
15. González, G., Evans, C.L.: Biomedical image processing with containers and deep learning: an automated analysis pipeline: data architecture, artificial intelligence, automated processing, containerization, and clusters orchestration ease the transition from data acquisition to insights in medium-to-large datasets. BioEssays **41**(6), 1900004 (2019). https://doi.org/10.1002/bies. 201900004
16. Chatterjee, S., Ghosh, S.K., Chaudhuri, R., Chaudhuri, S.: Adoption of AI-integrated CRM system by Indian industry: from security and privacy perspective. Inf. Comput. Secur. **29**(1), 1–24 (2021)

Understanding Human Behavior Through Smart Home IoT Data Analysis: Patterns and Insights

Md Israfil Biswas[1]([⊠]), Muhammad Atif Ur Rehman[2], Mohammed Al-Khalidi[2], and Ali Kashif Bashir[2]

[1] School of Computer Science and Technology, University of Bedfordshire, Luton 1 3JU, England
mdisrafil.biswas@beds.ac.uk
[2] Department of Computing and Mathematics, Manchester Metropolitan University, Manchester M15 6BH, UK
{m.atif.ur.rehman,m.al-khalidi}@mmu.ac.uk,
dr.alikashif.b@ieee.org

Abstract. This paper outlines the preprocessing methods and utilisation of clustering algorithms on a dataset [1] capturing individual tasks within a household (via energy consumption and reactive sensors). The analysis spans seven months that includes multi-sensor readings from a single household. In an effort to identify patterns through Human Activity Recognition (HAR), various clustering algorithms were applied to refined data to compare their respective outcomes. Hence, the paper examines multiple clustering algorithms suitable for the dataset exceeding 800,000 instances after preprocessing. It delves into the real-world applications of smart home data and conducts initial experiments where feasible, comparing results to uncover patterns indicative of user habits and changes therein. The study emphasises the potential for early intervention, particularly in identifying deviations to assist individuals such as those with dementia.

Keywords: Smart Home · IoT · data Analytics · Clustering

1 Introduction

A smart home, equipped with Internet of Things (IoT) devices, new wearables [2] collects and stores vast amounts of data regarding various aspects of household activities [3]. While this data-rich environment offers valuable insights into household dynamics, including behavioural patterns, this is important to recognise the limitations of Human Activity Recognition (HAR) analysis within this context. A significant challenge that arises in this area of research is the computational power limitations, particularly when dealing with clustering algorithms involving HAR for big data analytics. Much of the research usually relies on literature review and personal experimentation with clustering algorithms using a cloud-based platform. However, this platform imposes restrictions on

X. Feng et al. (Eds.): CloudComp 2024, LNICST 617, pp. 29–43, 2026.
https://doi.org/10.1007/978-3-031-92517-7_5

computational resources through paywalls and prioritisation, potentially necessitating data manipulation and resizing for exploration.

This issue is compounded by the fact that the dataset under study is categorised as big data, characterised by its diverse nature and substantial volume. Big data is also known for its rapid accumulation, often resulting in initial data structures that may lack coherence. Given the data-rich nature of smart home environments and the constant use of sensors, smart home data falls squarely within the realm of big data. Consequently, conventional non-industrial computers and cloud platforms may struggle to provide the necessary computing power to process smart home big data effectively. Even considering these factors, it's evident that the dataset's size exceeds the typical thresholds for big data classification.

This paper focuses on examining the processing and utilisation of IoT data for HAR. HAR holds significant applications across diverse fields, from healthcare to Artificial Intelligence (AI), all of which are explored in this work. Pattern recognition, whether identifying anomalous or repetitive patterns, represents one approach to studying HAR. In summary, the following are the core contributions of this paper.

- An overview discussing smart home data intricacies, alongside the application and analysis of clustering algorithms in relation to the dataset.
- Conduct data cleansing and feature engineering on the dataset to extract human activities derived from the provided IoT data.
- Utilise multiple clustering algorithms on the dataset; subsequently, assess their performance and impact by analysing differences in results.
- Ultimately, a comparative performance analysis is conducted to present all findings and determine the suitability of clustering algorithms for analysing human activity patterns.

The remainder of the paper is structured as follows. Section 2 presents a review of relevant literature on clustering algorithms, with a focus on their application within smart home environments. In Sect. 3, we explore the selected dataset using data parsing and visualisation techniques to assess vulnerabilities. Section 4 analyses the methodologies and outcomes of various clustering algorithms suitable for time-series data in smart home settings. Section 4.1 discusses the paper's findings, considering limitations and real-world use cases for implementing Internet of Things (IoT) smart home devices. Finally, Sect. 5 concludes the paper by outlining potential future research directions.

2 Background

Clustering is a widely employed data technique utilised across various industries to uncover potential categories within data, with an emphasis on dissimilarity [4]. This dissimilarity facilitates the identification and highlighting of distinct features within the dataset. Smart home data, in particular, offers the potential for such dissimilar categories, which may be discerned through various aspects including: the room in which tasks are performed, the timing of task execution, the sequence of task completion and human movement patterns throughout the day.

Data inherently contains a wealth of information, some of which is actionable while some may be extraneous. Data mining serves to extract and harness the actionable elements to align with user needs. One specific facet of data mining is data clustering, which encompasses a variety of clustering algorithms. These algorithms enable users to group data points together, thereby facilitating further classification [5].

There are three main types of clustering algorithms [6]: partitioning, hierarchical, and density-based methods. Partitioning methods evaluate a distance-based metric between data points to delineate clusters. While effective for classifying data with distinct features, these methods may struggle when features are less discernible. Hierarchical methods partition data into different levels based on features. This approach can be executed in two ways. Agglomerative algorithms proceed bottom-up, initially classifying the data before clustering it. Divisive algorithms, on the other hand, operate top-down, considering data relationships and distributions first [7]. Density-based algorithms assess the density of data points prior to clustering. Clusters are formed around denser regions, with less dense regions serving as separators. Each algorithm type is suited to different data types and situational requirements.

2.1 Potential Algorithms

The selected dataset comprises time-series data, encompassing two types of attributes: contextual and behavioural [6]. The behavioural element's value is temporally dependent on the contextual element, owing to the influence of time on value fluctuations. For instance, if a task is typically performed at a specific time each day, its completion is temporarily tied to that time. However, external factors like vacation may disrupt this cyclic task completion. Time-based clustering methods can be classified into two types: online analysis, where time is crucial, and offline analysis, where sequence holds significance. In smart home data, both approaches are applicable; time may indicate when a task is performed, highlighting patterns, while sequence could reveal task completion order, such as opening the fridge before using the microwave, suggesting meal preparation.

Multiple types of time-series clustering exist [8], including whole, subsequence, and time-point clustering. Whole clustering groups' individual series based on similarities, while subsequence clustering focuses on clustering within a single time series. Time-point clustering identifies clusters around specific points in time rather than the entire series. Time-series clustering typically explores dynamic changes, predictions, or data patterns, with applications spanning stock price analysis, weather forecasting, and sales pattern recognition.

Spark was chosen as the processing framework for its compatibility with Python and PySpark, along with its robust handling of big data. However, Spark's limited support for clustering algorithms prompted consideration of a select few models, including K-Means, Gaussian Mixture, Power Iteration Clustering, Latent Dirichlet Allocation, and Bisecting K-Means. Despite their utility, most of these algorithms are not optimised for time-series data. Unfortunately, the Pandas framework, which could support more suitable algorithms, was not feasible due to its inability to handle large datasets effectively. Attempts to use Pandas were hindered by framework limitations and likely constraints of cloud-based notebook capabilities.

2.2 Methodologies

In [9], various measures were considered during model evaluation. Initially, the time taken to execute each model was assessed. While this is a straightforward measure, it may not always indicate success. However, in certain industrial contexts, an algorithm that consumes excessive time may not be feasible. Additionally, the computational complexity of each model was examined using Big O notation, representing the worst-case scenario complexity. Although this is a basic measure, it may not necessarily correlate with model effectiveness, as a less complex algorithm could still yield suboptimal results.

The primary evaluation metrics utilised were Normalised Mutual Information (NMI) and Clustering Accuracy (AC). NMI quantifies the reduction in entropy between class labels and cluster labels, making it unsuitable for experiments involving unlabelled datasets. Similarly, AC relies on labelled data to assess the accuracy of cluster labels in comparison to class labels, rendering it inappropriate for these experiments. While manual labelling of data could address this issue, the dataset's size makes this approach impractical and eliminates the possibility of exploring unsupervised techniques. Moreover, manual labelling could introduce errors or biases stemming from personal life patterns influencing annotations.

In [4], the Adjusted Rand Index (ARI) and Fowlkes-Mallows Index (FMI) were employed to assess clustering models. However, both metrics rely on the presence of true clusters for calculation.

[10] explores unsupervised clustering and introduces three validation approaches: internal, external, and stability-based. Internal validation utilizes metrics to evaluate cluster quality based solely on the data used for clustering. External validation compares cluster effectiveness against true labels, providing some level of supervision for tuning hyperparameters based on accurate results. Stability-based analysis assesses algorithm reproducibility; consistent results indicate a stable model. However, conducting multiple executions for an ablation study can be time-consuming.

Spark offers built-in features that facilitate algorithm evaluation, including a cluster evaluator and cluster centres. The evaluator calculates the silhouette score, indicating cluster quality in terms of distinctiveness and overlap. A score of 1 signifies well-separated clusters, while 0 suggests the opposite. Negative scores may indicate misclassified clusters. Cluster centres provide visual insights by revealing the central points of clusters, aiding in identifying overlaps and discerning trends between clusters. Spark was chosen over alternatives like Pandas due to its capability to handle large datasets, which Pandas struggled with due to the sheer volume of instances.

Unsupervised technique exploration often lacks standardised success measures. While visualising clusters and analysing clustered readings can offer domain insights, human bias may influence the experiment. The overall process of how these experiments were conducted can be summarised as seen in Fig. 1 which shows the architecture of these methodologies.

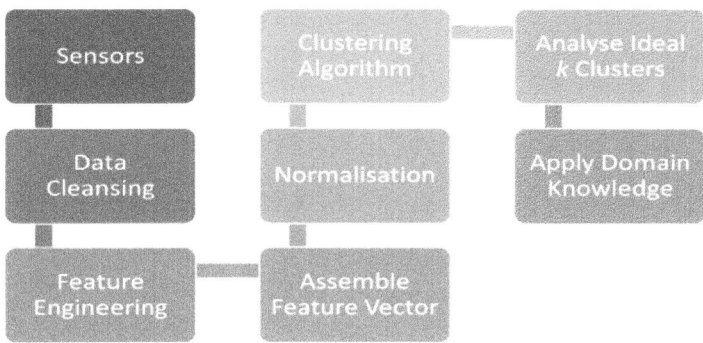

Fig. 1. Architecture of processing for clustering algorithms.

3 Dataset

In [1] raw data collected from 23 individual sensors strategically positioned within a residential setting to monitor daily human activities. This dataset offers an opportunity to explore unsupervised HAR by uncovering patterns inherent in the data. These patterns span from time-dependent activities, like sleeping and meals, to sequential activities, such as watching television before bedtime. The study was conducted in Sweden in 2020, prompting consideration of whether the results might differ from other HAR research due to the concurrent COVID-19 pandemic. Notably, Sweden did not enforce lockdown measures and maintained open borders during this period [11]. Thus, it is assumed that the dataset was not directly influenced by COVID-19. While individual resident choices may still impact the data, this remains speculative. Ideally, selecting a dataset from a different time period or comparing multiple datasets from the same time would provide more comprehensive insights. However, limited availability of smart home sensor data on a large scale constrained options, as discussed further in subsequent sections. The dataset is divided into three files: an integer file containing binary readings like the front door sensor, a float file containing continuous values such as fridge current, and a file correlating sensors with their IDs and respective rooms. The list file is displayed in Table 1 for reference throughout the paper.

3.1 Data Preparation

Pre-processing is a crucial step in any unsupervised machine learning task, as it enhances the quality and interpretability of results.

Data Cleansing. The dataset has been manually selected and thus requires thorough scrutiny for anomalies and errors. While published and reported data typically undergoes cleansing, it's noted that this dataset contains raw readings directly from the sensors [1]. Data cleansing involves various processes aimed at scanning and reformatting the data to detect and address issues.

One approach involves calculating the maximum and minimum values for each sensor to identify anomalies. For instance, a Sensor exhibits a negative minimum value

Table 1. A list of the sensors with their matching attributes.

Sensor ID	Type	Trigger	Room
5887	Stove	Light	Kitchen
5888	Door	Contact	Entrance
5889	Couch	Pressure	Living Room
5891	Ambience	Motion	Living Room
5892	Ambience	Motion	Bedroom
5893	Ambience	Motion	Kitchen
5894	Ambience	Motion	Corridor
5896	Bed	Pressure	Bedroom
6127	TV	Light	Living Room
6220	Door	Contact	Balcony
6222	Ambience	Humidity	Bathroom
6223	Ambience	Temperature	Bathroom
6253	Fridge	Contact	Kitchen
6632	Coffee Maker	Current	Kitchen
6633	Sandwich Maker	Current	Kitchen
6634	Dishwasher	Current	Kitchen
6635	Kettle	Current	Kitchen
6636	Washing Machine	Current	Bathroom
6686	Ambience (Under Bed)	Motion	Bedroom
6687	Weight Scale	Pressure	Bedroom
6896	Microwave	Current	Kitchen
7125	Ambience	Light	Bathroom
7139	iLifeRobot	Current	Corridor

Table 2. A table to show the unique sensor ids assigned to each cluster for K-means.

Cluster Group	Count of Sensors	Unique Sensors
0	318,513	5888,5891,5896,6223,5887,5893,6127,6222,5889,5892, 5894,6220,6253
1	498,898	6686,6632,6633,7125,6634,6636,6687,6896

that is the negative counterpart of the maximum value. This is an error, as the sensor measures current, which cannot be negative. Furthermore, only five instances of this negative measurement were found, and they were subsequently adjusted to reflect the correct positive values.

Table 3. The unique sensor ids assigned to each cluster for gaussian mixture.

Cluster Group	Count of Sensors	Unique Sensors
0	91,022	6127
1	92,465	5888,5891,5887,5893,5889,5892,5894
2	101,654	5896,5889
3	110,054	6223,6222
4	22,694	6687
5	284,220	7125
6	96,854	5887
7	7,980	6127,6222,6632,6633,6220,6253,6634,6636,6687,6896
8	1,356	6686
9	9,112	6633,6634,6636

Moreover, the sensors measuring current display unusually large maximum values. Upon examining percentiles ranging from a value of 1 to the original maximum, it was found that only 63 instances of current exceeded 2500. This represents a negligible fraction compared to the total number of readings. To address potential anomalies, data points beyond this threshold were filtered out, resulting in the adjusted maximum values. Additionally, another data cleansing step involves checking for null values in the dataset for removal. Upon inspection, it was found that there were no null values present in this dataset.

Feature Engineering. Since this data lacks labels, feature engineering is employed to derive a feature reflecting each sensor's status, indicating whether the device is in use for its intended task. For instance, sensor 5888, which detects front door usage, yields binary measurements, simplifying feature engineering. In contrast, sensor 6127, measuring lux from the television, produces varying lux values applicable to both artificial and natural light. Adjustments are necessary to distinguish when the sensor detects television usage amidst fluctuating light conditions. However, determining the threshold for accurate classification requires human intervention, which is impractical given time constraints. To ensure consistency, a modified minimum was adopted, representing a 25% increase from the original minimum for sensors measuring continuous values. The impact of this modification on classification distribution is illustrated in Figs. 2 and 3, displaying the before and after scenarios, respectively.

In Fig. 4, it is evident that the month of May has 24 sensor IDs recorded, while June, July, and August each have a count of 23. The additional sensor ID in May, labelled as 5895, specifically measured motion in the bathroom. Since this sensor was only active during May, it suggests that it may have been temporarily installed and later removed, possibly due to a technological issue. Additionally, considering that June, July, and August collectively utilize all 23 other sensors, the dataset was narrowed down to these three months. This adjustment enables a more comprehensive analysis with all sensors actively recording data. The discrepancy in the number of sensors across earlier months is likely attributed to the gradual addition of sensors to the residence throughout the experiment.

This indicates that some sensors exhibited repetitive anomalous readings, as evidenced by changes in density once the status was determined. However, this visualisation does not provide a clear depiction of the individual sensor distributions due to their global ranking. Additionally, the normalised distribution of sensor usage times can be visualised to gain insights into when certain sensors are most active throughout the day. Figure 5 illustrates this, highlighting instances where sensors are more frequently used during specific times. For example, sensor 5888, representing front door usage, shows increased activity during the afternoon and evening hours, which aligns with typical patterns of door usage. Similarly, sensors 6222 and 6223, monitoring bathroom temperature and humidity, respectively, demonstrate similar usage patterns during evening hours, likely associated with showering or bathing activities. In this visualisation, morning hours are categorised between 6:00 and 11:00, with subsequent time periods increasing in equal increments.

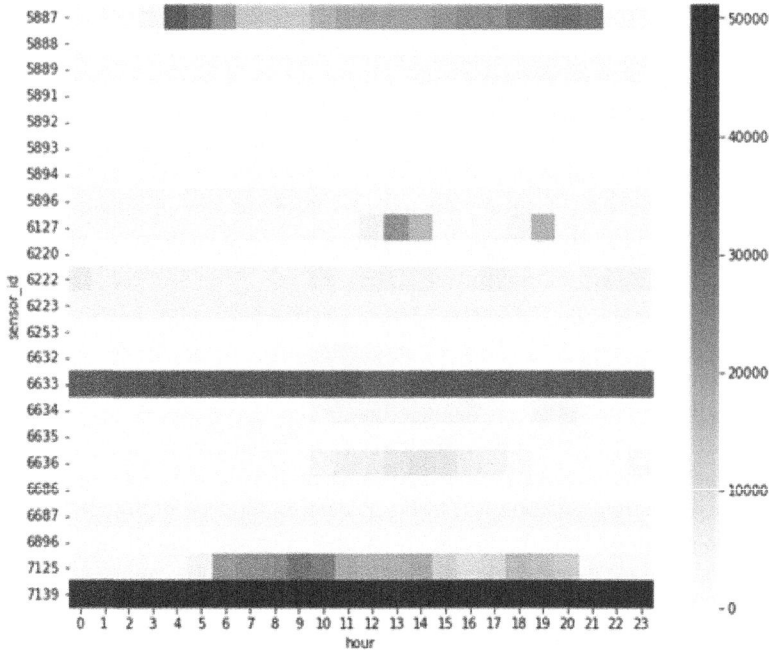

Fig. 2. The density distribution of sensors before modifying the minimum.

Standarsation or Normalisation. This is essential in machine learning to ensure consistent numeric data input. This process minimises fluctuations in integer or float values, reducing computation time and mitigating the risk of algorithm crashes mid-execution. Additionally, it helps prevent biases in results by ensuring equal treatment of features.

Failure to standardise or normalise data may lead to algorithmic favouritism towards certain features, potentially skewing results, particularly in clustering algorithms where

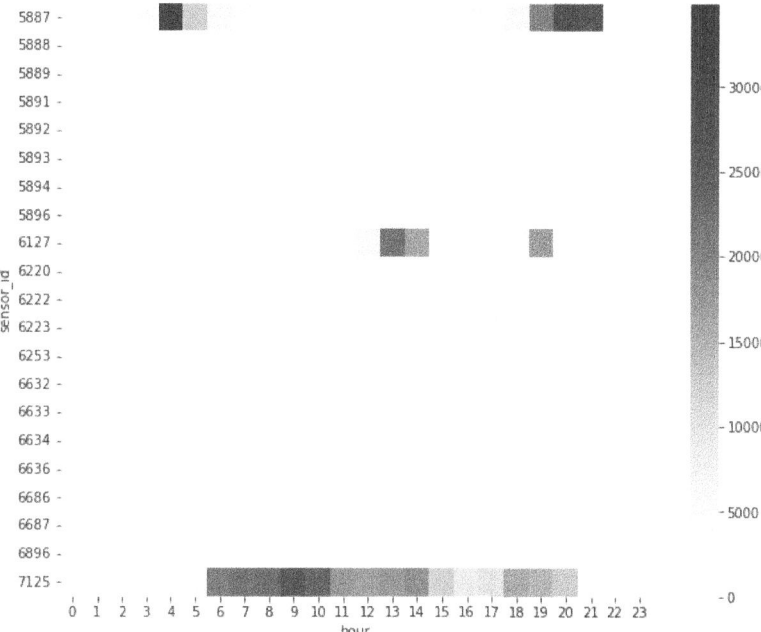

Fig. 3. The density distributions of sensors after modifying the minimum.

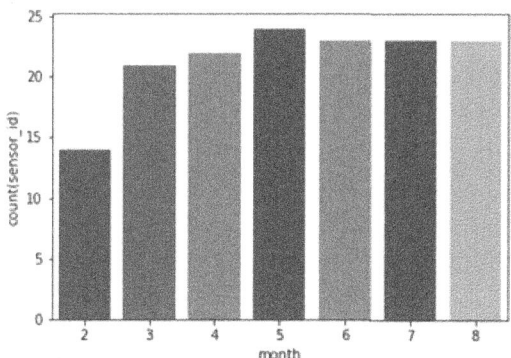

Fig. 4. A bar chart to show the count of unique sensor IDs in each month of the dataset.

scaled features facilitate distance metrics between data points. This enables algorithms to accurately determine relationships and identify clusters without being influenced by large differences in scales.

Various transformers are available for machine learning tasks, primarily focusing on standardising or normalising data. Standardisation involves rescaling values to achieve a mean of 0 and a standard deviation of 1, suitable when features operate on different scales but follow a normal distribution. On the other hand, normalisation scales data to

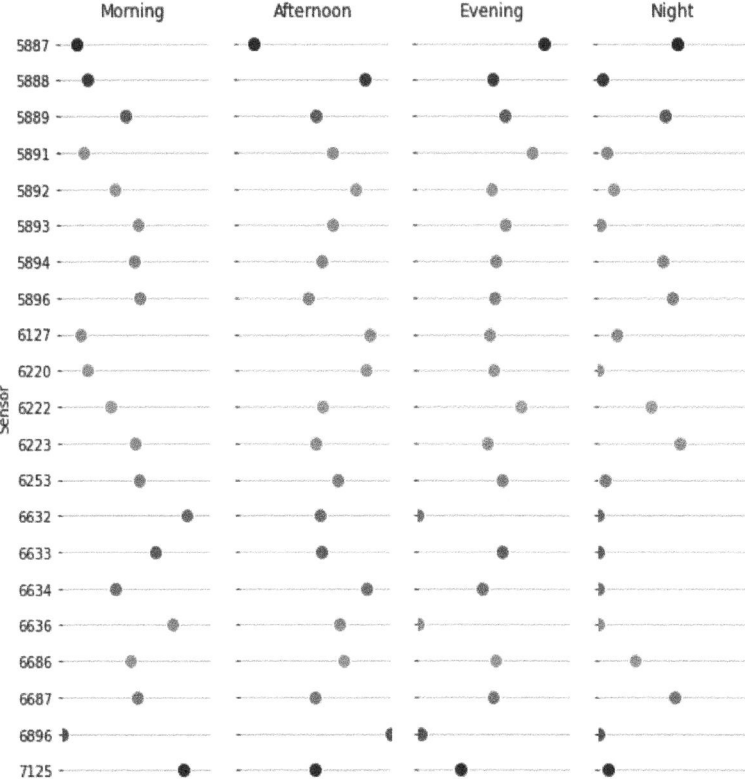

Fig. 5. The normalised distributions of sensors at different times in the day.

a range of 0 to 1, irrespective of distribution [12]. For this dataset, normalisation was chosen due to its non-normal distribution.

To facilitate smoother computational processing, the dataset underwent further reduction, focusing on a specific timeframe spanning three weeks from June 1st to June 21st. These dates were selected for their convenient duration of three weeks and because they encompassed instances captured by all sensors, as depicted in Fig. 6.

Choosing a date where all 23 sensors were operational, Fig. 7 displays the daily readings captured by these sensors. Notably, some readings align with expected patterns, such as sensor 6222, which monitors humidity in the bathroom.

It's plausible that this spike in humidity occurred around midday, coinciding with the use of the bath or shower, leading to an increase in room temperature.

Utilising Spark as the processing framework allowed for the inclusion of large datasets within the data frame. However, while Spark accommodated extensive data for algorithmic analysis, employing similarly large datasets for visual analysis (requiring conversion to a Pandas data frame) was constrained due to computational limitations. Nonetheless, the data frame still retained over 800,000 sensor readings.

Extensive research was undertaken to identify a suitable dataset initially intended for use with a random forest algorithm, later to be applied with clustering algorithms.

Given the project's focus on leveraging big data analytics in the realm of smart home data, the selected dataset needed to meet the criteria of being classified as big data while providing insights into real smart home environments.

Challenges arose when datasets were found to be too small or lacking in the requisite number of sensors to effectively capture meaningful activities. This type of data is often not readily available in open-source repositories, leading to a limited selection of suitable and accessible datasets.

The scarcity of openly available smart home data may be attributed to privacy concerns surrounding the nature of the data, potentially leading to its restricted access or commercial value due to its diverse applications.

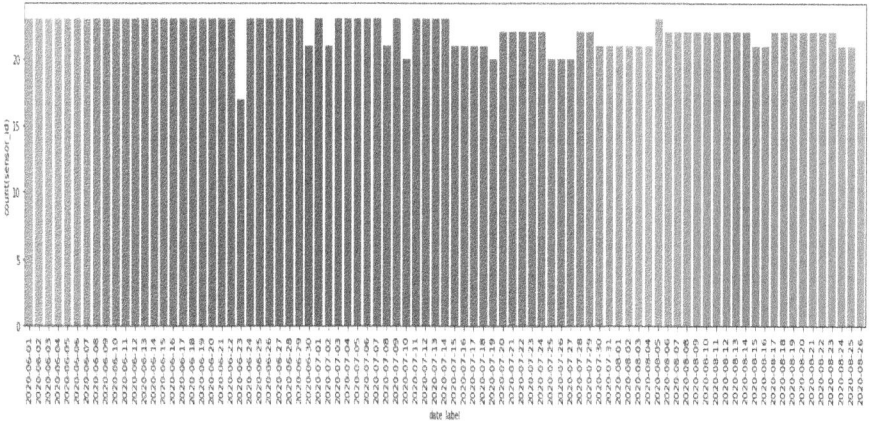

Fig. 6. A bar chart to show the count of unique sensor IDs for each day in June, July, and August.

4   Clustering Algorithms

Since algorithms cannot process datetime data directly, this feature has been deconstructed into its constituent components: the day of the year, day of the week, hour, and minute. This not only enables the algorithms to function but also facilitates the identification of similarities between instances based on these new features. For instance, tasks may occur around the same time each day or on the same day of the week. Initially, these algorithms typically require a feature vector. Spark provides the functionality to consolidate all attributes into a single vector using 'VectorAssembler'. Subsequently, data normalisation is necessary using 'MinMaxScaler' to prepare the data for model fitting. Additionally, most algorithms require a predetermined value for k, the number of clusters. Various methods exist for selecting k. One such approach is the elbow method, which involves iterating through different cluster sizes and analysing the sum of squared errors to identify a point where an elbow-shaped curve forms—the ideal k value corresponds to the middle point of this elbow. Another method is the silhouette method,

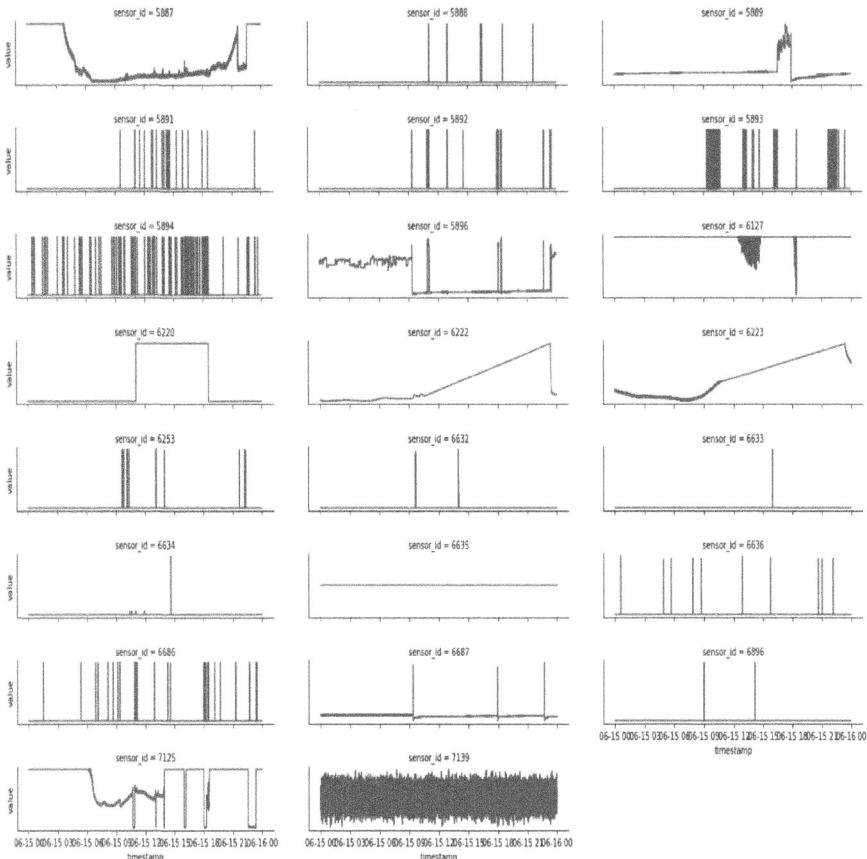

Fig. 7. Line charts to show the readings of each sensor in a single day.

which considers the silhouette score. A general rule of thumb for selecting k [13, 14], which is:

$$k = \sqrt{\frac{n}{2}},$$

Where n is the size of the sample. This results in a k size of 639 which is a lot larger than one would typically start at for determining cluster size, however the scaled and filtered dataset does contain 817,411 instances.

Conducting experiments to determine the optimal k value proved challenging due to the dataset's unsuitability for clustering analysis. The obtained results were inconsistent across repeated runs, and external logic failed to yield expected outcomes with this dataset. Attempting to set k at 639 resulted in a negative silhouette score, indicating poorly defined clusters. A gradual examination of k values from 2 to 10 did not consistently reveal a smooth elbow shape in the plot. Furthermore, the majority of scores were subpar, with many being negative. Realistically, exploring all possible k values would require substantial computational power and time.

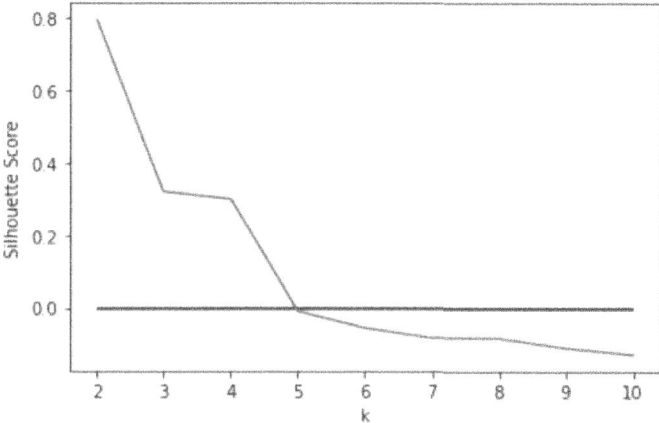

Fig. 8. A line plot to show the silhouette score from the k-means algorithm.

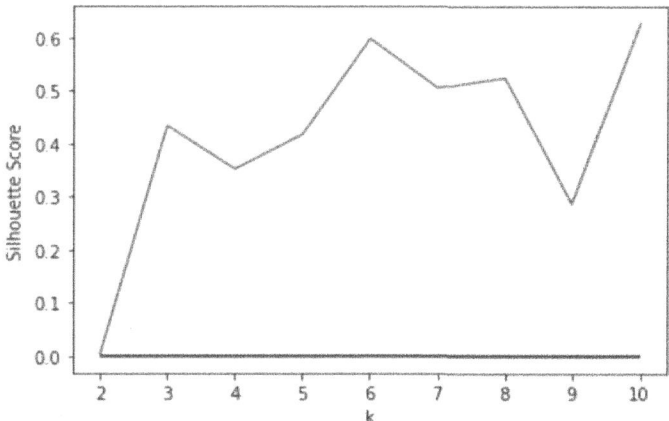

Fig. 9. A line plot to show the silhouette score from the Gaussian mixture algorithm.

This limitation underscores a drawback of clustering algorithms, particularly K-Means, which lacks a precise calculation for this metric. Figure 8 illustrates the brief gradual study conducted on the dataset to determine k. The unique sensor IDs assigned to each cluster for k-means.

4.1 K-Means

This indicates that a cluster size of 2 is the most optimal among the options, as it yields the highest non-negative silhouette score of 0.79 (rounded to 2 decimal places). Attempting a larger k size of 639, as suggested in [14], resulted in a negative silhouette score of -0.63 (rounded to 2 decimal places), indicating the formation of overlapping clusters at this size. However, a cluster size of 2 may not be ideal as it may not reveal prominent patterns in the data. This suggests that the data may not be well-suited for clustering, as the input features may not be the most appropriate. After opting to further investigate with a cluster size of 2, the cluster centres and the sensors contained within each cluster could be examined. Table 2 displays the unique sensors assigned to each cluster. There is no overlap between the lists because of the small size of k, indicating that these sensors possess distinct characteristics from the others. However, it is not immediately apparent from an external viewpoint what specific factors are responsible for distinguishing these sensors from one another. Regarding the cluster centres, they exist in six dimensions due to the six features used as input in the model. Visualising them proved challenging as they would need to be plotted simultaneously, which was not feasible due to Spark's complexity with array data frames.

4.2 Gaussian Mixture

Comparable experiments were carried out using the Gaussian Mixture clustering method [15]. Figure 9 below illustrates the examination of fewer clusters. The scores generally show improvement ask increases. However, computational constraints prevented the execution of the larger value of 639. This algorithm experienced longer run times as k increased, likely because it computed probabilities for all clusters, which strained the session for the cloud-based notebook. Consequently, additional analysis was performed using k set to 10, as it yielded the highest silhouette score..

Table 3 displays the sensors assigned to each cluster. The sizes of these clusters exhibit significant variation, potentially indicating distinct patterns identified by the algorithm. However, the presence of numerous singular sensor clusters is not an ideal outcome, as it fails to reveal meaningful patterns indicative of specific activities. For instance, Cluster 2 includes sensors measuring pressure from both the bed and couch, which logically should not be correlated. This discrepancy suggests that the algorithm may be matching the scales of the value element. Conversely, Cluster 3 accurately identifies the concurrent usage of temperature and humidity sensors in the bathroom, aligning with logical expectations regarding their simultaneous activation.

5   Conclusion and Future Work

The paper presented data pre-processing of data cleansing and manipulation methodologies while utilising clustering algorithms to identify and analyse HAR patterns for user habits within smart home applications IoT data. This work provided all the necessary information and data required to justify the proposed solution in terms of data cleaning of the utilised dataset, proper features for each sensor, and normalisation of the data to support the effective detection of anomalies, while analysing the methodologies followed through k-means and Gaussian mixture clustering with sufficient calculations, and presenting samples of the sensors' readings. Hence, a thorough presentation of the smart home infrastructure and the implemented IoT system is successfully achieved, while also providing an analysis of potential algorithms and strategies that can assist HAR patterns in other smart environments.

However, this work further aims to explore more attributes of the datasets with large size and computational complexity. This will extend the capabilities of the methods and frameworks for the analysis of HAR pattern research. More comprehensive exploration with extended comparison of methods on this scale will be conducted in future for the feasibility of this work. Given the opportunity to continue, a more precise investigation would be conducted, exploring a wider range of framework options rather than relying on smart home environments. The scale of the dataset, indicative of big data, will have extended resources available to further investigate this project considering HAR pattern analysis.

Acknowledgement. This work recognises Lewis Wright's contributions to the experiments conducted in developing the results presented in the paper.

References

1. Chimamiwa, G., Alirezaie, M., Pecora, F., Loutfi, A.: Multi-sensor dataset of human activities in a smart home environment. Data Brief **34**, 106632 (2021)
2. Vafeas, A., et al.: Wearable devices for digital health: the SPHERE wearable 3. In: European Conference/Workshop on Wireless Sensor Networks (2020)
3. Kim, S., Park, M., Lee, S., Kim, J.: Smart home forensics—data analysis of IoT devices. Electronics **9**(8), 1215 (2020)
4. Zhang, Y.: Advances in categorical data clustering, Doctor of Philosophy (PhD), Hong Kong Baptist University, https://scholars.hkbu.edu.hk/ws/portalfiles/portal/55045016/OA-0658.pdf. Accessed 12 Jan 2022
5. Raja, R.: Data mining and machine learning applications. Wiley; Scrivener Publishing, Hoboken (2019)
6. Aggarwal, C.C., Reddy, C.K.: Data clustering: algorithms and applications. CRC Press LLC, Philadelphia (2013)
7. Dey, D.: ML | Hierarchical clustering (Agglomerative and Divisive clustering). GeeksforGeeks. https://www.geeksforgeeks.org/hierarchical-clustering. Accessed 15 April 2024
8. Aghabozorgi, S., Shirkhorshidi, A.S., Wah, T.Y.: Time series clustering – a decade review. Inform. Syst. **53**, 16–38 (2015), ISSN0306-4379. https://doi.org/10.1016/j.is.2015.04.007
9. Luong, K.T.N.: Clustering methods for multi-aspect data. Doctor of Philosophy (PhD), Queensland University of Technology. https://eprints.qut.edu.au/131620/1/Thi%20Ngoc%20Khanh%20Luong%20Thesis.pdf. Accessed 1 Dec 2022
10. Unsupervised Learning and Clustering. January 2008 Lecture Notes in Applied and Computational Mechanics In: book: Machine Learning Techniques for Multimedia: Case Studies on Organization and Retrieval, pp. 51–90, Chapter: 3Publisher: SpringerEditors: Matthieu Cord and Pádraig Cunningham (2008).https://doi.org/10.1007/978-3-540-75171-7-3
11. Gordon, D.V., Grafton, R.Q., Steinshamn, S.I.: Cross-country effects and policy responses to COVID-19 in 2020: the Nordic countries. Econ. Anal. Policy **71**, 198–210 (2021)
12. Brownlee, J.: How to use standardscaler and minmaxscaler transforms in python. Machine Learning Mastery. https://machinelearningmastery.com/standardscaler-and-minmaxscaler-transforms-in-python. Accessed 4 Dec 2022
13. Mahendru, K.: How to determine the optimal K for K-means?: Medium. https://medium.com/analytics-vidhya/how-to-determine-the-optimal-k-for-k-means-708505d204eb. Accessed 4 Dec 2022
14. Ahmed, M., Mahmood, A.N.: Novel approach for network traffic pattern analysis using clustering-based collective anomaly detection. Ann. Data Sci. **2**(1), 111–130 (2015)
15. Understanding Gaussian Mixture Model. Great Learning. https://www.mygreatlearning.com/blog/gaussian-mixture-model. Accessed 4 Dec 2022

Blockchain in Space-Air-Ground Integrated Networks: A Critical Look

Wenbing Zhao[1](✉)(iD), Shunkun Yang[2](iD), and Xiong Luo[3](iD)

[1] Cleveland State University, Cleveland, OH, USA
wenbing@ieee.org
[2] Beihang University, 37 Xueyuan Rd, Beijing, China
ysk@buaa.edu.cn
[3] University of Science and Technology Beijing, Beijing, China
xluo@ustb.edu.cn

Abstract. In this paper, we provide a concise review on the use of blockchain in space-air-ground integrated networks (SAGIN). Our study is guided by several research questions. First, we identify the objectives of the blockchain-based solutions for SAGIN. Second, we investigate how the blockchain technology is used to achieve the objectives. Third, we evaluate the maturity levels of the proposed blockchain-based solutions. Our findings show that blockchain has been used in the areas of dynamic spectrum management, crowd-sensing, traffic offloading, computation offloading, geofencing for unmanned air vehicles, data sharing, authentication of various SAGIN-connected entities, security of air traffic management, data security, and trustworthiness of the network. All studies proposed some forms of custom blockchain instead of using an existing public blockchain platforms to achieve their intended objectives. Furthermore, most studies chose to use some traditional distributed consensus algorithms and other non-mainstream algorithms for the proposed blockchain solutions. Except for a couple of studies, in which Hyperledger was used as the basis for customization, none of the studies validated the proposed solution experimentally. In addition to the research questions, we highlight pervasive misconceptions and misunderstandings regarding the blockchain technology and provide a guideline on how to properly develop blockchain-based solutions for SAGINs.

Keywords: Blockchain · Space-air-ground integrated networks (SAGIN) · Smart contract · Decentralized consensus · Data immutability · Security and privacy · Trust · Hyperledger · Practical Byzantine fault tolerance (PBFT)

1 Introduction

The space-air-ground integrated network (SAGIN) refers to a future generation of communication system that promises full networking coverage of the entire

This work was supported in part by Beijing Natural Science Foundation under Grants L211020 and M21032.

X. Feng et al. (Eds.): CloudComp 2024, LNICST 617, pp. 44–56, 2026.
https://doi.org/10.1007/978-3-031-92517-7_6

planet Earth [7, 14, 21, 25]. The SAGIN would consist of three network segments, namely, space, aerial, and terrestrial. The space subnetwork offers wide coverage and can reach remote and sparsely populated regions, and is facilitated by geostationary earth orbiting satellite and low earth orbiting satellites. The aerial subnetwork can be set up to meet the increased demand of network traffic demand using communicating unmanned arial vehicles, airships, and balloons. The terrestrial subnetwork is powered by existing wireless networking infrastructures such as cellular base stations and other wireless facilitates.

The blockchain technology was pioneered by Bitcoin, the first cryptocurrency released in January 2009 [20, 26, 30]. Ethereum enriched the blockchain technology by supporting smart contracts in 2015 and by introducing an alternative consensus algorithm (*i.e.,* proof of state [32, 39]) in late 2022. While we have yet to see a killer app for the blockchain technology, the idea of having a decentralized global platform that ensures data immutability, decentralized consensus, atomic code execution (among many other desirable features) has attracted intensive research interests and industry support [1, 33, 34, 36, 37]. In general, blockchain has been proposed as the means to improve security and trust, avoid the single-point of failure, facilitate coordination and cooperation of multiple parties without having to trust any centralized entities [35].

Not surprisingly, numerous studies have proposed to use blockchain for SAGIN operations and SAGIN-based applications. We are aware of only one comprehensive review on the use of blockchain in SAGINs [25]. That study focused on the various applications of blockchain in Internet of Things (IoT) (asset management, access control, identity management, secure communication, data provenance, and auditing support) after first introducing an overview of security issues with IoT. A closer look at the included studies revealed that they are mostly about using blockchain in general IoT applications and very few are strictly within the scope of SAGIN. Consequently, the study may not inform how blockchain can be used to address the specific problems in SAGIN. Another comprehensive review on 6G IoT [21] also mentioned SAGIN and blockchain. Although relevant discussions on blockchain are specific to SAGIN, they lack depth because the subject matter is not the focus of the study. Hence, it is necessary to investigate how blockchain has been used specifically for SAGIN operations and SAGIN-based applications and provide discussion with sufficient technical depth.

In this paper, we organize our comprehensive review with the following research questions: (1) what are the objectives of the blockchain-based solutions for SAGIN? (2) How is the blockchain technology used to achieve the objectives? (3) what are the maturity levels of the proposed blockchain-based solutions? Our findings show that blockchain has been used to help manage dynamic spectrum dynamically, to help perform crowd-sensing, to facilitate traffic offloading, to enhance trustworthiness of the network, to facilitate computation offloading, to enable authentication of various SAGIN-connected entities, to improve the security of air traffic management, to facilitate data sharing, to enhance data security, and to enable geofencing for unmanned air vehicles. All studies proposed some form of custom blockchain instead of using an existing public blockchain such as Bitcoin and Ethereum to achieve their intended objectives for SAGIN. Except a couple of studies, in which Hyperledger was used as the basis for customization, none of the studies validated the proposed solution experimentally. Furthermore, most studies chose to use a traditional distributed consensus algorithm [30], namely, PBFT (short for practical Byzantine fault tolerance) [2], or some of its variation, as the consensus algorithm for the proposed blockchain solution. The proposed solutions are apparently in the very early stages of development, if any. In addition to the research questions, we highlight the issues that we have identified during the review. We point out pervasive misconceptions and misunderstandings regarding the blockchain technology [31].

2   Literature Collection

The Web of Science core collection was used for finding relevant publications because it is the most comprehensive yet selective source for academic publications. We used one search term: "space air ground blockchain". The search resulted 39 publications. The title and abstract of each of the publications were examined to filter out irrelevant papers. 17 papers were excluded (*i.e.*, 22 papers were retained) in this step. The full texts of the 22 papers were then retrieved for further evaluation. One of the papers was removed because it is the conference version of another journal article. Another paper was excluded because the main content is about blockchain operation rather than the application in SAGIN. Hence, this comprehensive review is based on 20 papers.

3   Objectives of Blockchain-Based Solutions

In this section, we report our findings for the first research question. For this research question, we exclude two studies that are comprehensive reviews. Key information regarding these 18 studies are provided in Table 1. As shown in Fig. 1, the objectives of blockchain-based solutions can be divided into two categories: (1) functional applications in SAGIN, and (2) non-functional applications. By functional applications, we mean the objectives are relevant for the operations of SAGIN, such as dynamic spectrum management. By non-functional applications, we mean the objectives are for improving the quality of services of SAGIN, such as for improving authentication, data security, and the trustworthiness.

3.1   Functional Applications of Blockchain for SAGIN

Two studies proposed to use blockchain to facilitate dynamic spectrum management for SAGIN [11,23]. One study proposed to use blockchain to help conduct crowd-sensing in vehicular networks [27]. In another study, blockchain is used to facilitate crowd-sourcing for indoor navigation as a case study [10]. In [9], blockchain is used to enable trusted data sharing. In [24], blockchain is used to

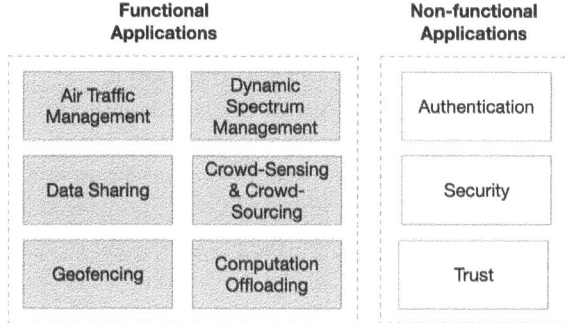

Fig. 1. Objectives of blockchain-based solutions for SAGIN.

enable trusted network traffic offloading. In [12], blockchain is used to facilitate computation offloading. Four studies from the same research group proposed to use blockchain to help air traffic management [15–18]. In [4], blockchain was proposed to facility geofencing of unmanned aerial vehicles (UAVs).

3.2   Non-Functional Applications of Blockchain for SAGIN

Three studies proposed to use blockchain to improve the trustworthiness of the SAGIN operation environment [3,5,22]. Three studies focused on using blockchain to facilitate the authentication of users for SAGIN and devices in SAGIN [8,13,19].

4   Technical Details of Blockchain-Based Solutions

In this section, we report our findings regarding the second research question on technical approaches. Some what surprisingly, no solution proposed to use any of the existing public blockchain platforms (such as Bitcoin and Ethereum). Two studies only mentioned some specific features of the blockchain for certain applications in SAGIN. In [4], an idea is proposed that the blockchain would be used to help the UAVs to reach consensus so that a particular region is granted to a particular UAV. Although the idea is intuitive, it is in fact not a viable solution for facilitating geofencing of UAVs. In blockchain such as Bitcoin and Ethereum, only blocks deep down in the blockchain can be regarded as immutable. The top few blocks may be changed due to the possibility of forks. In UAV operation, it is not practical for a UAV to wait for a long time before the block containing its request has been confirmed a sufficient number of times. In [22], the blockchain is credited to offer improved security and privacy, to facilitate automation due to support of smart contracts, and to enable efficient authentication. As we pointed out previously, the blockchain authentication mechanism is not a good fit for wireless sensors without additional mechanisms [36].

Table 1. Blockchain-based solutions for SAGIN.

Refs	Objective	Technical Approach	M
Li [11]	Dynamic spectrum management	Custom blockchain with a PBFT-inspired consensus algorithm	L3
Sun [23]	Dynamic spectrum management	Custom blockchain design only	L2
Zhao [27]	Vehicular crowd-sensing	Custom blockchain with proof of authority	L3
Li [10]	Crowdsourced indoor navigation	Custom blockchain design	L3
Li [9]	Data sharing	Custom blockchain with custom consensus algorithm	L3
Tang [24]	Trusted traffic offloading	Custom blockchain with a PBFT-inspired consensus algorithm	L3
Liao [12]	Computation offloading	Custom blockchain with no information about consensus	L3
Lu [16]	Air traffic management	Custom blockchain design only	L2
Lu [17]	Air traffic management	Custom blockchain with custom consensus	L2
Lu [18]	Air traffic management	Hyperledger with PBFT as consensus algorithm	L3
Lu [15]	Air traffic management	System design only	L2
Dasu [4]	Geofencing for UAVs	High level ideas only	L1
Du [5]	Increased trustworthiness	Custom blockchain with no information about consensus	L3
Pang [22]	Increased trustworthiness	No details	L1
Chen [3]	Increased trustworthiness	Custom blockchain that support smart contracts	L3
Luo [19]	Authentication of vehicles	Custom blockchain with custom consensus	L3
Li [8]	Authentication and service provision	Hyperledger with Conflux as consensus algorithm	L4
Liu [13]	Credential management for authentication	Hyperledger with a single ordering service	L4

All studies that have some forms of design and implementation follow a rather similar design, *i.e.*, a custom blockchain with a so-called lightweight consensus algorithm (compared with proof-of-work or proof-of-stake decentralized consensus algorithms). Furthermore, some key components in a SAGIN would participate consensus in the blockchain operation, ranging from UAVs [5] to ground stations [12].

We are very concerned about the approach of using so-called lightweight blockchains. Most important of all, this trend fails to understand what makes the various benefits of the blockchain technology, which we have elaborated previously [31, 40]. For a decentralized open system to offer data immutability and other associated properties, the only way is to enact a barrier for changing existing data, *i.e.,* the blockchain, maintained by the system. For proof-of-work based blockchains, the barrier can be achieved via the difficulty of the puzzle and the scale of the system (*i.e.,* large number of competing mining nodes). For proof-of-stake based blockchains, this is accomplished via staking requirements and slashing rules, although we have strong concerns about this approach (discussion on this issue is out of scope of this paper). A blockchain with only a few nodes cannot offer the well-hyped benefits of the blockchain technology because the barrier cannot possibly high enough to mitigate attacks that aim to change the data maintained by the system. Therefore, a private or consortium blockchain cannot offer data immutability and other benefits beyond those of a centralized system.

Also pervasive in the studies is the belief that PBFT is a viable lightweight alternative to proof-of-work or proof-of-stake consensus algorithms. Although the full PBFT has been proven to be correct, it is not a good fit for an open decentralized system. First, PBFT assumes a static membership, which is not realistic for an open system where the nodes are not known beforehand. Second, PBFT is not scalable with respect to the number of nodes. Third, PBFT does not guarantee a consensus can be reached within a given time frame due to the famous FLP impossibility result [6]. Despite numerous claims of high throughput achieved by PBFT, the algorithm works well only when the number of nodes is small and the operating environment is fault free and very synchronous. Regarding PBFT, a popular technical mistake permeated in the academic literature is that PBFT is only a 3-phase commit protocol (*i.e.,* pre-prepare, prepare, and commit), and it will always complete. In fact, the 3-phase commit protocol can be completed only when the primary does not fail and the environment is sufficiently synchronous. When the conditions are not met, the protocol would fail and a view change will have to be initiated. The view change protocol is very complex and one view change attempt might not lead to a stable membership if the environment is not sufficiently synchronous [29].

In [18], the PBFT is used as the consensus algorithm. However, there is no discussion regarding the potential impact if view change takes place. In [11], a PBFT-inspired algorithm was proposed, which consists at most two phrases. The paper then demonstrated via simulation that it has better performance than PBFT. Unfortunately, the proposed algorithm will not work correctly when the primary fails during the consensus process or when the network is sufficiently asynchronous. In [24], the PBFT is extended with the possibility of adding a new node or removing a node, and the normal operation three-phase commit protocol is assumed to be the PBFT as its entirety. Again, it is a mistake to regard PBFT as only the three-phrase commit. In [12], the PBFT three-phase commit protocol for normal operation is reported as the consensus algorithm.

In [8], the Conflux algorithm is used as the consensus algorithm. This algorithms is a graph-based algorithm that aims to derive a total order of all transactions. It is said to have better performance than PBFT (even when during normal operation). However, this algorithm has not been rigorously analyzed theoretically for its correctness.

In [27], the so-called proof-of-authority consensus algorithm is used. In proof-of-authority, one or a small set of validators who have been pre-approved to create new blocks. This is completely against the decentralization goal of the blockchain technology. As such, the solution is not decentralized and it cannot possibly offer stronger security than traditional centralized systems.

In [19], instead of any consensus algorithm, Kafka distributed message processing is used for block creation and verification. Again, this is essentially a centralized solution, which is against the design principle of the original blockchain technology. Furthermore, the paper compared the performance of Kafka and PBFT. Kafka can only tolerate crash fault while PBFT is designed to tolerate Byzantine faults. Hence, the comparison is meaningless.

In [17], another validator-based consensus algorithm is adapted as the consensus in the proposed solution. The argument for better security is based on the fact that the validators have stronger credibility and are endorsed by the government. First, this argument is sound because the endorsement by a government does not necessarily mean the nodes are more trustworthy. Second, even if the claim is true, the thought is directly against principle of decentralization, which means no node is trusted.

In [9], a committee of validators are used and the node that has the highest credit would create the block. How the committee is selected not elaborated in the paper. In [3], a custom blockchain is described as part of the proposed solution. However, there is no elaboration on how consensus is reached.

In [13], a single ordering service is used for consensus despite the claimed goal of ensuring data immutability and trustworthiness. The experimental validation was also carried using a single computer.

In [23], only high level ideas about a custom consortium blockchain are provided. In particular, smart contracts would play a big role in spectrum management.

5   Maturity Levels of Blockchain-Based Solutions

In this section, we report our findings for the third research question. Considering the very early stages of the proposed solutions, we propose the following five-level scale: (1) L1: conceptual without detailed design; (2) L2: design only; (3) L3: partial validation with simulation; (4) L4: partial validation with experimentation; (4) L5: thorough validation with theoretical proof and experimentation, as shown in Fig. 2.

At the L1 level, only high level discussions are presented regarding the potential benefits. At the L2 level, the design of the proposed solution is described, not necessarily complete. At the L3 level, a portion of the proposed solution is demonstrated using simulation. At the L4 level, the proposed solution is implemented and validated using at least one computer. At the L5 level, the proposed solution is thoroughly validated with both theoretical proof of correctness and

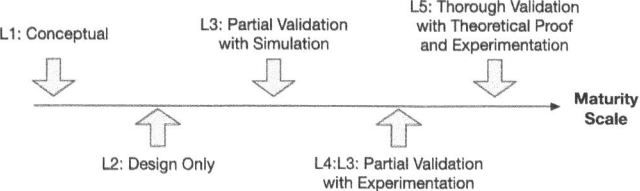

Fig. 2. The proposed five-level maturity scale.

experimentation. The maturity levels of the proposed blockchain solutions for SAGIN are illustrated in Fig. 3. The individual rating is provided in Table 1. The studies are ranked at the L1 level [4, 22]. Four studies are ranked at the L2 level [15–17, 23]. Ten studies are ranked at the L3 level, which means that these studies repented some forms of simulation results [3, 5, 9–12, 18, 19, 24, 27]. Only two studies are ranked at the L4 level, with some form of actual experimentation using a computer [8, 13].

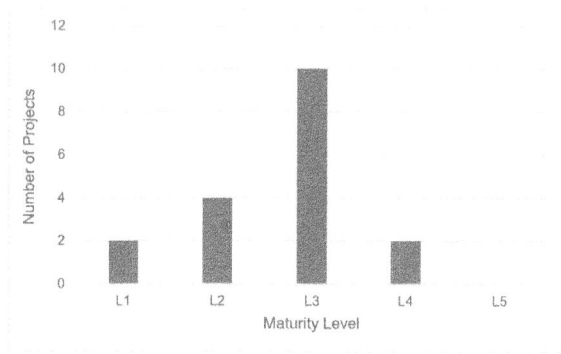

Fig. 3. The distribution of maturity levels among the proposed blockchain solutions.

6 Discussions

As we have elaborated in the previous section, there exists apparent misconceptions regarding the blockchain technology. The most obvious is equating blockchain to data immutability, decentralization, and trust. As we have pointed out in previous publications [31, 40], such well-known properties can only be achieved in large public blockchains such as Bitcoin and Ethereum. For an open decentralized system to protect itself for data immutability, the only way is to enact a high barrier to modify existing data maintained by the system, which requires a sound consensus algorithm and a large scale of the system. In principle, the consensus must incur a substantial cost each each competing node and the number of competing nodes must be sufficiently large [31,38,40]. Although it might not be obvious, data immutability also hinges on decentralization. Without decentralization, such as a private or a consortium blockchain, the owner or owners of the blockchain could impose arbitrary changes to the blockchain, which include the change of existing data. Unfortunately, in the context of this review, all proposed solutions with a specific design choose to use a private or a consortium blockchain.

It is worth noting traditional distributed consensus algorithms such as PBFT assume a predefined known membership, which preclude their use in a decentralized system [28,30]. PBFT is one of the most favorite consensus algorithms for private or consortium blockchains, citing its good performance. Unfortunately, the cited good performance is achievable only during fault-free and synchronous environments.

Yet another misconception about blockchain is that to use blockchain, one would have to set up nodes to participate in the consensus process. The misconception is perhaps due to the publicity of a key innovation in the blockchain technology, *i.e.,* decentralized consensus. First, the blockchain technology does not require a regular user to participate in the consensus process. In fact, there are two types of participants in a blockchain system: (1) regular users who do not participate in the consensus process; (2) miners (*i.e.,* stake holders of the system) must make substantial investment in order to have the capability of participating in the consensus process. Regular would use the services provided by the system by paying a transaction fee. Miners would support the operation of the system and help secure the system by participating in the consensus process. Miners are incentivized by collecting block rewards and transaction fees. The regular users are essentially the customers of the blockchain system. The miners are stake holders of the system. This is an incredibly smart design that is conducive for the open decentralized systems to be usable and to grow. As such, we do not see any need for any components in SAGIN to directly participate in the consensus process.

A related issue that we have noticed is the attempt to directly use consensus in the blockchain for the operation of SAGIN. While there is nothing wrong for the desire of using a consensus service for SAGIN operation, it should not be the primary reason for using the blockchain technology as we know. According to the design of the blockchain technology, consensus is used to ensure a single copy of the system state (*i.e.,* the blockchain) and to enact a barrier for changing the system state (which is know as data immutability), and consensus is not exposed to regular users. On the other hand, Hyperledger offers the possibility of constructing custom systems that integrate application logic with a custom consensus algorithm. As such, custom solutions for SAGIN can be developed where consensus is used for the operation of SAGIN. Although Hperledger-based systems are often referred to as a private or consortium blockchain, the term "blockchain" is really a misnomer because such a system is neither a decentralization system nor does it offer any data immutability or trust at the level of Bitcoin.

Considering the pervasive misunderstanding and misconception about the blockchain technology, it is useful to provide a guideline on when to use a public blockchain, and when to use a private or consortium blockchain based on the application needs.

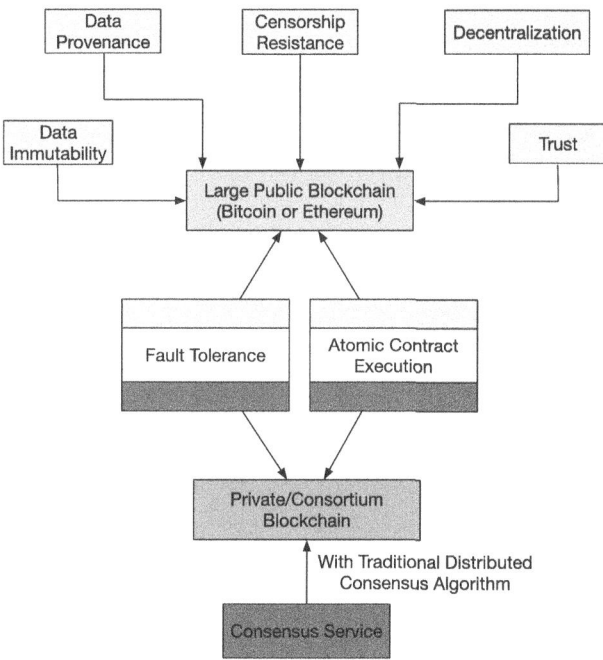

Fig. 4. A guideline on when to use public and private/consortium blockchain based on the need of the application.

If the application needs any of the following features: data immutability, data provenance, censorship resistance, decentralization, and trust, then a large public blockchain such as Bitcoin or Ethereum should be used. On the other hand, if the application requires a consensus service for its operations, then a private or consortium with a traditional distributed consensus algorithm such as PBFT (note that both the normal operation protocol and the view change protocol must be implemented) should be used. If the application requires fault tolerance or atomic contract execution, then either public blockchain or private/consortium blockchain may be used. We note that it is not a good idea to rely on a public blockchain for reaching consensus because of the probabilistic nature in decentralized consensus algorithms.

7   Conclusion

In this paper, we provided a comprehensive review on the use of blockchain in space-air-ground integrated networks. Our study is guided by several research questions. First, we identified the objectives of the blockchain-based solutions for space-air-ground integrated networks. Second, we investigated how the blockchain technology is used to achieve the objectives. Third, we evaluated the maturity level of the proposed blockchain-based solution. Our findings show that blockchain has been used to help manage dynamic spectrum dynamically, to help perform crowd-sensing, to facilitate traffic offloading, to enhance trustworthiness of the network, to facilitate computation offloading, to enable authentication of various SAGIN-connected entities, to improve the security of air traffic management, to facilitate data sharing, to enhance data security, and to enable geofencing for unmanned air vehicles. All studies proposed some form of custom blockchain instead of using an existing public blockchain such as Bitcoin and Ethereum to achieve their intended objectives for SAGIN. Except a couple of studies, in which Hyperledger was used as the basis for customization, none of the studies validated the proposed solution experimentally. Furthermore, most studies chose to use a traditional distributed consensus algorithm, namely, PBFT, or its variations, as the consensus algorithm for the proposed blockchain solution. The proposed solutions are apparently in the very early stages of development, if any. In addition to the research questions, we highlighted the issues that we have identified during the review. We pointed out pervasive misconceptions and misunderstandings regarding the blockchain technology.

References

1. Aldyaflah, I.M., Zhao, W., Upadhyay, H., Lagos, L.: The design and implementation of a secure datastore based on Ethereum smart contract. Appl. Sci. **13**(9), 5282 (2023)
2. Castro, M., Liskov, B.: Practical byzantine fault tolerance and proactive recovery. ACM TOCS **20**(4), 398–461 (2002)
3. Chen, M., Tan, C., Zhu, X., Zhang, X.: A blockchain-based authentication and service provision scheme for internet of things. In: 2020 IEEE Globecom Workshops (GC Wkshps), pp. 1–6. IEEE (2020)
4. Dasu, T., Kanza, Y., Srivastava, D.: Geofences in the sky: herding drones with blockchains and 5G. In: Proceedings of the 26th ACM SIGSPATIAL International Conference on Advances in Geographic Information Systems, pp. 73–76 (2018)
5. Du, J., Lv, J., Lu, G.: Economical revenue maximization in mobile edge caching and blockchain enabled space-air-ground integrated networks. J. Cloud Comput. **12**(1), 98 (2023)
6. Fischer, M.J., Lynch, N.A., Paterson, M.S.: Impossibility of distributed consensus with one faulty process. JACM **32**(2), 374–382 (1985)
7. Guo, F., Yu, F.R., Zhang, H., Li, X., Ji, H., Leung, V.C.: Enabling massive IoT toward 6G: a comprehensive survey. IEEE Internet Things J. **8**(15), 11891–11915 (2021)
8. Li, B., Liang, R., Zhou, W., Yin, H., Gao, H., Cai, K.: LBS meets blockchain: an efficient method with security preserving trust in SAGIN. IEEE Internet Things J. **9**(8), 5932–5942 (2021)
9. Li, D., Guo, Q., Yang, C., Yan, H., et al.: Trusted data sharing mechanism based on blockchain and federated learning in space-air-ground integrated networks. Wirel. Commun. Mobile Comput. **2022**, 5338876 (2022)

10. Li, W., Su, Z., Li, R., Zhang, K., Wang, Y.: Blockchain-based data security for artificial intelligence applications in 6G networks. IEEE Netw. **34**(6), 31–37 (2020)
11. Li, Z., Wang, W., Guo, J., Zhu, Y., Han, L., Wu, Q.: Blockchain-empowered dynamic spectrum management for space-air-ground integrated network. Chin. J. Electron. **31**(3), 456–466 (2022)
12. Liao, H., et al.: Blockchain and semi-distributed learning-based secure and low-latency computation offloading in space-air-ground-integrated power IoT. IEEE J. Sel. Top. Sig. Process. **16**(3), 381–394 (2021)
13. Liu, D., Wu, H., Huang, C., Ni, J., Shen, X.: Blockchain-based credential management for anonymous authentication in SAGVN. IEEE J. Sel. Areas Commun. **40**(10), 3104–3116 (2022)
14. Liu, J., Shi, Y., Fadlullah, Z.M., Kato, N.: Space-air-ground integrated network: a survey. IEEE Commun. Surv. Tutorials **20**(4), 2714–2741 (2018)
15. Lu, X., Dong, R., Wang, Q., Zhang, L.: Information security architecture design for cyber-physical integration system of air traffic management. Electronics **12**(7), 1665 (2023)
16. Lu, X., Wu, Z.: ATMCC: design of the integration architecture of cloud computing and blockchain for air traffic management. In: 2021 IEEE International Conference on Parallel & Distributed Processing with Applications, Big Data & Cloud Computing, Sustainable Computing & Communications, Social Computing & Networking (ISPA/BDCloud/SocialCom/SustainCom), pp. 37–43. IEEE (2021)
17. Lu, X., Wu, Z., Wu, Y., Wang, Q., Yin, Y.: ATMChain: Blockchain-based solution to security problems in air traffic management. In: 2021 IEEE/AIAA 40th Digital Avionics Systems Conference (DASC), pp. 1–8. IEEE (2021)
18. Lu, X., Wu, Z., et al.: ATMChain: Blockchain-based security framework for cyber-physics system in air traffic management. Secur. Commun. Netw. **2022** (2022)
19. Luo, G., Shi, M., Zhao, C., Shi, Z.: Hash-chain-based cross-regional safety authentication for space-air-ground integrated VANETs. Appl. Sci. **10**(12), 4206 (2020)
20. Nakamoto, S.: Bitcoin: a peer-to-peer electronic cash system (2008). https://bitcoin.org/bitcoin.pdf
21. Nguyen, D.C., et al.: 6G internet of things: a comprehensive survey. IEEE Internet Things J. **9**(1), 359–383 (2021)
22. Pang, Y., Wang, D., Wang, D., Guan, L., Zhang, C., Zhang, M.: A space-air-ground integrated network assisted maritime communication network based on mobile edge computing. In: 2020 IEEE World Congress on Services, pp. 269–274. IEEE (2020)
23. Sun, Z., Liang, W., Qi, F., Dong, Z., Cai, Y.: Blockchain-based dynamic spectrum sharing for 6G UIoT networks. IEEE Netw. **35**(5), 143–149 (2021)
24. Tang, F., Wen, C., Luo, L., Zhao, M., Kato, N.: Blockchain-based trusted traffic offloading in space-air-ground integrated networks (SAGIN): a federated reinforcement learning approach. IEEE J. Sel. Areas Commun. **40**(12), 3501–3516 (2022)
25. Wang, Y., Su, Z., Ni, J., Zhang, N., Shen, X.: Blockchain-empowered space-air-ground integrated networks: opportunities, challenges, and solutions. IEEE Commun. Surv. Tutorials **24**(1), 160–209 (2021)
26. Wood, G., et al.: Ethereum: a secure decentralised generalised transaction ledger. Ethereum Proj. Yellow Pap. **151**(2014), 1–32 (2014)
27. Zhao, R., Yang, L.T., Liu, D., Deng, X., Mo, Y.: A tensor-based truthful incentive mechanism for blockchain-enabled space-air-ground integrated vehicular crowdsensing. IEEE Trans. Intell. Transp. Syst. **23**(3), 2853–2862 (2022)
28. Zhao, W.: Optimistic byzantine fault tolerance. Int. J. Parallel Emergent Distrib. Syst. **31**(3), 254–267 (2016)

29. Zhao, W.: Performance optimization for state machine replication based on application semantics: a review. J. Syst. Softw. **112**, 96–109 (2016)
30. Zhao, W.: From Traditional Fault Tolerance to Blockchain. Wiley, Hoboken, NJ, USA (2021)
31. Zhao, W.: On Blockchain: design principle, building blocks, core innovations, and misconceptions. IEEE Syst. Man Cybern. Mag. **8**(4), 6–14 (2022)
32. Zhao, W.: On Nxt proof of stake algorithm: a simulation study. IEEE Trans. Dependable Secure Comput. **20**(4), 3546–3557 (2022)
33. Zhao, W., Aldyaflah, I.M., Gangwani, P., Joshi, S., Upadhyay, H., Lagos, L.: A blockchain-facilitated secure sensing data processing and logging system. IEEE Access **11**, 21712–21728 (2023)
34. Zhao, W., Aldyaflah, I.M., Zheng, Z., Luo, X.: A Blockchain-based academic degree attestation system. Int. J. Parallel Emergent Distrib. Syst., 1–15 (2024)
35. Zhao, W., Jiang, C., Gao, H., Yang, S., Luo, X.: Blockchain-enabled cyber-physical systems: a review. IEEE Internet Things J. **8**(6), 4023–4034 (2020)
36. Zhao, W., Qi, Q., Zhou, J., Luo, X.: Blockchain-based applications for smart grids: an umbrella review. Energies **16**(17), 6147 (2023)
37. Zhao, W., Qi, Q., Zhou, J., Luo, X.: Industry-led blockchain projects for smart grids: an in-depth inspection. In: 2023 IEEE Symposium Series on Computational Intelligence (SSCI), pp. 240–245. IEEE (2023)
38. Zhao, W., Yang, S., Luo, X.: On consensus in public blockchains. In: Proceedings of the 2019 International Conference on Blockchain Technology, pp. 1–5. ACM, Honolulu, Hawaii, USA (2019)
39. Zhao, W., Yang, S., Luo, X., Zhou, J.: On Peercoin proof of stake for blockchain consensus. In: 2021 The 3rd International Conference on Blockchain Technology, pp. 129–134 (2021)
40. Zhao, W., Yang, S., Luo, X., Zhou, J.: Dos and don'ts in Blockchain research and development. In: Proceedings of the 4th International Conference on Blockchain Technology, pp. 37–43 (2022)

Empowering HEIs Through LLMs and Cloud Computing: Strategies for Seamless Integration and Sustainable Transformation

Mohamed Diab Idris[1]([✉]) [iD], Xiaohua Feng[1], and Vladimir Dyo[2] [iD]

[1] School of Computer Science and Technology, University of Bedfordshire, University Square, Luton 1 3JU, UK
mohamed.idris@study.beds.ac.uk, xiaohua.feng@beds.ac.uk
[2] Department of Electronic Engineering, Royal Holloway, University of London, Egham TW20 0EX, UK
vladimir.dyo@rhul.ac.uk

Abstract. Large Language Models (LLMs) have demonstrated significant potential to revolutionize higher education, prompting a need for strategic guidance on leveraging their benefits while addressing associated challenges [1]. This paper reaches into the critical role of cloud computing in enabling the smooth integration and sustainable transformation of Higher Education Institutions (HEIs) through LLMs. By examining the mutually beneficial relationship between LLMs and cloud technologies, this paper highlights how the cloud empowers HEIs to utilize the full potential of LLMs, overcoming challenges related to scalability, accessibility, and cost-effectiveness. The paper presents a comprehensive framework for the strategic integration of LLMs and cloud computing within HEIs, addressing key considerations such as data privacy, security, interoperability, and ethical governance. Through a systematic review of case studies and best practices, the paper offers actionable insights and recommendations for HEIs to navigate the complexities of LLM deployment in the cloud era. The findings emphasize the importance of a holistic, collaborative approach that engages diverse stakeholders, prioritizes data management, and aligns with the core values of higher education. By incorporating the merging of LLMs and cloud computing, HEIs can unlock new limits in personalized learning, research innovation, and societal impact, ultimately redefining the landscape of higher education in the Artificial Intelligence (AI)-driven era.

Keywords: Large language models · higher education institutions · cloud · Integration · LLMs · HEIs

1 Introduction

The previously published paper in the IEEE Access journal by the1st author has confirmed that Large Language Models (LLMs) have significant potential for transforming Higher Education Institutions (HEIs) across various domains. These include teaching

© ICST Institute for Computer Sciences, Social Informatics and Telecommunications Engineering 2026
Published by Springer Nature Switzerland AG 2026. All Rights Reserved
X. Feng et al. (Eds.): CloudComp 2024, LNICST 617, pp. 57–73, 2026.
https://doi.org/10.1007/978-3-031-92517-7_7

and learning, as well as research and innovation [1]. However, the successful integration and sustained impact of LLMs in HEIs depends upon another critical technology: cloud computing. The cloud serves as the backbone for the deployment, scaling, and accessibility of LLMs, enabling HEIs to utilize their power in a cost-effective, flexible, and secure manner [2]. The integration of LLMs and cloud computing represents a transformative shift in how HEIs approach the development and delivery of educational services. The cloud provides the computational infrastructure and tools necessary to train, fine-tune, and deploy LLMs at scale, allowing HEIs to leverage these advanced LLMs technologies without the worry of substantial upfront investments in hardware and maintenance [3]. Moreover, the cloud enables seamless collaboration and data sharing among researchers, educators, and students across institutional boundaries, promoting an energetic environment of innovation and knowledge exchange [4]. However, the integration of LLMs and cloud computing within HEIs is not without challenges. Issues related to data privacy, security, interoperability, and ethical governance must be carefully navigated to ensure the responsible and sustainable adoption of these technologies [5]. HEIs must also address the complex relationship between the technical affordances of LLMs and the academic, social, and cultural dimensions of education, ensuring that the deployment of these tools aligns with the main values and missions of higher education [6].

The research presented herein aims to bridges the gap between LLMs' transformative potential and their practical cloud-era implementation in Higher Education Institutions (HEIs). By proposing a comprehensive framework for integrating LLMs and cloud computing, it offers evidence-based recommendations for HEIs to navigate complexities and leverage opportunities. Drawing from case studies and best practices, the study provides a roadmap prioritizing data management, ethical governance, and stakeholder engagement. Unlike technology-focused approaches, the proposed framework addresses multifaceted challenges including governance, ethics, infrastructure, skills development, pedagogy, and research innovation. This holistic strategy equips HEIs with a comprehensive plan to leverage these technologies for educational transformation.

This paper is structured as follows: Sect. 2 provides background research, including a taxonomy of LLMs' impacts on HEIs (Fig. 1). Section 3 discusses the symbiotic relationship between LLMs and Cloud Computing. Section 4 outlines a framework for strategic integration of LLMs and Cloud Computing in HEIs (Fig. 2). Section 5 presents case studies and best practices, while Sect. 6 compares cloud-based and stand-alone solutions. Section 7 analyses case studies and solution comparisons. Section 8 offers a framework analysis of LLMs and Cloud in HEIs. Finally, Sect. 9 concludes the paper and suggests future directions.

2 Background

Large Language Models (LLMs) like GPT-4 and Gemini are increasingly impacting Higher Education Institutions (HEIs), offering potential benefits in teaching and learning while also presenting significant challenges. Current research often focuses on specific applications rather than broader implications across diverse educational settings. To address this gap, a comprehensive analysis of LLMs' impact on HEIs is required, examining ten critical areas: HEIs as knowledge gatekeepers, credential providers, research centres, innovation incubators, social change drivers, and employers; as well as academic integrity, the future of higher education, intellectual property, and public perception. Understanding these impacts can inform strategies for effective and responsible LLM adoption in HEIs, guiding policy and practice. Key findings indicate that LLMs have transformative potential in personalized learning, research innovation, and knowledge democratization. However, challenges include verifying LLM-generated content accuracy, developing ethical use guidelines, and preventing biases. To address these issues, HEIs must adopt proactive approaches, including clear policies, faculty training, and interdisciplinary research on long-term implications.

Practical implications for HEIs are multifaceted and require a strategic approach. Primarily, HEIs need to develop comprehensive institutional strategies for the responsible integration of LLMs. This involves creating clear guidelines for LLM use in various academic contexts, from teaching and research to administrative functions. Establishing robust oversight mechanisms is crucial to ensure compliance with these guidelines and to monitor the impact of LLMs on educational outcomes and institutional integrity.

Policymakers have a vital role to play in shaping the landscape of LLM use in education. Their focus should be on creating overarching frameworks that govern the ethical deployment of LLMs across the education sector. This includes developing regulations that protect student privacy, ensure equitable access to LLM technologies, and maintain academic standards. Investing in research is another critical area for policymakers, as it can help uncover both the potential and pitfalls of LLM integration in educational settings.

Collaboration between policymakers, HEIs, and industry partners is essential for establishing best practices in LLM use. This collaborative approach can lead to the development of standards that balance innovation with ethical considerations. By fostering open dialogue and shared learning, stakeholders can create a more robust and adaptable framework for LLM integration.

Addressing these aspects comprehensively enables HEIs and policymakers to maximize LLMs' benefits while mitigating potential risks in higher education. This balanced approach ensures that LLM integration enhances the quality and integrity of higher education, preparing students for an AI-driven future [1]. The strategy fosters an educational environment that leverages Artificial Intelligence (AI) technologies to improve learning outcomes and institutional efficiency, while maintaining ethical standards and academic rigor.

3   LLMs and Cloud Computing: A Symbiotic Alliance

The successful deployment and impact of Large Language Models (LLMs) within Higher Education Institutions (HEIs) is deeply connected with the capabilities and affordances of cloud computing. The cloud provides the foundational infrastructure and services necessary to unleash the full potential of LLMs, enabling HEIs to overcome challenges related to scalability, accessibility, and cost-effectiveness [7]. Figure 2 shows details Framework for Strategic Integration of LLMs and Cloud Computing in HEIs.

Fig. 1. The taxonomy of impacts (Positive and Negative) of LLMs within HEIs [1]

3.1   Scalability and Elasticity

One of the key advantages of cloud computing is its ability to provide scalable and elastic resources for the deployment of LLMs. The training and fine-tuning of these models require vast amounts of computational power and storage capacity, which can be expensive and complex for HEIs to setup and maintain on-premises [2]. Cloud platforms offer a flexible and on-demand infrastructure that can seamlessly scale up or down based on the needs of LLM workloads, allowing HEIs to efficiently allocate resources and avoid over-provisioning [8].

3.2   Accessibility and Collaboration

Cloud computing enables the democratization of access to LLMs by providing a centralized and universal platform for hosting and sharing these models. Educators, researchers, and students can access LLMs from anywhere, at any time, using a variety of devices and interfaces, breaking down barriers to collaboration and knowledge exchange [9]. The cloud also facilitates the creation of shared repositories and marketplaces for LLMs, enabling HEIs to discover, adapt, and contribute to a growing ecosystem of Artificial Intelligence (AI)-powered educational resources [10].

3.3   Cost-Effectiveness and Optimization

The adoption of cloud computing for LLM deployment allows HEIs to significantly reduce the total cost of ownership associated with AI infrastructure. By taking advantages of the economies of scale and the pay-as-you-go pricing models offered by cloud providers, HEIs can avoid the substantial upfront investments in hardware, software, and maintenance required for on-premises solutions [11]. Moreover, cloud platforms provide a range of optimization tools and services, such as auto-scaling, spot instances, and serverless computing, that enable HEIs to fine-tune their resource utilization and minimize waste [12].

3.4   Agility and Innovation

The cloud provides a rich ground for experimentation and innovation in the development and application of LLMs in higher education. The rapid provisioning, flexible configuration, and easy integration capabilities of cloud services allow HEIs to quickly prototype, test, and deploy new LLM-powered solutions, accelerating the pace of pedagogical and research breakthroughs [13]. The cloud also enables HEIs to tap into an extensive ecosystem of AI services, frameworks, and pre-trained models, lowering the barriers to entry and promoting a culture of innovation [14].

4   Strategic Framework: Integrating LLMs and Cloud in HEIs

Maximizing the revolutionary capabilities of Large Language Models (LLMs) and cloud computing in higher education requires a holistic and methodical approach. This section introduces a comprehensive strategic framework designed to navigate the complex landscape of challenges and opportunities inherent in their integration. The proposed framework is built on six critical pillars: ethical governance, data stewardship, technological infrastructure and compatibility, talent cultivation and workforce readiness, innovative pedagogy and instructional design, and advancement in research and creative inquiry. By addressing these interconnected dimensions, Higher Education Institutions (HEIs) can create a robust foundation for the responsible and effective adoption of LLMs and cloud technologies, promoting an environment of innovation, efficiency, and academic excellence.

4.1 Governance and Ethics

The integration of LLMs and cloud computing in HEIs must be guided by a robust governance framework that ensures the responsible and ethical use of these technologies. This involves establishing clear policies, guidelines, and oversight mechanisms that address issues such as data privacy, security, fairness, transparency, and accountability [15]. HEIs should also promote a culture of ethical awareness and engage diverse stakeholders, including students, faculty, staff, and external partners, in the development and implementation of LLM and cloud strategies [16].

4.2 Data Management

Effective data management is critical for the successful deployment of LLMs in the cloud. HEIs must develop comprehensive data governance policies and practices that cover the entire lifecycle of data, from acquisition and storage to processing and sharing [17]. This includes implementing secure and compliant data infrastructures, establishing data quality and interoperability standards, and ensuring the privacy and confidentiality of sensitive information, such as student records and research data [18].

4.3 Infrastructure and Interoperability

The strategic integration of LLMs and cloud computing requires a flexible and interoperable infrastructure that can seamlessly connect diverse systems, platforms, and services. HEIs should adopt open standards and architectures that enable the easy integration and portability of LLM workloads across different cloud environments, avoiding vendor lock-in and ensuring long-term sustainability [19]. Moreover, HEIs should invest in robust network and security infrastructures that can support the high-bandwidth and low-latency requirements of LLM applications [20].

4.4 Skills and Workforce Development

The successful adoption of LLMs and cloud computing in HEIs relies upon the availability of a skilled and adaptive workforce. HEIs must invest in the continuous professional development of faculty, staff, and students, equipping them with the technical, pedagogical, and ethical competencies necessary to effectively leverage these technologies [21]. This involves integrating LLM and cloud skills into curricula, providing hands-on training and certification programs, and promoting a culture of lifelong learning and upskilling [22].

4.5 Pedagogy and Learning Design

The integration of LLMs and cloud computing within HEIs presents new opportunities and challenges for pedagogy and learning design. Educators must rethink traditional approaches to teaching and learning, leveraging the capabilities of LLMs to create personalized, interactive, and adaptive learning experiences [23]. This involves designing new pedagogical models and frameworks that blend human and machine intelligence, promoting active and collaborative learning, and empowering students to take ownership of their learning journeys [24].

4.6 Research and Innovation

The convergence of LLMs and cloud computing opens new frontiers for research and innovation in higher education. HEIs should establish interdisciplinary research centres and programs that bring together experts from diverse fields, such as computer science, linguistics, education, and social sciences, to explore the frontiers of LLM and cloud technologies [25]. Moreover, HEIs should promote collaborations with industry partners, government agencies, and community organizations to co-create innovative solutions that address real-world challenges and drive societal impact [26].

5 Case Studies and Best Practices

To illustrate the practical application of the strategic integration framework, this section presents a selection of case studies and best practices from Higher Education Institutions (HEIs) that have successfully leveraged Large Language Models (LLMs) and cloud computing to transform their operations and enhance their impact.

5.1 Carnegie Mellon University: OpenSimon Toolkit

Carnegie Mellon University's OpenSimon Toolkit is a prime example of how HEIs can utilize the power of LLMs and cloud computing to create open and accessible educational resources. The toolkit provides a suite of Artificial Intelligence (AI)-powered tools and services, including intelligent tutoring systems, chatbots, and adaptive learning platforms, that can be easily integrated into various educational contexts [27]. By leveraging cloud infrastructure and Application Programming Interfaces (APIs), the OpenSimon Toolkit enables educators and researchers to rapidly develop and deploy LLM-powered applications, promoting energetic ecosystem of innovation and collaboration [28].

5.2 Georgia Institute of Technology: Jill Watson

The Georgia Institute of Technology's Jill Watson project demonstrates how LLMs, and cloud computing can be used to create intelligent teaching assistants that enhance the learning experience. Jill Watson is an AI-powered chatbot that uses natural language processing and machine learning to answer student questions and provide personalized feedback in online courses [29]. By leveraging cloud services for text analysis and speech recognition, Jill Watson can engage in human-like conversations and adapt to the diverse needs of students, freeing up instructors to focus on higher-level tasks [30].

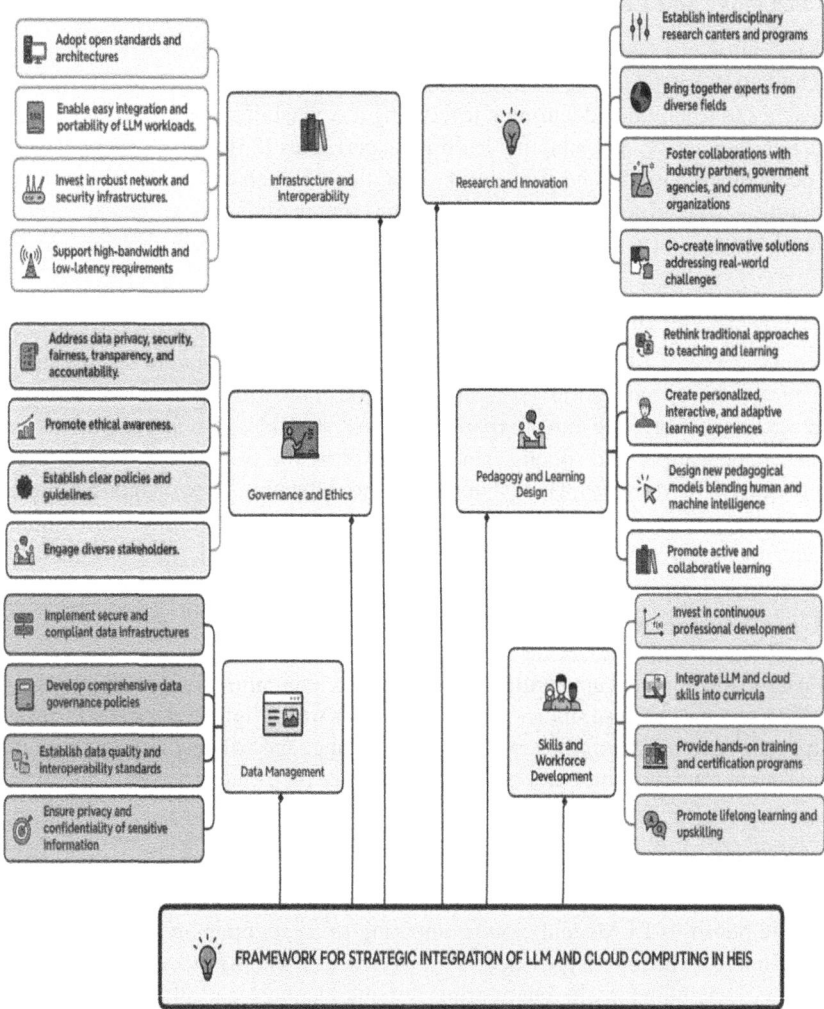

Fig. 2. A Framework for Strategic Integration of LLMs and Cloud Computing in HEIs

5.3 University of Michigan: CROMA

The University of Michigan's CROMA (Coursera Research and Analysis) project show-cases how LLMs, and cloud computing can be used to gain insights into student learning patterns and optimize course design. CROMA uses natural language processing and machine learning algorithms to analyse massive datasets of student interactions and performance on the Coursera platform, identifying key factors that influence learning outcomes [31]. By leveraging cloud-based data analytics and visualization tools, CROMA enables researchers and educators to make data-driven decisions and continuously improve the quality and effectiveness of online education [32].

6   Comparison of Cloud-Based and Stand-Alone Solutions

As Higher Education Institutions (HEIs) contemplate the integration of Large Language Models (LLMs), a critical evaluation of cloud-based versus traditional stand-alone implementations becomes essential. This comparative analysis serves as a cornerstone for HEIs in formulating well-informed, strategic decisions regarding their LLM deployment approaches. By examining the distinct characteristics, advantages, and potential drawbacks of each implementation method, HEIs can align their choices with their specific needs, resources, and long-term technological vision. This thoughtful consideration ensures that the adopted LLM solution not only meets current educational demands but also positions the institution for future technological advancements and pedagogical innovations. Below is a comparison on seven aspects:

1. Scalability and Flexibility: Cloud-based solutions offer superior scalability, allowing HEIs to easily adjust resources based on demand. Stand-alone solutions have fixed capacity and require significant planning and investment to scale [33].
2. Cost Structure: Cloud solutions typically follow a pay-as-you-go model, which can be more cost-effective for irregular or growing usage. Stand-alone solutions involve high upfront costs but may be more economical for consistent, high-volume workloads over time [34].
3. Maintenance and Updates: Cloud providers handle most maintenance and updates, reducing the burden on IT staff. Stand-alone solutions require in-house expertise and resources for maintenance, updates, and troubleshooting.
4. Accessibility and Collaboration: Cloud-based LLMs can be accessed from anywhere with an internet connection, facilitating remote work and collaboration. Stand-alone solutions are typically limited to on-premises access, which can hinder remote collaboration and accessibility [35].
5. Security and Data Control: Stand-alone solutions offer complete control over data and security measures but require significant expertise to implement properly. Cloud solutions provide robust security features but involve sharing some control with the provider [36].
6. Performance and Latency: Stand-alone solutions can offer lower latency for on-premises users, which can be crucial for certain real-time applications. Cloud solutions may introduce some latency but often provide higher overall performance due to advanced infrastructure [37].
7. Reliability and Redundancy: Cloud providers typically offer high reliability and built-in redundancy across multiple data centres. Stand-alone solutions require careful planning and additional investment to achieve similar levels of reliability and redundancy [37].

7   Analysis of Case Studies and Solution Comparison

7.1   Insights from Higher Education LLM Implementations

The examination of three prominent case studies—Carnegie Mellon University's Open-Simon Toolkit, Georgia Institute of Technology's Jill Watson, and the University of Michigan's CROMA—reveals valuable insights into the practical implementation of

Large Language Models (LLMs) in Higher Education Institutions (HEIs). These implementations share common technological foundations, primarily leveraging cloud computing, Natural Language Processing (NLP), and Machine Learning (ML) to deliver innovative educational solutions. A key trend observed across these case studies is the emphasis on personalization. The OpenSimon Toolkit provides adaptive learning platforms, Jill Watson offers personalized feedback to students, and CROMA enables data-driven customization of online courses. This focus on personalization demonstrates the potential of LLMs to address individual student needs at scale, a long-standing challenge in education.

Another significant commonality is the drive towards efficiency. By automating routine tasks such as answering common student queries (Jill Watson) or analysing large datasets (CROMA), these LLM implementations free up valuable time for instructors and researchers. This efficiency gain allows educators to focus on higher-value activities such as complex problem-solving and personalized mentoring. The role of cloud computing emerges as a crucial enabler in all three cases. Cloud infrastructure provides the necessary scalability to handle large numbers of users and process vast amounts of data. It also facilitates real-time interactions and updates, critical for responsive educational tools. Moreover, the cloud's inherent accessibility promotes collaboration and allows these tools to reach a wider audience, breaking down geographical barriers in education [29–31].

7.2 Cloud vs. On-Premises LLMs: A Comparison

When considering the implementation of LLMs in HEIs, institutions face a critical decision between cloud-based and stand-alone solutions. Our analysis reveals that cloud-based solutions generally offer significant advantages, particularly in areas crucial for the effective deployment of LLMs in educational settings. Scalability emerges as a primary advantage of cloud-based solutions. The ability to easily adjust resources based on demand is particularly valuable in educational contexts, where usage can fluctuate dramatically based on academic calendars or specific events. This scalability ensures that LLM-powered educational tools can handle peak loads without significant upfront investment. Cost flexibility is another area where cloud-based solutions excel. The pay-as-you-go model aligns well with the often unpredictable or cyclical nature of educational resource usage. This can be particularly beneficial for HEIs with limited budgets or those looking to experiment with LLM implementations without committing to large capital expenditures.

In terms of maintenance and updates, cloud-based solutions offer clear advantages. With providers handling most maintenance tasks, HEIs can focus their IT resources on value-added activities rather than routine upkeep. This is particularly important given the rapid pace of advancement in LLM technologies, where frequent updates may be necessary to maintain state-of-the-art performance. However, stand-alone solutions maintain an edge in data control and security. For HEIs dealing with sensitive student data or protective research, the ability to maintain complete control over data and security measures can be crucial. Stand-alone solutions also offer potential advantages in terms of latency for on-premises users, which could be important for certain real-time applications [38].

To provide a quantitative comparison of cloud-based and stand-alone solutions, Table 1 shows a scoring system based on key factors relevant to LLM implementation in HEIs. The scoring is on a 1–5 scale.

Table 1. Comparison of Cloud-Based and Stand-Alone Solutions performance (5 represents the best performance)

No	Factor	Cloud-Based	Stand-Alone
1	Scalability	5	2
2	Cost Flexibility	4	2
3	Maintenance Ease	5	2
4	Accessibility	5	2
5	Data Control	3	5
6	Security	4	5
7	Collaboration	5	2
	Total Score	**31**	**20**

This comparison illustrates the overall advantage of cloud-based solutions in most areas, particularly in scalability, cost flexibility, maintenance ease, and accessibility. However, stand-alone solutions maintain an edge in data control, which can be crucial for certain institutions.

Figure 3 visually represent this comparison, in a radar chart (spider chart), it illustrates the relative strengths of cloud-based and stand-alone solutions across these key factors.

The chart emphasizes that cloud-based solutions generally score higher across most factors, forming a larger overall shape. However, it also clearly shows the spike in the stand-alone solution's score for the Data Control factor, highlighting this key advantage. The choice between cloud-based and stand-alone solutions ultimately depends on the specific needs and constraints of each institution. Cloud-based solutions offer superior scalability, cost flexibility, and ease of maintenance, making them an attractive option for many HEIs, especially those looking to rapidly deploy and scale LLM applications. These advantages align well with the dynamic nature of educational environments and the fast-paced evolution of LLM technologies. On the other hand, stand-alone solutions provide greater control over data and potentially lower latency for on-premises applications. This makes them a viable option for institutions with strict data governance requirements or specific performance needs that are best met by on-premises infrastructure.

In conclusion, while cloud-based solutions offer significant advantages for LLM implementations in HEIs, the optimal choice depends on each institution's specific circumstances. Factors such as scalability, budget, data sensitivity, and long-term strategy should be carefully considered. By evaluating these factors against each approach's strengths and weaknesses, HEIs can make informed decisions that best support their educational missions and strategic goals in the era of Artificial Intelligence (AI)-enhanced education.

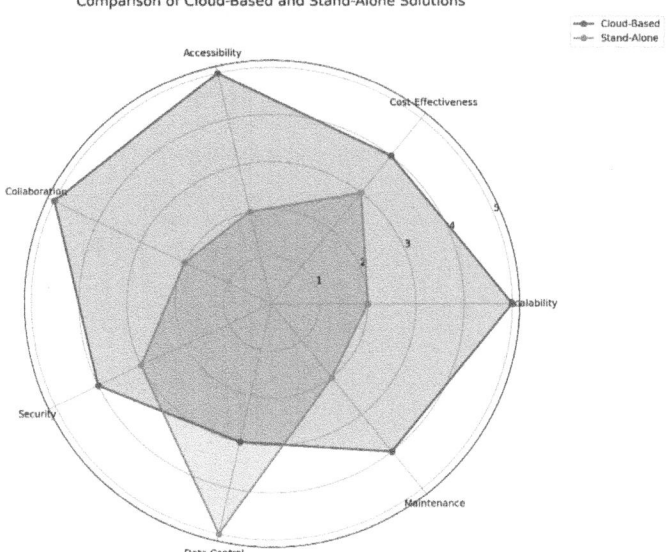

Fig. 3. Radar Chart Comparison of Cloud-Based and Stand-Alone Solutions

7.3 Decision Framework for HEIs

Based on this analysis, below is a proposed decision framework for HEIs considering LLM implementations:

1. Assessment of the current resource, HEIs should evaluate their existing IT infrastructure, expertise, and budget. Those with limited IT resources may find cloud-based solutions more manageable.
2. Analysis of the usage patten: Institutions should analyse their expected usage patterns. Those with highly variable demand or plans for rapid scaling may benefit more from cloud-based solutions.
3. Evaluation of data sensitivity: HEIs must carefully consider their data security requirements. Those with highly sensitive data or strict regulatory requirements may lean towards stand-alone solutions.
4. Performance Requirements: Institutions should assess their performance needs, particularly in terms of latency. Applications requiring the lowest possible latency may be better served by on-premises, stand-alone solutions.
5. Long-term Strategy Alignment: The choice should align with the institution's long-term technology strategy, considering factors such as future scalability needs and potential for inter-institutional collaboration.

In conclusion, while cloud-based solutions offer significant advantages for most LLM implementations in HEIs, the optimal choice depends on each institution's specific circumstances and requirements [39].

8   Framework Analysis: LLMs and Cloud in HEIs

The strategic framework for integrating Large Language Models (LLMs) and cloud computing in Higher Education Institutions (HEIs) consists of six key pillars, as outlined in Sect. 4 and Fig. 2 of the paper: Governance and Ethics, Data Management, Infrastructure and Interoperability, Skills and Workforce Development, Pedagogy and Learning Design, and Research and Innovation.

These pillars address various aspects of implementation, from establishing clear policies and guidelines to fostering innovative research collaborations. They emphasize the importance of data governance, open standards, continuous professional development, adaptive learning experiences, and interdisciplinary research.

To analyse this framework, we conducted several assessments, including Pillar Importance Analysis, Interdependency Matrix, Implementation Difficulty Assessment, Stakeholder Impact Analysis, Time Horizon Classification, and Resource Allocation Suggestion. Table 2 shows pillars importance using a scale of 1–10 (10 being most important) and implementation difficulty using a scale of 1–5 (5 being most difficult to implement).

Table 2. Pillar Importance and Implementation Difficulty

Pillar Name	Importance (1–10)	Implementation Difficulty (1–5)
Governance and Ethics (G&E)	9	4
Data Management (DM)	8	4
Infrastructure and Interoperability (I&I)	7	3
Skills and Workforce Development (SWD)	9	5
Pedagogy and Learning Design (PLD)	10	5
Research and Innovation (R&)	8	4

This analysis suggests that Pedagogy and Learning Design, along with Governance and Ethics and Skills and Workforce Development, may require the most focus and resources. It also indicates that Skills and Workforce Development and Pedagogy and Learning Design are the most challenging to implement.

The Interdependency Matrix Table 3 shows interconnections among the pillars:0 = no dependency,1 = weak dependency and 2 = strong dependency.

This matrix shows strong interdependencies, particularly between Data Management and other pillars, and Research & Innovation with all other pillars.

The stakeholder impact analysis and time horizon are shown in Table 4 below.

This analysis shows that all stakeholders are significantly impacted, with students and faculty most affected by the pedagogical and skill development aspects. The time horizon classification suggests a phased approach, with infrastructure changes happening

Table 3. Interdependency Matrix

	G&E	DM	I&I	SWD	PLD	R&I
G&E	0	2	1	1	1	1
DM	2	0	2	1	1	2
I&I	1	2	0	1	2	2
SWD	1	1	1	0	2	2
PLD	1	1	2	2	0	2
R&I	1	2	2	2	2	0

Table 4. Stakeholder Impact and Time Horizon

Pillar	Students	Faculty	Admin	Time Horizon
G&E	Medim	High	High	Medium-Term
DM	Medim	Medim	High	Medium-Term
I&I	Low	Medim	High	Short-Term
SWD	High	High	Medim	Long-Term
PLD	High	High	Medim	Long-Term
R&I	High	High	Medim	Medium-Term

first, followed by governance and data management, and finally the long-term goals of skills development and pedagogical changes.

Based on these analyses, a suggested resource allocation could prioritize Skills and Workforce Development (25%), Governance and Ethics (20%), Pedagogy and Learning Design (20%), Data Management (15%), with Infrastructure and Interoperability and Research and Innovation each receiving 10%.

These analyses provide a comprehensive view of the strategic framework, highlighting the complexities and interdependencies involved in integrating LLMs and cloud computing in HEIs. They suggest that while all pillars are important, particular attention should be paid to developing skills, redesigning pedagogy, and ensuring strong governance and ethical frameworks. The high level of interdependency also emphasizes the need for a holistic, well-coordinated approach to implementation.

9   Conclusions and Future Directions

The integration of Large Language Models (LLMs) and cloud computing represents a significant transformative shift in how Higher Education Institutions (HEIs) approach the development and delivery of educational services. By employing the scalability, accessibility, and cost-effectiveness of the cloud, HEIs can unleash the transformative potential of LLMs, enabling personalized learning, research innovation, and societal impact at an unprecedented scale. However, the successful adoption of LLMs and cloud computing in HEIs requires a strategic and holistic approach that addresses the multifaceted challenges and opportunities associated with their integration. The framework presented in this paper provides a roadmap for HEIs to navigate the complexities of governance and ethics, data management, infrastructure and interoperability, skills and workforce development, pedagogy and learning design, and research and innovation.

As HEIs embark on this transformative journey, it is crucial to engage diverse stakeholders, prioritize data stewardship, and align the deployment of LLMs and cloud computing with the core values and missions of higher education. By promoting a culture of collaboration, experimentation, and continuous learning, HEIs can position themselves at the forefront of the digital transformation of education, shaping the future of learning and discovery in the age of Artificial Intelligence (AI).

The research presented in this paper contributes to the field by proposing a novel, comprehensive framework that bridges the gap between theoretical potential and practical implementation of LLMs and cloud computing in higher education. By addressing both technological and organizational aspects, this study offers new insights into the sustainable and ethical integration of these technologies in HEIs.

Future research in this field should focus on several key areas. Developing new pedagogical models that leverage LLMs to create immersive and personalized learning experiences is crucial. Exploring the potential of these technologies to support lifelong learning and workforce development will be vital in bridging the gap between formal education and professional practice. Investigating the social, cultural, and ethical implications of LLM and cloud adoption in higher education will ensure these technologies promote equity and inclusion. Additionally, there is a pressing need to collect more comprehensive data on the implementation and impact of LLMs and cloud computing in various HEI contexts. This data collection should encompass a wider range of institutions, disciplines, and geographical regions to provide a more nuanced understanding of the challenges and opportunities presented by these technologies. Such data will be invaluable in refining the strategic framework and developing more targeted, effective integration strategies. Finally, promoting interdisciplinary collaborations to create innovative solutions addressing real-world challenges will be essential in driving societal impact.

References

1. Idris, M.D., Feng, X., Dyo, V.: Revolutionizing higher education: unleashing the potential of large language models for strategic transformation. IEEE Access **12**, 67738–67757 (2024). https://doi.org/10.1109/ACCESS.2024.3400164
2. Narayanan, D., et al.: Efficient large-scale language model training on GPU clusters using Megatron-LM. In: Proceedings of the International Conference for High Performance Computing, Networking, Storage and Analysis (SC), pp. 1–15 (2021)
3. Abadi, M., et al.: TensorFlow: a system for large-scale machine learning. In: Proceedings of the 12th USENIX Symposium on Operating Systems Design and Implementation (OSDI '16), pp. 265–283. USENIX Association (2016)
4. Wang, L., Li, M., Zhang, Y., Ristenpart, T., Swift, M.: Peeking behind the curtains of serverless platforms. In: Proceedings of the 2018 USENIX Annual Technical Conference (USENIX ATC '18), pp. 133–146. USENIX Association (2018)

5. Bender, E.M., Gebru, T., McMillan-Major, A., Mitchell, S.: On the dangers of stochastic parrots: can language models be too big? In: Proceedings of the 2021 ACM Conference on Fairness, Accountability, and Transparency (FAccT '21), pp. 610–623. ACM, New York (2021). https://doi.org/10.1145/3442188.3445922

6. Torrey, L., Shavlik, J.: Transfer learning. In: Handbook of Research on Machine Learning Applications and Trends: Algorithms, Methods, and Techniques, pp. 242–264. IGI Global, Hershey (2010)

7. Yi, S., Hao, Z., Qin, Z., Li, Q.: Fog computing: platform and applications. In: 2015 Third IEEE Workshop on Hot Topics in Web Systems and Technologies (HotWeb), pp. 73–78. IEEE, Piscataway (2015)

8. Dean, J., Ghemawat, S.: MapReduce: simplified data processing on large clusters. Commun. ACM **51**(1), 107–113 (2008). https://doi.org/10.1145/1327452.1327492

9. Baldassarre, M.T., Caivano, D., Dimauro, G., Gentile, E., Visaggio, G.: Cloud computing for education: a systematic mapping study. IEEE Trans. Educ. **61**(3), 234–244 (2018). https://doi.org/10.1109/TE.2018.2796558

10. Radford, A., Narasimhan, K., Salimans, T., Sutskever, I.: Language models are unsupervised multitask learners. OpenAI Blog (2019). https://cdn.openai.com/better-language-models/lan guage_models_are_unsupervised_multitask_learners.pdf. Accessed 20 Aug 2024

11. Breck, E., Cai, J., Chandler, J., Sculley, D.: The ML test score: a rubric for ML production readiness and technical debt reduction. In: 2017 IEEE International Conference on Big Data (Big Data), pp. 1123–1132. IEEE, Piscataway (2017)

12. Ben-Nun, T., Hoefler, T.: Demystifying parallel and distributed deep learning: an in-depth concurrency analysis. ACM Comput. Surv. **52**(4), 1–43 (2019)

13. Dean, J., Corrado, G., Monga, R., Pardoe, D., Tung, D.: Large scale distributed deep networks. In: Advances in Neural Information Processing Systems (NeurIPS), pp. 1223–1231 (2012)

14. Ribeiro, M., Wu, T., Guestrin, C., Singh, S.: Beyond accuracy: Behavioral testing of NLP models with CheckList. In: Proceedings of the 58th Annual Meeting of the Association for Computational Linguistics (ACL 2020), pp. 4902–4912. Association for Computational Linguistics, Stroudsburg (2020)

15. Floridi, L., Cowls, J., Beltrametti, M., Chatila, R., Dupont, Y., Oksanen, J.: AI4People—an ethical framework for a good AI society: opportunities, risks, principles, and recommendations. Mind. Mach. **28**(4), 689–707 (2018)

16. Jobin, A., Ienca, M., Vayena, E.: The global landscape of AI ethics guidelines. Nat. Mach. Intell. **1**(9), 389–399 (2019). https://doi.org/10.1038/s42256-019-0088-2

17. Puthal, D., Sahoo, B.P.S., Mishra, S., Swain, S.: Cloud computing features, issues, and challenges: a big picture. In: Proceedings of the 2015 International Conference on Computational Intelligence and Networks (CINE), pp. 116–123. IEEE, Piscataway (2015). https://doi.org/10.1109/CINE.2015.31

18. Saltz, J., Shamshurin, I.: Exploring the process of doing data science via an ethnographic study of a media advertising company. In: 2016 IEEE International Conference on Big Data (Big Data), pp. 2098–2105. IEEE, Piscataway (2016)

19. Jacksi, K., Abass, S.M.: Development history of the World Wide Web. Int. J. Sci. Technol. Res. **8**(9), 75–79 (2019)

20. Chandramouli, R., Iorga, M., Chokhani, S.: Cryptographic key management issues & challenges in cloud services. In: Jajodia, S., Kant, K., Samarati, P., Singhal, A., Swarup, V., Wang, C. (eds.) Secure Cloud Computing, pp. 1–30. Springer, New York (2014). https://doi.org/10.1007/978-1-4614-9278-8_1

21. Bughin, J., Chui, M., Manyika, J., Woetzel, J., Batra, P., Aharon, D.: Skill shift: Automation and the future of the workforce. McKinsey Global Institute, New York (2018). https://www.mckinsey.com/featured-insights/future-of-work/skill-shift-automation-and-the-future-of-the-workforce. Accessed 20 Aug 2024

22. Stergiou, C., Psannis, K.E., Gupta, B.B., Ishibashi, Y.: Security, privacy & efficiency of sustainable cloud computing for big data & IoT. Sustain. Comput. Inform. Syst. **19**, 174–184 (2018). https://doi.org/10.1016/j.suscom.2018.06.003

23. Qiu, J., Liu, X., Li, J., Han, J.: A survey of machine learning for big data processing. EURASIP J. Adv. Sign. Process. **2016**(1), 1–16 (2016)

24. Zhai, Y., Ong, Y., Tsang, I.: The emerging "big dimensionality." IEEE Comput. Intell. Mag. **9**(3), 14–26 (2014)

25. Kshetri, N.: Big data's impact on privacy, security and consumer welfare. Telecommun. Policy **38**(11), 1134–1145 (2014)

26. Agrawal, A., Gans, J., Goldfarb, A.: Prediction machines: the simple economics of artificial intelligence. Harv. Bus. Rev. **96**(3), 58–59 (2018)

27. Topol, E.: High-performance medicine: the convergence of human and artificial intelligence. Nat. Med. **25**(1), 44–56 (2019). https://doi.org/10.1038/s41591-018-0300-7

28. Ilomäki, L., Paavola, S., Lakkala, M., Kantosalo, A.: Digital competence—an emergent boundary concept for policy and educational research. Educ. Inf. Technol. **21**(3), 655–679 (2016)

29. Goel, A., Polepeddi, L.: Jill Watson: a virtual teaching assistant for online education. Georgia Institute of Technology (2016). https://smartech.gatech.edu/handle/1853/59104. Accessed 20 Aug 2024

30. Deterding, S., et al.: Mixed-initiative creative interfaces. In: Proceedings of the 2017 CHI Conference Extended Abstracts on Human Factors in Computing Systems, pp. 628–635. ACM, New York (2017). https://doi.org/10.1145/3027063.3027072

31. Siemens, G., Baker, R.S.J.D.: Learning analytics and educational data mining: towards communication and collaboration. In: Proceedings of the 2nd International Conference on Learning Analytics and Knowledge (LAK 2012), pp. 252–254. ACM, New York (2012)

32. Ruipérez-Valiente, J.A., Muñoz-Merino, P.J., Kloos, C.D.: Detecting and clustering students by their gamification behavior with badges: a case study in engineering education. Int. J. Eng. Educ. **33**(2-B), 816–830 (2017)

33. Fox, A., et al.: Above the clouds: A Berkeley view of cloud computing. University of California, Berkeley, Tech. Rep. UCB/EECS-2009-28 (2009). https://www2.eecs.berkeley.edu/Pubs/TechRpts/2009/EECS-2009-28.html. Accessed 20 Aug 2024

34. Marston, S., Li, Z., Bandyopadhyay, S., Zhang, J., Ghalsasi, A.: Cloud computing—the business perspective. Decis. Support Syst. **51**(1), 176–189 (2011)

35. Botta, A., de Donato, W., Persico, V., Pescapé, A.: Integration of cloud computing and Internet of Things: a survey. Futur. Gener. Comput. Syst. **56**, 684–700 (2016). https://doi.org/10.1016/j.future.2015.09.021

36. Subashini, S., Kavitha, V.: A survey on security issues in service delivery models of cloud computing. J. Netw. Comput. Appl. **34**(1), 1–11 (2011). https://doi.org/10.1016/j.jnca.2010.07.006

37. Armbrust, M., Fox, A., Griffith, R., et al.: A view of cloud computing. Commun. ACM **53**(4), 50–58 (2010). https://doi.org/10.1145/1721654.1721670

38. Sultan, N.: Cloud computing for education: a new dawn? Int. J. Inf. Manage. **30**(2), 109–116 (2010)

39. Pardeshi, V.H.: Cloud computing for higher education institutes: architecture, strategy and recommendations for effective adaptation. Procedia Econ. Finan. **11**, 589–599 (2014)

Identifying the 'Gaps' Where Cloud Computing Can Help Computer Laws in Curbing Cyber Bullying and Cyber Stalking in India

Ameema Miftha[✉], Marc Conrad, and Marcia Gibson

Institute for Research in Applicable Computing, The University of Bedfordshire, University
Square, Luton, Bedfordshire, UK
ameema19@gmail.com

Abstract. This paper tries to identify cloud computing as an aid to the existing computer law on cyber stalking and cyber bullying in India. The computer laws are there in the country for over two decades, but they still fail to truly identify the tort and its remedial measure. A secondary study is therefore being conducted, as evidential support, to the applicability of cloud computing in computer laws on cyber stalking and cyber bullying. The findings go on to support the claim that the interconnectedness, inoperability and ubiquity of cloud can create various opportunities to nab Cyberstalker and also remove the ambiguity out of the law.

Keywords: Cybercrime · Computer laws · Cyberstalking · Cyberbullying · Cloud · Computing

1 Introduction

This research study uses a doctrinal (non-empirical), descriptive, and definitive methodology to assess the role of cloud computing in limiting the effect of cyber bullying and cyber stalking in India. Secondary sources are the sources consulted for this paper. The Bare Acts, articles, news reports, and e-sources are the main types of the sources, The assessment includes excerpts from the Indian Penal Code of 1860 and the Information Technology Act of 2000. The researcher has attempted to clarify a few portions of the Indian Penal Code and the Information Technology Act that are related to this offense, and an explanation of the relationship between the provisions and the crime has been provided.

2 Defining the Terms

Before delving deeper into the subject, a quick overview of some basic terms that will be used often is provided, such as "cyberspace". Cyber space is a phrase refers to the setting in which online conversation occurs (Hashmi 2023). On the other hand, Cyberbullying and cyber-harassment are often used interchangeably. Cyberbullying is included in the

© ICST Institute for Computer Sciences, Social Informatics and Telecommunications Engineering 2026
Published by Springer Nature Switzerland AG 2026. All Rights Reserved
X. Feng et al. (Eds.): CloudComp 2024, LNICST 617, pp. 74–82, 2026.
https://doi.org/10.1007/978-3-031-92517-7_2

more general concept of online harassment. Any harassment that takes place online, on a mobile phone, or on another device is referred to as cyberbullying (Errakot & Rahoof 2023). Technology-enabled aggressive behavior, such texting and making offensive comments online, is utilized to cause harm to other people. Bullies publicly harass individuals on social media. To make matters worse, it is widely visible and creates a digital trail, which negatively impacts the victim's mental health (Education 2021). Social media has evolved to the point that anyone can harass someone else by posting hurtful messages or remarks. The absence of just laws has made cyberbullying victims more susceptible and allowed bullies to persist in their abusive behaviour (Table 1).

Table 1. Tabular: Representation of 'legal remedies' to cybercrimes in India (Freelaw 2023).

Indian Penal Code	Information Technology Act	Indian Penal Code
Section 292	Section 43(a-h)	Section 419,420
Section 354C	Section 65	Section 465,
Section 354D	Section 66(a-f)	Section 468,469
Section 379	Section 67(a-b)	Section 500,504
Section 411		Section 506,509

3   Bringing Cloud Computing and Cyber-Bullying Together on the Same Platform

Cloud computing has all the potential to play a crucial role in preventing cyberbullying in India by offering scalable and efficient solutions to monitor, detect, and mitigate online harassment.

Technology	How this curbs cyber-bullying?
Real-Time Monitoring and Detection	Automated Monitoring Tools: Cloud platforms enable the deployment of automated tools that monitor online interactions in real-time, detecting harmful content, such as hate speech or abusive language, using machine learning algorithms (Chaitra K.M 2019)
	AI-Powered Content Filtering: Advanced AI models hosted on the cloud can analyse vast amounts of data from social media platforms, forums, and messaging apps to identify potential cases of cyberbullying
	Sentiment Analysis: Cloud-based sentiment analysis tools can assess the tone of conversations and flag negative or aggressive behaviour, allowing for early intervention (Errakot & Rahoof 2023)

(continued)

(continued)

Technology	How this curbs cyber-bullying?
Data Collection and Analysis	Big Data Analytics: Cloud computing supports big data analytics, which can be used to analyse patterns and trends in cyberbullying cases. This helps in understanding the prevalence and impact of cyberbullying across different demographics (Education 2021) Anonymized Reporting: Cloud-based systems can collect and store data on reported cyberbullying incidents while ensuring user privacy through anonymization techniques (Gawade 2021)
Collaboration and Reporting	Integrated Reporting Systems: Cloud platforms can facilitate the creation of integrated systems where victims or witnesses can report cyberbullying incidents easily. These reports can be automatically directed to the relevant authorities or support services (Arora 2020) Cross-Platform Collaboration: Cloud-based services enable collaboration between different social media platforms, educational institutions, and law enforcement agencies, ensuring a coordinated approach to tackling cyberbullying (Shivashankar B. 2018)
Educational Resources and Support	-Learning Platforms: Cloud computing supports the development of e-learning platforms that can offer resources, training, and awareness programs on cyberbullying prevention for students, teachers, and parents (Errakot & Rahoof 2023) 24/7 Support Services: Cloud-hosted chatbots and support systems can provide round-the-clock assistance to victims of cyberbullying, offering guidance, counselling, and resources (Thakur 2016)
Scalability and Accessibility	Scalable Solutions: Cloud computing allows for the deployment of scalable solutions that can handle the growing number of online users in India, ensuring that anti-cyberbullying measures are accessible to all (Errakot & Rahoof 2023) Accessibility Across Regions: Cloud services can be accessed from any location, making
Legal and Ethical Compliance	cyberbullying prevention tools available to users across urban and rural areas in India (Freelaw 2023) Data Protection and Privacy: Cloud providers often have robust data protection policies in place, ensuring that the personal information of users, especially minors, is securely handled Compliance with Regulations: Cloud computing platforms can help organizations and schools in India comply with national and international regulations on data privacy and cyberbullying prevention (Kashmira 2014)

One might therefore argue that cloud computing offers powerful tools to combat cyberbullying in India by enabling real-time monitoring, facilitating data-driven analysis, supporting collaborative efforts, and providing accessible resources. These cloud-based solutions are essential in creating a safer online environment for all users, particularly vulnerable groups such as children and teenagers.

4   Identifying the 'GAPS'

4.1   Cloud Computing and Cyber Bullying: Analysing the 'Turf'

Combining cloud computing with efforts to prevent cyberbullying in India presents several practical challenges and problems:

In India, the deployment of cloud computing across various platforms often involves complex hybrid and multi-cloud environments. Managing these systems can be challenging due to a lack of standardization and the difficulty of integrating different cloud platforms (Chaitra K.M 2019). This complexity can hinder the seamless operation of anti-cyberbullying tools and services across different cloud environments, leading to inefficiencies and potential gaps in service.

While cloud computing offers scalable resources, it also introduces significant security challenges, particularly concerning data protection and compliance with regulations like the IT Act, 2000, and emerging data localization laws. Ensuring that sensitive information related to cyberbullying incidents is stored and processed securely in the cloud is critical, yet difficult, especially when using public cloud services that may not fully comply with local regulations (Gawade 2021).

Cyberbullying prevention often involves the use of multiple applications and platforms, which need to be interoperable across different cloud services. However, cloud providers may use proprietary technologies, leading to vendor lock-in and making it difficult to integrate and manage these applications effectively across different platforms (Khachatryan 2022). This lack of interoperability can impede the responsiveness and flexibility of cyberbullying prevention strategies.

The effectiveness of cloud-based cyberbullying prevention tools is heavily dependent on a stable and fast internet connection. In many parts of India, especially rural areas, internet connectivity remains unreliable (Khachatryan 2022). This can significantly affect the deployment and accessibility of cloud-based solutions, limiting their reach and effectiveness in preventing cyberbullying across the country.

There is a notable skills gap in India regarding cloud computing. Many IT professionals lack the necessary expertise to effectively implement and manage cloud-based solutions, including those aimed at combating cyberbullying (Narnolia 2024). This lack of knowledge can lead to poor deployment, underutilization of cloud resources, and ultimately, ineffective cyberbullying prevention.

Addressing these challenges requires a multi-faceted approach, including improving internet infrastructure, enhancing cloud security measures, fostering better interoperability among cloud services, and investing in the training and upskilling of IT professionals.

4.2   Cloud and the 'Inconsistencies' of the Law

There are no specific laws that address the problem of cyberstalking for guys (Keswani 2017). One can witness this with just 500+ cases being booked against women offenders against 25000+ male offenders, despite the fact that the victim ratio is reaching 50:50 in India (Basuroy 2023).

The Indian Penal Code's Section 354D contains numerous flaws, including the fact that it solely recognizes "women" as victims while ignoring the possibility of male victims as well. According to this section, it is illegal to attempt to track how a woman uses the internet, email, or any other kind of electronic communication. This practice is known as cyberstalking. It is evident that it solely concentrates on women. It is legislation that is prejudiced against women. Second, the "method of monitoring" has not been brought up by the legislators. It is possible that even though someone does not intend to stalk, their behaviours still qualify as such (UNODC 2024) (Fig. 1).

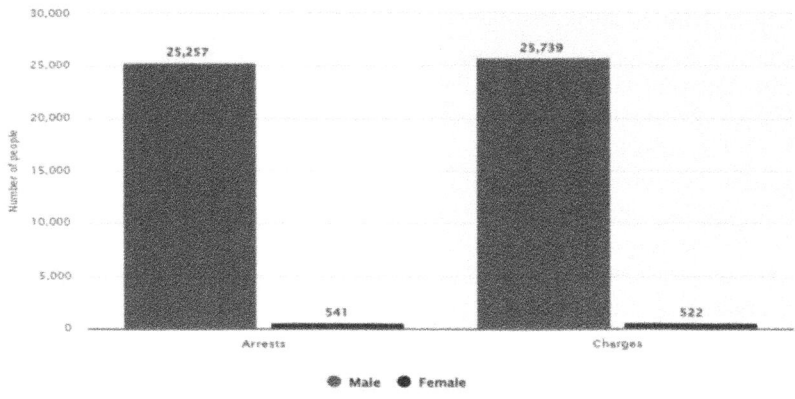

Fig. 1. Gender Discrimination in India (Basuroy 2023)

Considering Sections 507, 292 and 509, it can be argued that they have numerous flaws. Among these are the following: it is a gender-biased clause that exclusively emphasizes a woman's modesty, ignoring the reality that this crime of cyberstalking is gender neutral, men can also become victims of these crimes (Arora 2020). The law mentions that it is necessary to speak, hear, or see the words, sound, or gesture in this section. Because words cannot be spoken, gestures cannot be seen, and sounds cannot be heard over the internet, Cyberstalker can thus easily avoid the punishment outlined in this section. Finally, it is not possible to infer from online discussions that the woman's modesty is being insulted (Narnolia 2024).

Secure Access Control and Compliance:

In such a scenario, cloud computing platforms offer vast repositories of data, analytical software and compliance frameworks to 'decode' data in explanatory terms to ensure regulatory compliance (Gawade 2021). Law enforcement agencies can implement 'clarity' while making FIRs (first information registered), evaluate digital evidence, prevent ambiguity, and maintain chain of custody throughout the investigation process (Hasan 2023). Cloud providers also adhere to industry standards and regulations, such as GDPR and HIPAA, to ensure data protection and privacy.

4.3   Inadequate Enforcement Mechanisms

Even if cyberbullying and cyberstalking cases are reported, the enforcement mechanisms under current computer laws may be insufficient to address these offenses. Law enforcement agencies lack specialized training, resources, or expertise to investigate and prosecute such cases effectively.

The majority of the time, authorities have been unable to obtain, maintain, produce, or prove electronic evidence. The police almost never register cybercrimes, even when they are reported, because they are unsure if they will be able to solve the case. When it comes to crimes that are committed physically, the police feel more at ease with the old laws. The capacity of law enforcement organizations is not being increased. Therefore, the most of these instances end in an acquittal.

The anonymity of the stalker is one of the characteristics of cyberstalking. It has been suggested that there be limitations on maintaining the anonymity of the identity. However, it seemed like this was a contentious issue because virtually all national laws guarantee the right to free speech, and limiting one's ability to remain anonymous would be against that right. The court concluded in the cases of *Sahara India Real Estate Corp. Ltd.* v. *Securities & Exchange Board of India* and In *Ramlila Maidan Incident* v. *Home Secretary* that the freedom of speech and expression guaranteed by Article 19(1)(a) is not an unqualified right (ETCISE 2023).

Also, the Indian Constitution's Article 14 guarantees "equality before the law." Although it is evident from the Constitution that equality is guaranteed, reading the legislative requirements reveals that there is also significant gender disparity (ETCISE 2023). Since women are viewed as the weaker member of society, the regulations are geared more toward their protection. But given the current circumstances, such gender imbalance is untenable. Law enforcement finds it rather confusing while doing the investigation.

Improved Data Management and Storage:

When it is about strong enforcement, cloud computing offers scalable and secure data storage solutions, allowing law enforcement agencies to efficiently manage and store vast amounts of digital evidence related to cyber stalking and cyberbullying cases (Chaitra K.M 2019). By centralizing data storage on cloud platforms, investigators can access and analyse evidence more effectively, facilitating swift and thorough investigations.

4.4   Jurisdictional Challenges

The borderless nature of the internet presents jurisdictional challenges when it comes to prosecuting cyberbullying and cyberstalking cases, especially if the perpetrator and victim are located in different jurisdictions. This can further complicate legal proceedings and hinder the delivery of justice.

Neither the Information Technology Amendment Act of 2008 nor the Information Technology Act of 2000 adequately addressed the primary issue of territorial jurisdiction (Education 2021). The Cybercrimes are crimes done using computers as a tool. For example, it can be challenging to identify the P.S. of an individual who hacks into the email account of someone who is located in a different state or nation. Due to jurisdictional issues, many police personnel attempt to avoid acknowledging the victim's allegations in these situations. Since cybercrimes have no territorial boundaries, it is necessary to resolve the jurisdictional question and identify all pertinent factors to take into account in these kinds of circumstances.

The primary issue is when national laws clash with those of another nation. It could happen that stalker behaviour is illegal in one nation but not in another. be considered illegal in a different nation (Kashmiria 2014). The term "jurisdictional issue" describes this. In these situations, the issue of enforcement also comes up. Cooperation between the two nations is required in such a scenario. This is the point at which extradition laws are relevant.

Real-time Collaboration and Information Sharing:

To meet out jurisdictional challenges, cloud-based collaboration platforms enable realtime communication and information sharing among law enforcement agencies, government organizations, victim support groups, and other stakeholders involved in combating cyber stalking and cyberbullying (Chaitra K.M 2019). By leveraging cloudbased communication tools, investigators can coordinate efforts, share intelligence, and collaborate on cases more efficiently, leading to quicker response times and better outcomes for victims (Khachatryan 2022).

4.5 Limited Awareness and Support

There may be limited awareness among the general public, law enforcement agencies, and legal professionals about the prevalence and impact of cyberbullying and cyberstalking. Additionally, victims of these offenses may face challenges in accessing support services and legal recourse due to social stigma or fear of retaliation.

The common perception that cyberstalking is less harmful than physical stalking could arise from the fact that it doesn't require direct physical interaction (Shivashankar & Rajan 2018). This isn't always the case. As the Internet grows, the stalkers can profit from the convenience of contact and the easier access to personal information in both personal and professional life. While a potential stalker might not feel comfortable approaching a victim face-to-face or over the phone, he or she might not think twice about sending threatening or harassing emails to the victim. Similar to physical stalking, cyberbullying and intimidation can serve as a precursor to more severe actions, such as assaults.

Clearly, cybercrimes and online abuse have not received the priority they deserve in India. These crimes are seen as relatively small due to the mindset. According to data, India has generally been unable to secure the necessary convictions for cybercrimes, and the quantity of these offenses is increasing, according to cyberlaw specialist and attorney for the Supreme Court Pavan Duggal (Arora 2020).

Several criminologists have recommended that the best way to combat cyberstalking is not to use laws to prove guilt and finally impose penalties for physical stalking, but rather to establish a new system of protection against Cyberstalker that takes into account the two fundamental components of crime—actus reus and mens rea—and addresses issues with jurisdiction, evidence collection, and crime identification (Thakur 2016).

5 Conclusion

Indian laws can punish customary offenses in the physical world and are skilfully crafted. A few laws designed to penalize cybercrimes are well-crafted to ensure justice is served. One intriguing feature of the internet is that it is expanding and changing in contrast to actual space. For the same reason, it is yet unclear exactly how crimes will manifest themselves; cyberbullying is one such instance. It can occur in a variety of ways and be tested under various sections of current legislation but doing so will influence how cyber laws in India develop. Since cybercrime offenses differ in their mode, effects, gravity, and likely targets, distinct laws must be defined for each. In such a complex scenario, cloud computing can help overcome loopholes in computer laws related to cyber stalking and cyberbullying by providing advanced technology solutions, enhancing collaboration, ensuring data security and compliance, and offering cost-effective alternatives for law enforcement agencies to investigate and address online harassment incidents more effectively.

References

1. Arora, S.: Cyberbullying laws in India. Int. J. Law Manage. Human. **3**(6), 351 (2020)
2. Basuroy, T.: Number of arrests and charges for cyber-crimes across India 2022, by gender (2023). https://www.statista.com/statistics/1118320/india-per sonsarrestedand-charged-for-cyber-crimes-by-gender/#:~:text=Premium%20statist ics,Number%20of%20arrests%20and%20charges%20for,across%20India%202022% 2C%20by%20gender&text=In%202022%2C%20over%2025%20tho
3. Bhattacharjee, G.: Issues and challenges of cyber crime in india: an ethical perspective. IJCRT **9**(9), ISSN: 2320-2882 (2021)
4. Chaitra K.M, Tiwari, S.: Authentication mechanisms for preventing cybersecurity and providing safety in cloud. Int. J. Innov. Technol. Explor. Eng. (2019)
5. Economic times. Problem of cybercrime troubling everyone, policing system needs to be reformed: HC (2024). https://economictimes.indiatimes.com/news/india/problem-ofcybercr ime-troubling-everyone-policing-system-needs-to-be-reformedhc/articleshow/106901065. cms?from=mdr
6. Education, J.O.: Issues and challenges to control cyber crimes in India. J. Adv. Scholar. Res. Allied Educ. (2021)
7. Errakot, S., Rahoof, V.: Cyber bullying: the need for separate provision in India. GLS Law J. **05**(01) (2023)
8. ETCISE. Countering cybercrime in India: experts share challenges and approaches (2023). https://ciso.economictimes.indiatimes.com/news/ot-security/countering-cybercrime-inindia-experts-share-challenges-and-approaches/103059611
9. Freelaw. Punishments for Cyber Crime Under Indian Constitution (2023). https://www.fre elaw.in/legalarticles/Punishments-for-Cyber-Crime-Under-IndianConstitution
10. Gawade, R.: Cloud computing and cyber crimes. Anveshana's Int. J. Res. Region. Stud. Law Soc. Sci. (2021)
11. Halder, D., Jaishankar, K.: Cyber gender harassment and secondary victimization: a comparative analysis of the United States, the UK, and India. Victims Offend. **6**, 386–398 (2011)
12. Hasan, M.Z.: Impact of cybercrime on enterprises in cloud computing environment: a review. In: 2023 IEEE International Conference on Emerging Trends in Engineering, Sciences and Technology (ICES&T) At: India (2023)

13. Hashmi, A.: The rise of cybercrime in India: reasons, impacts, and safety measures (2023). https://www.linkedin.com/pulse/rise-cybercrime-india-reasons-impactssafetymeasures-adil-hashmi/
14. Iqbal, J., Beigh, M.: Cybercrime in India: trends and challenges. In: International Conference on Advancements and Innovations in Engineering, Technology& Management ICAIETM-2017At: Joginpally B.R. Engineering College, Hyderabad, India (2017)
15. Joseph, V., Jain, M.: India: anti-cyber bullying laws in India - an analysis (2020). https://www.mondaq.com/india/crime/989624/anti-cyber-bullying-laws-in-india---ananalysis
16. Kashmiria, S.: Mapping cyber crimes against women in India. Int. Res. J. Commerce Law **1**(5) (2014)
17. Keswani, H.: Cyber stalking: a critical study. Bharati Law Review (2017)
18. Khachatryan, G.: Analysis of cybercrime investigation problems in the cloud environment. IJCSNS **22**(7) (2022)
19. Kshetri, N.: Cybercrime and cybersecurity in India: causes, consequences and implications for the future". Crime Law Soc. Chang. **66**(3), 313–338 (2016)
20. Narnolia, N.: Cyber Crime in India: an overview (2024). https://www.legalserviceindia.com/legal/article-4998-cybercrime-in-india-an-overview.html
21. NCRB. National Crime Research Bureau (NCRB) Report (2015)
22. Harassment/Cyberstalking Statistics. Shivashankar, B., Rajan, A.: A critical analysis of cyber bullying in India-with. Int. J. Pure Appl. Math. **119**(17), 18111822 (2018)
23. Thakur, A.: Cyberstalking: a crime or a tort (2016)
24. UNODC. India: Promoting internet safety amongst 'netizens' (2024). https://www.unodc.org/southasia/frontpage/2012/May/india_-addressingthe-rise-of-cybercrime-amongst-children.html

SecureCloud: A Cross-Platform Encrypted File Sharing Solution with Forensic Imaging Capability

Arunpaul Muthupandian^(✉), Mahmoud Artemi, Xiahua Feng, and Marc Conrad

School of Computer Science and Technology, University of Bedfordshire, Luton, UK
arunpaul.muthupandian@study.beds.ac.uk, {Mahmoud.artemi,
xiaohua.feng,marc.conrad}@beds.ac.uk

Abstract. In this age of AI dominating the digital panorama, the way we deal with, and procedure records has grown to be a sensitive circumstance. As individuals' percentage sensitive non-public information and files over the net, a veil of uncertainty shrouds the adventure of those files, leaving us brooding about how inclined the device is to ability misused with the aid of malicious actors. This uncertainty extends to the protection of facts saved on our devices and how securely online provider companies manipulate our documents. Amid these issues, enterprise giants like Apple and Microsoft have taken proactive steps to deal with this issue. Notably, Apple, a brand recognised for its trustworthiness and successful products, has launched the latest marketing campaign squarely centred on improving privacy. Acknowledging the evolving panorama, they have committed to bolstering the security features of their gadgets. Yet, this begs the question of how different platforms are responding to privacy and security-demanding situations.

Keywords: Encryption · Decryption · Crypto · React Native · Cross-Platform · Virtual Disk · Agile · Kanban · Waterfall Model · AES XTS 128 · AES CTR 128 · Apple FileVault · Microsoft BitLocker · Proton Drive · Nord Locker

1 Introduction

In today's paced world our growing reliance on information has led to an increased demand for reliable data transmission and storage. As a result, there is a need for an encoding process that can ensure the safety and integrity of our data when transferring it through electronic mediums [13]. Using advanced encryption techniques that guarantees your files remain confidential and shielded from prying eyes during transit and storage. In an era defined by interconnectedness and data mobility, safeguarding sensitive information while ensuring effortless collaboration is of paramount importance. Though we have multiple options to keep the files secured we are not sure if confidentiality is lost or not. Because the application or software we use to secure the file might be saved in their database, or the encryption method they used for securing them might not be strong. And, while sharing the secured file with others there will be a loss of confidentiality. It

X. Feng et al. (Eds.): CloudComp 2024, LNICST 617, pp. 83–102, 2026.
https://doi.org/10.1007/978-3-031-92517-7_3

might get hacked by the hackers if less security is added. A solution for this problem is securing the files by encrypting the entire file. Even if it gets hacked or lost, only authorised people who have the decryption key to view files can only be able to see it. The same applies to sharing the file as well. I developed an application called SecureCloud which provides enhanced security to your files. Whether you are a business professional sharing confidential documents or an individual preserving cherished memories, Secure-Cloud stands as a sentinel of protection that ensures your data remains in your control. It allows users to share files with security continuously. In an age where cyber threats loom large, and privacy breaches can wreak havoc [17].

This paper presents SecureCloud, a cross-platform application designed to secure files in cloud storage by providing secure file sharing. SecureCloud offers a solution by encrypting entire files to counteract security vulnerabilities during both storage and transit. The main goals of this application are to improve data security through encryption mechanisms to store files in secure cloud storage by providing enhanced security for files and ensure compatibility across various devices like tablets, mobile phones, and laptops regardless of the operating system (e.g., Android, iOS, Microsoft Windows, MAC, etc). The foundation of SecureCloud lies in our commitment to offering a higher level of security for your files. With our cloud storage integration, collaboration knows no bounds as your shared records remain protected in the cloud and accessible worldwide. Your secured file finds a home in the cloud, easily accessible from any corner of the world with an internet connection. It allows the users to share the encrypted files in the private vault with other users across other applications in the device, and it will ensure the data will not leak hence it is encrypted and cannot be read until the valid key is entered.

Below are the core objectives that drive SecureCloud's mission:

1. To ensure data security and privacy, the uploaded files in this application will be stored in secured cloud storage and will be encrypted by using strong encryption algorithms.
2. To commit to data security extends from the moment you start sharing files, so from sender to receiver encryption remains unchanged to ensure that there will be no loss of confidentiality.
3. Files uploaded in the SecureCloud vault are kept encrypted, so they cannot be viewed, downloaded, or shared without proper permission.
4. One of the main objectives is to make an application work irrespective of the platforms (operating system) it installed, so the authorised users can access their files from anywhere across the world by using any device like Smartphone, Laptop, Desktop computer, Tablet, etc.
5. To provide convenient secure cloud storage with strong access controls and extra layers of protection, advanced privacy, and robust security measures to ensure that while your data remains at your fingertips well, it is also secure from unauthorised access in the absence of decryption keys.

SecureCloud aims to provide a solution for sharing encrypted files across platforms with imaging capability, emphasising user convenience and data protection. The implementation utilises XTS-AES-128 encryption algorithms for file encryption and RSA for end-to-end encryption using Generate Key Pair Sync for secured file sharing.

2 Related Concepts

2.1 Cross-Platform Application

The protection of storage devices is crucial. Requires versatile encryption software. To tackle this issue cryptographic software that works across platforms allows for real-time encryption safeguarding against malware and unauthorised access. This application, compatible with operating systems is a solution to prevent the loss of user's private data stored on personal computers and removable storage devices [10]. The authors specifically addressed the growing concern surrounding the security of information on devices, particularly within the Android ecosystem which has become an attractive target for cyberattacks [10].

2.2 Encryption/Decryption and File Sharing

To guarantee the security of user data one effective approach is to implement real-time encryption. This involves applying an encryption/decryption algorithm during the recording and reading processes when transferring data, between a PC and a storage medium [20]. According to Apple, they guarantee security by encrypting all data using the Advanced Encryption Standard using 128-bit keys. However, there is limited technical information, beyond this statement. The only other known fact is that encrypted volumes, also known as disk images, are utilised for this purpose [19]. Both encryption and decryption, in the method, are conducted using a single key referred to as a private key, also known as a secret key. To securely share this key between the sender and receiver [2]. This will be achieved using Symmetric key cryptographic algorithms (Fig. 1).

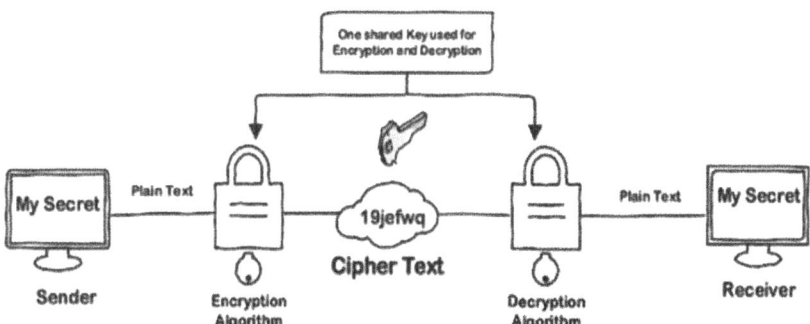

Fig. 1. Symmetric Encryption [2]

Many existing methods for storing data (whether by encrypting during transmission or on the storage device) require data creators to trust the storage server. This means trusting that the server will control access to the data for all users and ensure its integrity. Most of these storage systems are designed for users and a few enable secure sharing of data beyond simply sharing a password. Of encrypting and decrypting files every time they are transferred over the network a scalable solution is to precompute encryption only when data is updated. This approach distributes the cost of encryption and decryption, among users without involving the server [9]. Through the exploration of file sharing mechanisms, in scenarios where multiple users are engaged in storage activities, we can devise a system [16].

3   Analysis of XTS–AES-128 Encryption Algorithm

XTS uses a pair of keys; one for encryption and the other as a tweak key, which serves a similar purpose as in LRW. In XTS keys act as secondary keys for the ciphers [5]. XTS techniques have applications in disk encryption extending beyond disk encryption to encompass mobile device encryption and network encryption that incorporates location information for enhanced security. Block cipher, making it versatile and compatible, with various cryptographic algorithms using the XTS mode [3]. The unique adjustments made in XTS mode make it highly resistant to attacks and manipulation of text since changes made to one block of encrypted content will not affect the decryption process of blocks [3, 12].

XTS AES 128 encryption, also referred to as XEX-based Tweaked Codebook mode, with AES 128 is a type of encryption specifically designed for block ciphers like AES. It plays a role in file storage and sharing solutions as it provides benefits in safeguarding data stored in disk sectors. This algorithm combines techniques to ensure privacy, security, and protection against types of attacks. In XTS mode the data is divided into blocks. Processed separately which enhances security and enables processing [3] (Fig. 2).

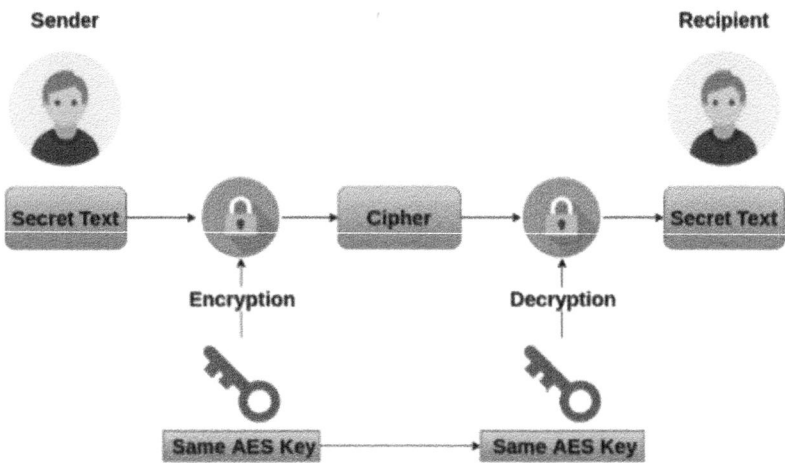

Fig. 2. Encryption and Decryption Process of XTS-AES using the Same Key [24]

AES XTS is a block cipher that utilises 128-bit (or its multiples) for encrypting data by incorporating the AES block cipher as a subroutine. AES XTS efficiently tackles issues such as tampering with ciphertext and copy-and-paste attacks all the while enabling processing and streamlining in cipher executions [24] (Figs. 3 and 4).

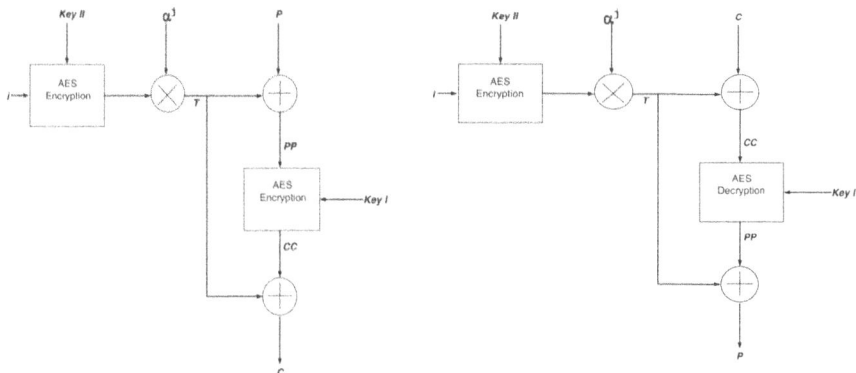

Fig. 4. AES-XTS Block Decryption [24]

Fig. 3. AES-XTS Block Encryption [24]

The AES XTS standard is used for encrypting a data stream that needs to be divided into contiguous data units before encryption is applied to it. The term "data stream", in this context refers to the information stored in a device that requires encryption. An integer value called the value is assigned to each data unit. Tweak values begin with an integer and are assigned consecutively. The adjustment amount is then transformed into a byte array, in format and encrypted using the AES algorithm.

The method, for encrypting a 128-bit block using AES-XTS mode is as follows:

$$C \leftarrow AESXTS\_Enc(K, P, i, j) \tag{1}$$

The encrypted message is generated using a sequence of actions in which the key is seen as a combination of two keys denoted as $key_1 \mid key_2$ [24]

$$T \leftarrow AESenc\,(key_2, i) \otimes \alpha^j \tag{2}$$

$$PP \leftarrow P \oplus T \tag{3}$$

$$CC = AES\,enc\,(key_1,\ PP) \tag{4}$$

$$C = CC \oplus T \tag{5}$$

The decryption process, for a 128-bit block, in AES XTS mode proceeds in a manner; the plaintext is derived through specific steps utilising the corresponding decryption formula:

$$C \leftarrow XTS - AES - Block_{dec}(key,\ C,\ i,\ j) \tag{6}$$

The plaintext is calculated as [24]:

$$T \leftarrow AES - dec\,(key_2,\ i) \otimes \alpha^j \tag{7}$$

$$CC \leftarrow C \oplus T \tag{8}$$

$$PP = AES - dec\,(key_1,\ CC) \tag{9}$$

$$P = PP \oplus T \tag{10}$$

4   Analysis of Generate Key/Pair Sync End-To-End Encryption Using RSA Algorithm

End-to-end encryption guarantees that data is securely sent from the sender to the recipient without any unauthorised third parties being able to view or alter it. In this method, the sender encodes the information and only the intended recipient can decode it. The data stays encrypted throughout the transfer process ensuring that it stays private and cannot be accessed by anyone. One employed method for achieving this is, through the RSA algorithm. RSA encryption is based on number theory. Involves using math to create two keys. A key and a private key; one, for encrypting data that is shared openly and another for decrypting the data which is kept private and confidential throughout the process of sending and receiving messages securely [4]. It is important to note that the private key cannot be derived from the key ensuring its secrecy is maintained. While anyone can use the user's key to send messages only the user, with their key can decrypt those messages (Fig. 5).

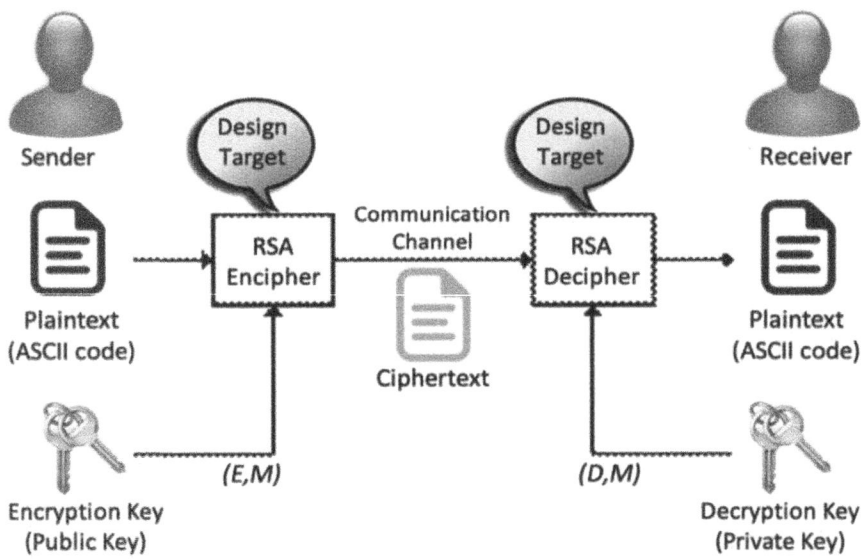

Fig. 5. RSA Algorithm Architecture [22]

RSA is commonly used to send shared keys, in cryptography that are later utilised for encrypt and decrypt amounts of data efficiently and securely, over time the RSA encryption algorithm has become widely accepted for ensuring the safe transmission of data in the context of public cryptosystems the RSA algorithm continues to be highly respected [5, 23]. Continuous research efforts focus on enhancing its security and performance to increase complexity, reliability, and encryption/decryption speed. To experiment with this, a 64-bit i7 processor is used with 8GB of RAM. PyCharm IDE was selected to develop Windows applications to run the simulation. It takes advantage of interpreter settings to execute the algorithms written in Python. Some essential software components comprise the Cryptography package with tools and the PyCryptodome Python package offering cryptographic features and improvements in addition to fixes and additions to the existing ones available within the library suite. Another useful tool is the Psutil library which functions seamlessly across platforms to gather details on processes and system performance metrics like CPU usage and memory consumption along with disk operations monitoring network data flow status and sensor readings [4].

The equation for calculating the process time *(Tx)* is given by subtracting the finish time *(Tx2)* from the time *(Tx1)*.

Where,

$$Start\ time\ =\ Tx1\ (ms) \tag{11}$$

and,

$$Finish\ time\ =\ Tx2\ (ms), \tag{12}$$

The time taken for the entire process,

$$(Tx) = Tx2 - Tx1 \tag{13}$$

The encrypted output of each file is used as input, for decryption. Throughout the study, input files are used to ensure memory and processor conditions for all cryptographic algorithms use cases. It is important to note that cryptographic algorithms consume system resources such as CPU time, memory, and computation time [4].

In the encryption process for file sharing is used in a method that employs the AES encryption key to secure the original file and generate the ciphertext (ciphertext 1). Next, the RSA key is used along with the AES encryption key to encrypt this ciphertext and create a second ciphertext (ciphertext 2). Even if ciphertext 2 is compromised, accessing data encrypted using the RSA key would require a matching RSA key. The decryption process is simply the reverse of encryption. By utilising the RSA key to decrypt ciphertext 2. Obtain both ciphertext 1 and the AES encryption key. Finally, by using this AES encryption key we decrypt ciphertext 1 to retrieve our source file (plaintext). AES enables encryption and decryption of data sets, with security in mind while the RSA algorithm focuses solely on safeguarding the encryption key and ciphertext for heightened protection against breaches of data integrity. In scenarios where multiple recipients need access to data sets securely encrypted using the AES encryption key and ciphertext 1 copies of both the ciphertext 1 and AES key are shared among them. Each recipient is required to utilise their public RSA key to encode the AES encryption key along with ciphertext 1 prior to transmitting it across the network.

5   System Design

The blueprint for the SecureCloud application is illustrated in this design phase.

5.1 System Architecture

The architecture of SecureCloud is designed to outline how its various elements function and interact within the application. Its primary objective is to create a user environment, for sharing encrypted files. SecureCloud relies on a server infrastructure based on cloud technology for tasks such as file storage, user account management and client communication. Additionally, it utilises a database to store user information such as credentials, access controls and metadata associated with shared files (Fig. 6).

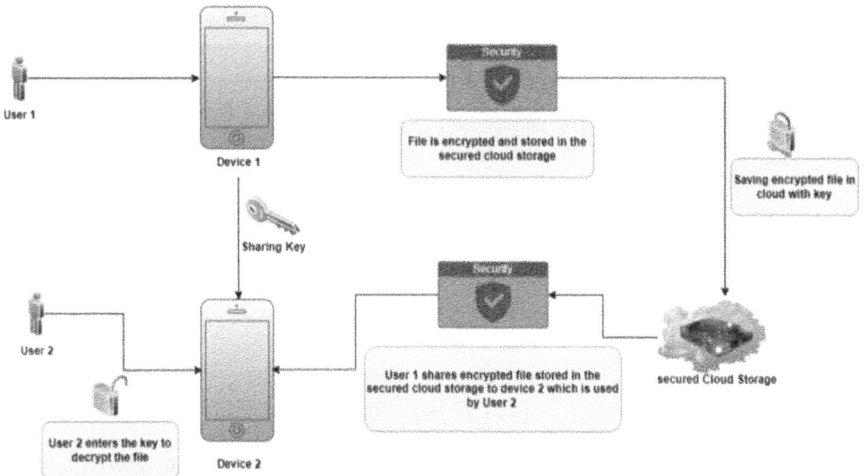

Fig. 6. High-Level System Architecture

5.2 User Management and User Access Control

In the application, there are two roles: the User and the Admin. The User is responsible for performing file operations such as uploading or removing files as sharing encrypted files and their corresponding keys, with other authorised users. On the other hand, the admin oversees both the User and the entire application having access to view all operations carried out by the User.

5.3 File Management

To access, upload or delete files, in the SecureCloud application users must log in with their username and password. After authentication users will be directed to the dashboard where they can find a folder containing files. Within the folder page users have the option to upload files and delete uploaded encrypted files from their secure cloud storage. If users wish to share a file with others, they can provide them with the RSA key required for decryption of both the file and its encryption.

5.4   Secured Cloud Storage

When users upload files, they are securely stored in cloud storage. The backend API uses the XTS AES 128-bit algorithm to encrypt the files during the uploading process. Additionally, a key is generated using the RSA algorithm for decrypting the files. The decrypted file is then stored reactively and asynchronously. Once this process is complete the encrypted file is securely saved in cloud storage.

6   Implementation of Encryption and File Sharing Algorithms

The SecureCloud application has been designed to work across platforms, including mobile and PC. To achieve this development, I carefully selected a stack that supports all these platforms (Fig. 7).

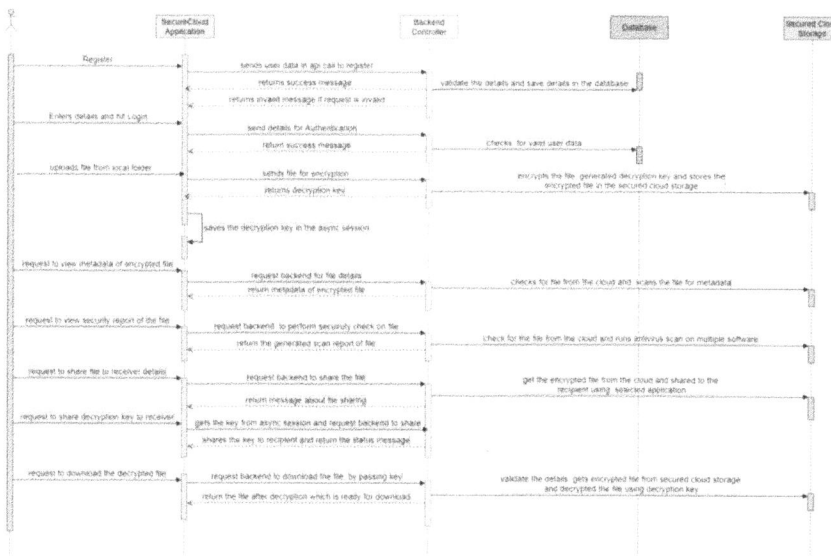

Fig. 7. Sequence Diagram of SecureCloud

The main part of the entire development is implementing encryption algorithms to encrypt the file and share the encrypted files from the secured cloud storage.

- Only authenticated users can access the application. To create an account user, need to navigate to the login page and provide the information.
- Users will be directed to a home page Fig. 9 with successful authentication, where they can view a list of encrypted files. In the Private Vault screen, Fig. 8 users can upload files which will be encrypted and stored in cloud storage. The files can then be shared along with a decryption key.
- Furthermore, users have access to see the history of the file operations in the application, they can also see the antivirus scan report of the encrypted file.

- Users also have the capability to remove files and share them with individuals using level 1 encryption (Fig. 10).

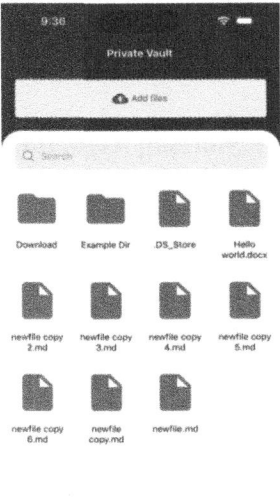

Fig. 8. Private Vault screen

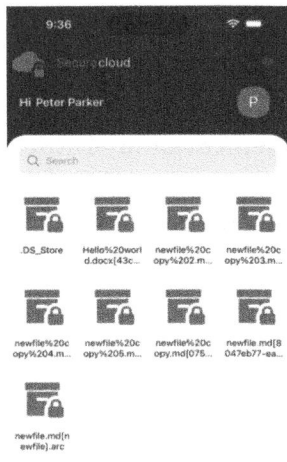

Fig. 9. Home Screen with Encrypted files

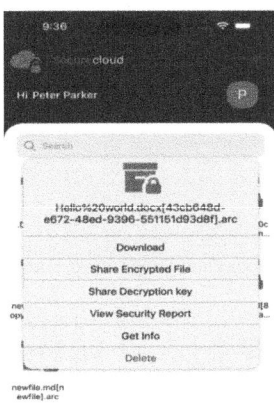

Fig. 10. File click operations list on the Home Screen

7 Comparison with Other Products

7.1 Apple's FileVault

Apple's FileVault is a disk encryption application that works on Mac OS X 10.3 and later. It uses the user's login password as the encryption passphrase and is implemented by using XTS-AES-128 encryption to prevent unauthorised access to information on disks. It employs full disk encryption, which means encrypts the entire disk including all user data, system files, and even the swap files used by the OS. It decrypts the user's data when the user logs in because the login password is the decryption key. It provides a Recovery key to the user, so if the user forgets the password by using the recovery key, they can unlock the disk. They also implemented a kill switch, if the application turns off, it erases the encryption key and the data on the disk is kept encrypted and impossible to recover. Because of its hardware acceleration, the performance impact is less (Fig. 11).

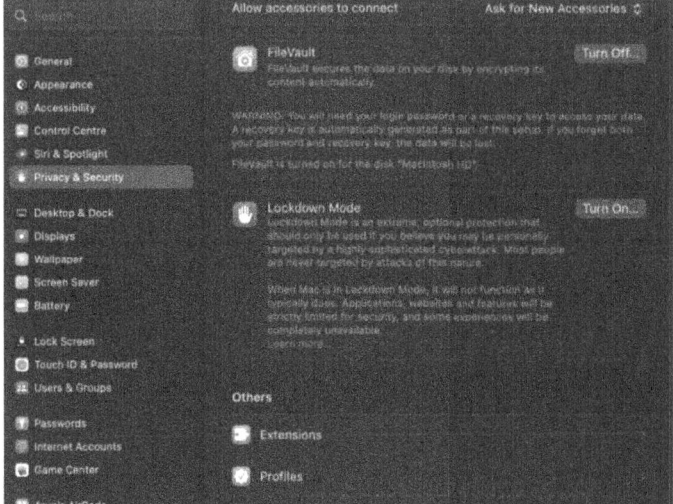

Fig. 11. Apple's FileVault

There could be a permanent data loss and no way to recover the encrypted data if the user forgets Apple's login password and recovery key [19]. It also takes a lengthy process to get the encrypted files back by contacting Apple Support, it does not guarantee the full recovery of the files. Though it has less performance impact, users may suffer slow read and write speeds when the FileVault is enabled during the initial encryption process because it takes a significant amount of time. It also provides external drive encryption with FileVault, but it will not work on non-MAC devices. There will be a loss of data if the login password gets leaked or hacked or kind of activities like phishing allow unauthorised people to gain access to your encrypted data [7]. By comparing SecureCloud with Apple's FileVault, they are using the XTS algorithm to encrypt the entire disk and use the login password to decrypt the drive, this leads to a major impact of loss of data. In SecureCloud we encrypt each and the decryption key for each file is generated by the same XTS algorithm. Whether the users know the password or not it remains encrypted and stored securely in the cloud storage, there will be no loss of confidentiality and unauthorised access to that file will not happen, because no one knows the key to decrypt the file, even the user who uploaded it. It is saved in the UI's async session and retrieved from the async session whenever there is a need to decrypt the encrypted file. We also provide a password recovery option to the users, whether during the password recovery, log off, or if the application goes off in the device. It will not affect the encrypted files because they are stored in the cloud securely.

The use of disk-based encryption, such as Apple's FileVault, is effective in securing data on individual devices employing the AES-256 encryption. However, there are limitations compared to cloud-based solutions like SecureCloud. A static encrypted key would be a liability if compromised for hard-drive-based encryption that depends on one device's security and has no advanced access controls, lacks real-time threat monitoring and data redundancy. On the other side, SecureCloud provides a better security framework when compared with that of any other solution in the market. It improves protection against data tampering by using AES-XTS 128-bit encryption and guarantees end-to-end transmission protection through RSA. Moreover, it offers dynamic key management which involves regular rotation of encryption keys as a measure towards tightening its security. Furthermore, SecureCloud can reduce risks associated with data loss via multiple locations wherein data is stored redundantly.

Looking at all these aspects of SecureCloud's layered and comprehensive approach to security; it can easily be concluded that it is a more robust and reliable alternative for keeping sensitive information safe in comparison to traditional disk-based encryption solutions such as FileVault.

7.2   Microsoft BitLocker

BitLocker is also a full-disk encryption available in Microsoft Windows OS, designed to protect data on a computer's hard drive or other storage devices including operating system, user data and system files using AES. It ensures data is protected when the device is turned off or in a hibernation state. BitLocker requires users to enter a PIN or provide a USB key before the computer can boot up; this is added for an extra layer of security. BitLocker can work in combination with TPM (Trusted Platform Module), an embedded hardware component, which stores the decryption key and ensures the system has not been tampered with without access. It also provides a recovery key to unlock the drive like Apple's FileVault if the user forgets the PIN. The combination of UEFI (Unified Extensible Firmware Interface) and Secure Boot protects data against boot-level attacks. It provides an option to store the recovery key in Microsoft Azure Active Directory (Fig. 12).

BitLocker is only available in Windows Pro, Enterprise, and Education editions not available in the home edition. It cannot provide complete security without a combination with TPM, PIN or USB Key, any of these should be combined with BitLocker for security. If any other hardware lacks TPM or security boot, BitLocker will not work in that system. It only encrypts Windows System drive (C:), it does not provide security

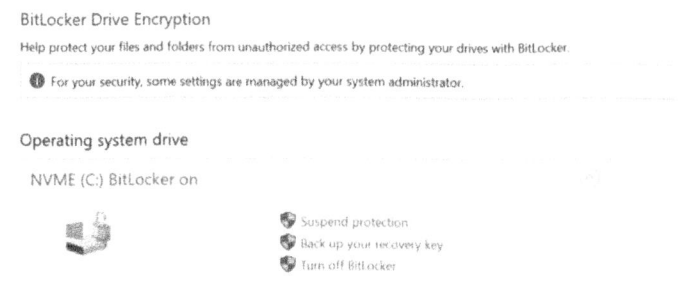

Fig. 12. Windows's BitLocker

support for other drives. It has limited Cross-Platform compatibility, OS other than Windows cannot access the BitLocker's encrypted drive [8]. As with Apple's FileVault, if you forget your BitLocker PIN or recovery key, then you can permanently lose access to your data, we might need to contact customer service to recover the files. It is vulnerable to cold boot attacks, which means that when the device is powered off, attackers can try to physically access the files, leading to starting up the device from scratch. If the device is capable of DMA (network card, or USB device), they will have access to the memory and start to copy all the data including encrypted files.

We cannot share the files in the encrypted drive to other devices, it keeps products in Windows and can be viewed when the PIN or key is entered, to store the key they are providing the option to store it in Azure [8]. But in SecureCloud we do not require any external application for the support, it works independently on providing security to the files encrypted and when sharing the encrypted files.

7.3 Proton Drive

Proton drives end-to-end encryption using Swiss Vault ensuring that no one including the creator of that application can access your files. All files, along with their names and folder names are encrypted both when they are stored and when they are transmitted to your cloud. Moreover, this application provides a file-sharing feature that guarantees encryption not only for folders but also for any associated metadata ensuring comprehensive protection. This application is available at https://proton.me/drive. Proton application allows the users to create a Swiss vault only if they have a Proton Mail email address. This shows that the users should create a proton email account like Gmail to access the proton drive. This application is developed by utilising PGP, which combines public key encryption with encryption also known as symmetric encryption. Asymmetric encryption uses a pair of keys, for encrypting and decrypting data. These keys are created in tandem. Have a connection with each other. They are often known as the key and the private key. The public key is specifically employed to encrypt data ensuring that it can only be deciphered using its corresponding key [18] (Fig. 13).

Proton Drive has access to your encrypted files, but it does not offer end-to-end encryption by default, which means there will be a loss of security if the file gets hacked. This does not provide a file sharing feature so you cannot have your encrypted confidential data with others. This is not a cross-platform application, you can access your

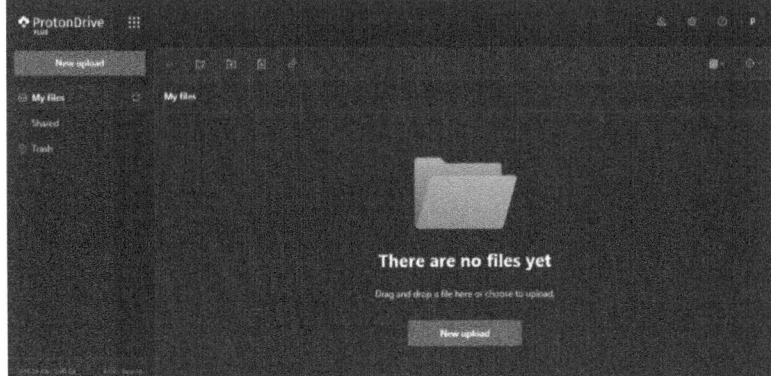

Fig. 13. Proton Drive UI

files only on a desktop computer or laptop. Proton drive has also been criticised for its slow performance and lack of features. PGP should be used when sharing information across an open network, but it can be slower, and not recommended to process a group of files. They are using a private cloud vault (Swiss vault) there might be a chance of losing data.

Our application uses a symmetric encryption key for end-to-end encryption during file sharing, only one key is generated and that will be used for encryption and decryption. AES works best with closed systems and large databases that lean towards performance. The generated key will be stored in the user's device. During file decryption, the decryption key will be sent to the backend in the API call which will be used for decrypting the file. We provided a kill switch if something goes off, in such cases the user will be required to upload the same file again.

7.4 NordLocker

NordLocker is also a cross-platform application that protects data from cybercriminals, surveillance, and malware. It also secures data, and backup, and allows accessing files via a private file vault on the web or desktop and mobile apps. This application uses secure cloud storage for storing the files available at https://nordlocker.com/.

They also used asymmetric encryption methods, by generating two keys (public and private key). Limitations of these asymmetric encryptions are they cannot provide complete protection for the application, it might require PIN, pattern, or multi-factor authentication like these kinds of additional layers of security [17]. There are some other limitations in this application when compared with SecureCloud. NordLocker does not offer a zero-knowledge encryption option which means that this application has access to your encryption key for your files. So that this application could be potentially compromised if it gets hacked. In case of an internet connection lost in between, your files could be left unencrypted because it does not have a kill switch. There is no password recovery option, if you forget your password, you will not be able to access your encrypted files. They do not provide file sharing and collaborating features (Fig. 14).

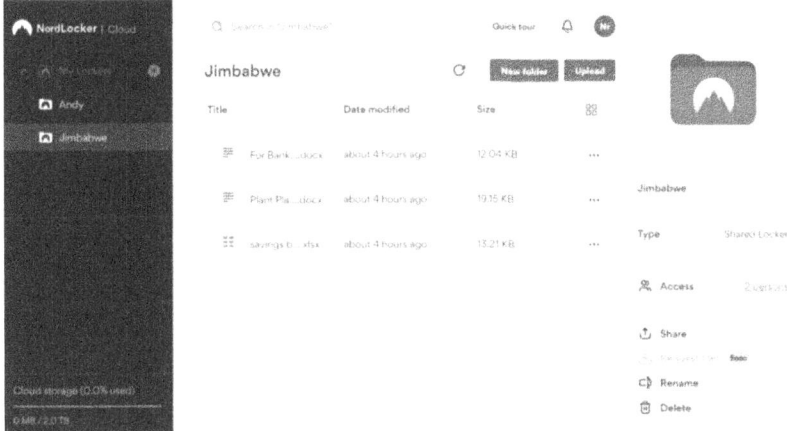

Fig. 14. NordLocker UI

Based on the limitations and specifications added above, NordLocker is a secure file encryption tool, but the limitations it has might be important for some users. If you are looking for a file encryption application with a zero-knowledge encryption tool, a kill switch, and a recovery vault, then SecureCloud is the best choice for you, because the encryption algorithm we use generates the decryption key. We are not storing the key anywhere in DB or cloud, it will be stored in the application session. During file decryption, the decryption key will be sent to the backend from the UI which will be used for decrypting the file they requested. We provided a kill switch if something goes off, in such cases the user will be required to upload the same file again. SecureCloud application is user-friendly, if they forget the password, they can recover the password at any instance and there will not be a loss of security in such cases.

In the above-mentioned existing products, the files can be shared only within that domain account. For Proton, the users should have a Proton email account so that they can be able to add files to the Swiss vault and they can be able to share their files only to another Proton account. In the same way, Nord locker files are only transmitted from one Nord locker account to another Nord locker account. But the current project is not like this, during sharing we are providing an option for the users to select other applications like messages, mail, etc. Only the encrypted data is shared, not the original content, to decrypt the data, the user should enter the decryption key.

SecureCloud is compared to existing products like Proton Drive and Nord Locker. These products also offer secure file storage and sharing but have limitations, such as the requirement for specific email addresses or the use of asymmetric encryption methods. SecureCloud distinguishes itself by providing complete end-to-end encryption and enabling file sharing with other applications. Users have the flexibility to share encrypted data securely with others, enhancing the platform's usability.

7.5 Comparative Performance Analysis

A major part of the SecureCloud application is file encryption. It is achieved by using the AES-XTS-128 encryption algorithm, which provides a high level of security for the encryption compared with the other AES algorithms and this algorithm performs faster compared with other algorithms because of the tweaked key implementation in the XTS AES-128 encryption.

The bigger the files, the longer it usually takes to perform file encryption and decryption, and finding which key or algorithm is suitable can be difficult. Bitwise encryption also adds a layer of security by operating on data one bit at a time, making unauthorised access more difficult. Reducing the bits of an image file using Image quantization is often applied to colour spaces to obtain a reduced number of colour bins [25]. Quantum algorithms have made this process much faster, reducing the time needed from a huge amount to a more manageable one.

In this section, I have covered the evaluation of XTS-AES-128 encryption algorithms by comparing them with other algorithms. I developed a JavaScript code to perform file encryption of a 10.5MB PDF file with text and image. This code contains the above-mentioned algorithms implemented. Based on the 100 iterations the results of each algorithm are aggregated and added to Fig. 15.

Mode	Security	Efficiency	Latency (in milliseconds)	Throughput (in KB/s)	Time (in Seconds)
AES XTS 128	Very high	High	28	377	0.028
AES CBC 128	High	High	37	280	0.037
AES CTR 128	High	Very high	24	424	0.024
AES CFB 128	High	Medium	47	221	0.047
AES OFB 128	High	Low	42	250	0.042
AES ECB 128	Medium	Low	24	426	0.024

Fig. 15. Evaluation procedure results

This covers the levels of security and efficiency provided by the above-mentioned algorithms, latency, throughput, and the time each algorithm took to perform file encryption.

To perform this, the device I used is.

- Test Bench Environment: Apple M1, 3.2GHz, 8 cores, 16GB
- Dataset Source: FREETESTDATA.COM

To begin with the evaluation, I chose top AES 128 encryption algorithms which are the best in the market [14]. Those algorithms are AES XTS, CBS, CTR, CFB, OFB, and ECB. The reason for choosing XTS 128 is illustrated below.

The Apple Silicon M1(and M2) chip is an AArch64 architecture also known as ARM64, hence it is an ARM architecture. Based on the results we captured from the above table; the pictorial representation of the results is given below using a Line chart and Bar chart (Figs. 16 and 17).

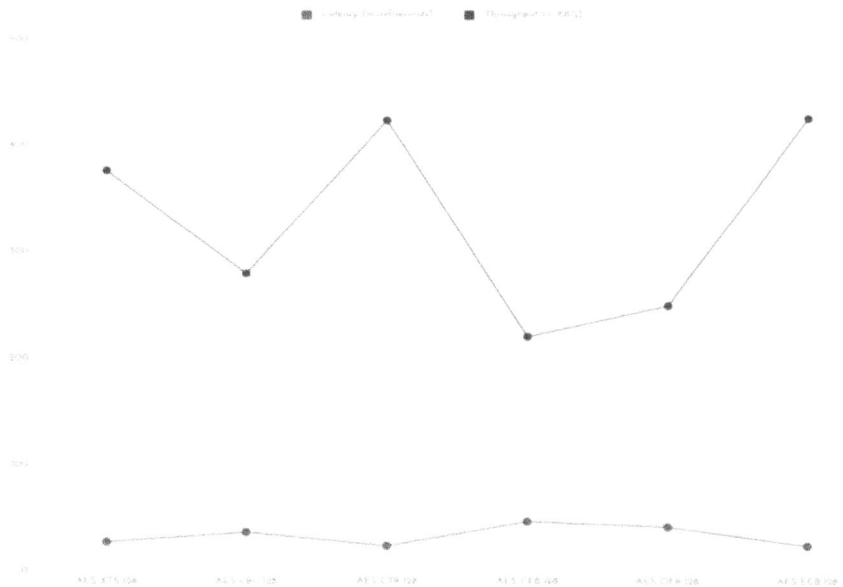

Fig. 16. Line Chart - Comparison of AES- XTS, CTR, CBC, CFB, OFB, ECB

This chart shows the CTR has high throughput and efficiency. But it has less security when compared with the XTS algorithm. Our application's main concern is security as we are providing a high level of security for the user files. The resulting efficiency of the top 5 algorithms is shown in the below chart (Fig. 18).

This result shows the CTR is higher than the algorithm we chose XTS. However, the problem with the CTR is that it performs encryption processes sequentially, so it will take more time for execution. But XTS performs the execution parallel thus this results in faster encryption with a higher level of security. Because XTS is specifically designed to enhance data security in storage scenarios in disk encryption applications [15]. It operates at the block level by treating each data block as an entity for encryption purposes. This approach effectively prevents attackers from identifying patterns or repetitions in the data ensuring confidentiality. This is a reason for choosing XTS for SecureCloud application development as a file encryption mechanism.

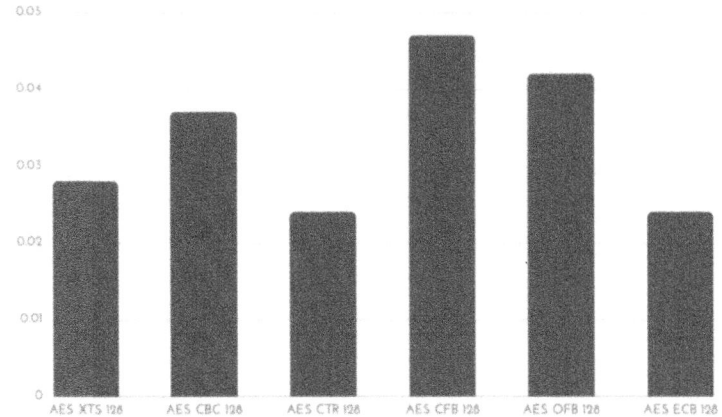

Fig. 17. Bar Chart - Latency Comparison of AES- XTS, CTR, CBC, CFB, OFB, ECB

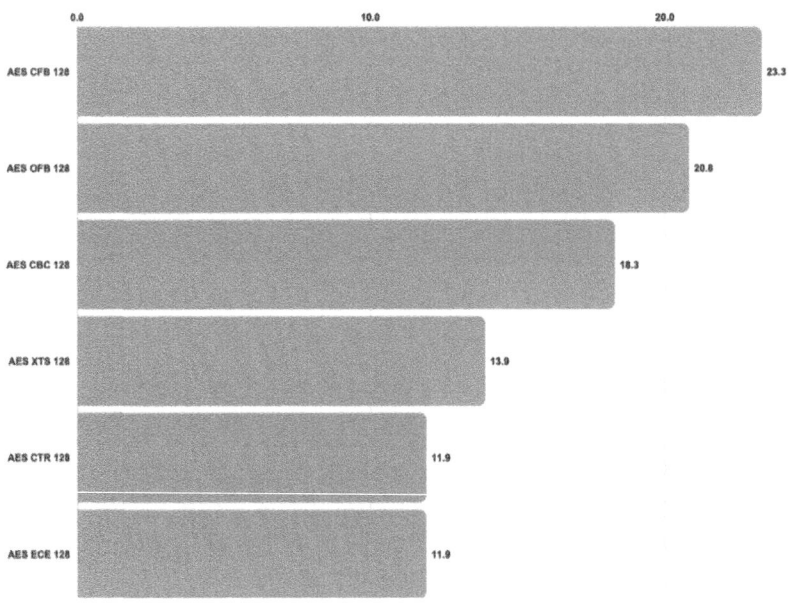

Fig. 18. Bar Race Chart - Efficiency Comparison of AES- XTS, CTR, CBC, CFB, OFB, ECB

8 Summary

This paper highlights how SecureCloud stands out as a file-sharing platform that puts the needs of its users first ensuring both top-notch security and efficiency. What sets SecureCloud apart from other products is its adaptability and user-friendly design. It excels at providing end-to-end encryption allowing users to securely share encrypted data across applications. This flexibility makes SecureCloud an excellent choice for individuals and organisations looking for customised communication solutions. To summarise SecureCloud's commitment to testing protocols continuous focus on improving user experience and unwavering dedication to data security establish it as a trailblazer in the field of cloud-based applications with an emphasis on security.

Though we have multiple algorithms to encrypt and decrypt files or data, the comparative analysis showed that AES-XTS is faster and more efficient than other encryption algorithms in terms of time and memory. Usually, the time taken to decrypt or encrypt the file increases as the size of the file increases and there are multiple possibilities in terms of binary without proper key and the algorithm. The introduction of quantum algorithms potentially reduced the time complexity from exponential to potential. By using the most advanced quantum algorithm for file encryption/decryption and file sharing by maintaining confidentiality SecureCloud represents a significant advancement in data protection.

References

1. Ahmed, S., Samsudin, K., Ramli, A.R., Rokhani, F.Z.: Advanced Encryption Standard-XTS implementation in field programmable gate array hardware. Secur. Commun. Networks **8**, 516–522 (2015)
2. Alenezi, M.N., Alabdulrazzaq, H., Mohammad, N.Q.: Symmetric encryption algorithms: review and evaluation study. Int. J. Commun. Networks Inform. Secur. **12**, 256–272 (2020)
3. An, S., Seo, S.C.: Designing a new XTS-AES parallel optimisation implementation technique for fast file encryption. IEEE Access **10**, 25349–25357 (2022)
4. Blaise, O.O., Awodele, O., Yewande, O.: An understanding and perspectives of end-to-end encryption. Int. Res. J. Eng. Technol. (IRJET) **8**, 1086 (2021)
5. Broz, M., Matyas, V.: The truecrypt on-disk format–an independent view. IEEE Secur. Priv. **12**, 74–77 (2014)
6. Demir, L., Thiery, M., Roca, V., Tenkes, J.-M., Roch, J.-L.: Optimising Dm-crypt for XTS-AES: getting the best of atmel cryptographic co-processors (long version). In: SECRYPT 2020–17th International Conference on Security and Cryptography, pp. 1–11 (2020)
7. Heinrich, A., Hollick, M., Schneider, T., Stute, M., Weinert, C.: AirCollect: efficiently recovering hashed phone numbers leaked via Apple AirDrop. In: Proceedings of the 14th ACM Conference on Security and Privacy in Wireless and Mobile Networks, pp.. 371–373 (2021)
8. Junaid Gul, M., Rabia, R., Jararweh, Y., Rathore, M.M., Paul, A.: Security flaws of operating system against live device attacks: a case study on live linux distribution device. In: 2019 Sixth International Conference on Software Defined Systems (SDS), pp. 154–159. IEEE (2019)
9. Kallahalla, M., Riedel, E., Swaminathan, R., Wang, Q., Fu, K.: Plutus: scalable secure file sharing on untrusted storage. In: 2nd USENIX Conference on File and Storage Technologies (FAST 03) (2003)
10. Loginova, N., Trofimenko, E., Zadereyko, O., Chanyshev, R.: Program-technical aspects of encryption protection of users' data. In: 2016 13th International Conference on Modern Problems of Radio Engineering, Telecommunications and Computer Science (TCSET), pp. 443–445. IEEE, (2016)
11. Malvai, H., et al.: Parakeet: Practical key transparency for end-to-end encrypted messaging. Cryptology ePrint Archive (2023)
12. Milidonis, A., Hatzidimitriou, E., Kakarountas, A.P.: A survey on throughput-efficient architectures for IEEE P1619 for shared storage media (2011)

13. Muttaqin, K., Rahmadoni, J.: Analysis and design of file security system AES (advanced encryption standard) cryptography based. J. Appl. Eng. Technol. Sci. **1**, 113–123 (2020)
14. Nadeem, A., Javed, M.Y.: A performance comparison of data encryption algorithms. In: 2005 International Conference on Information and Communication Technologies, pp. 84–89. IEEE (2005)
15. Sanida, T., Sideris, A., Dasygenis, M.: Accelerating the AES algorithm using opencl. In: 2020 9th International Conference on Modern Circuits and Systems Technologies (MOCAST), pp. 1–4. IEEE (2020)
16. Shu, J., Shen, Z., Xue, W.: Shield: a stackable secure storage system for file sharing in public storage. J. Parallel Distrib. Comput. **74**, 2872–2883 (2014)
17. Stephens, K.: Healthcare sector named a top target for ransomware attacks. AXIS Imaging News (2021)
18. Velàsquez Melenciano, X.: Design and implementation of an end-to-end encrypted cloud backup service for disk partitions (2020)
19. WEINMANN, R.-P. Dissecting Apple's FileVault. 5. Krypto-Tag–Workshop über Kryptographie Universität Kassel, 2006. 10
20. Zadereyko, A., Troyanskiy, O.: Program and technical aspects of cryptographic defence of data storage. Інформатика та математичні методи в моделюванні, pp. 347–352 (2015)
21. Kakarountas, A., Hatzidimitriou, E., Milidonis, A.: A survey on throughput-efficient architectures for IEEE P1619 for shared storage media, pp. 758–763 (2011). https://doi.org/10.1109/ISCC.2011.5983931
22. Bodur, H., Kara, R.: Secure SMS encryption using RSA encryption algorithm on android message application (2015)
23. Imam, R., Areeb, Q.M., Alturki, A., Anwer, F.: Systematic and critical review of RSA based public key cryptographic schemes: past and present status. IEEE Access **9**, 155949–155976 (2021)
24. Ahmed, S., et al.: Advanced Encryption Standard-XTS implementation in field programmable gate array hardware. Secur. Commun. Netw. **8.3**, 516–522 (2015)
25. Artemi, M., Liu, H.: Image optimization using improved gray-scale quantization for content-based image retrieval. In: 2020 IEEE 6th International Conference on Optimization and Applications (ICOA), pp. 1–6. Beni Mellal, Morocco (2020). https://doi.org/10.1109/ICOA49421.2020.9094507

Wireless Networks; Network Security

Network Intrusion Detection by Adaptive Deep Metric Learning

Yanpeng Qu[1], Qi Zhang[1], Mingxiao Zheng[1], and Longzhi Yang[2(✉)]

[1] Dalian Maritime University,Dalian, China
{yanpengqu,qizhang,zhengmingxiao}@dlmu.edu.cn
[2] The University of Northumbria at Newcastle,Newcastle upon Tyne, U.K.
longzhi.yang@northumbria.ac.uk

Abstract. In the realm of network security, advancements like 5G, IoT, and cloud computing have expanded network environments and real-time traffic complexity, accompanied by a rise in diverse and sophisticated cyber-attacks. This paper introduces a self-adaptive discriminative autoencoder (SADAE) method which is developed through deep metric learning aiming to effectively detect various network intrusions. SADAE integrates K local autoencoders and one global autoencoder: the former captures diverse data distributions, whilst the latter governs network traffic representation scale. Through effective self-adaptive metric learning, the proposed SADAE is able to identify and extract discriminative features to automatically detect various network traffic classes, enhancing data separability and improving detection accuracy. For validation and evaluation, the proposed approach was applied to the binary NSL-KDD datasets and multi-class CSE-CIC-IDS2018 datasets. The experimental results demonstrate SADAE's effectiveness in detecting and categorising network intrusion anomalies in reference to other popular deep learning and metric learning approaches.

Keywords: Intrusion detection for computer networks · Deep learning · Metric learning · Autoencoder network

1 Introduction

Thanks to the rapid development of IoT, cloud computing, and the next generation of communication technologies, the expanding scale of the network environment and the rising complexity of real-time traffic will inevitably lead to potential threat to network security. To effectively address this, Network Intrusion Detection System (NIDS) [1], as a key defence barrier after the firewall [34], assumes the important responsibility of accurate identification of malicious behaviours, implementing real-time monitoring, adopting dynamic defence strategies and formulating corresponding measures [21,25,37]. From a more macroscopic perspective, NIDS can essentially be conducted as a classification task, to classifying

This work was jointly supported by the Fundamental Research Funds of Educational Department of Liaoning Province of China (JYTMS20230162) and the Industry-University-Research Innovation Fund for Chinese Universities (2024HY028).

X. Feng et al. (Eds.): CloudComp 2024, LNICST 617, pp. 105–117, 2026.
https://doi.org/10.1007/978-3-031-92517-7_8

network connections either normal or attack as a binary classification problem, or further subdividing attack types as a multi-classification problem.

In [29], a preliminary investigation into utilizing machine learning for monitoring network anomalies during the intrusion detection process is presented, aiming to identify attack behaviors and subsequently recognize the detected attacks. In [13,27,36], support vector machine (SVM) algorithms are employed in NIDS to enhance their efficiency and accuracy by correctly identifying normal and malicious traffic. In [9,19,23,33], Convolutional Neural Networks (CNNs) are utilized to perform feature extraction on raw data for the classification of network traffic. In [32], a deep stacked network (DSN) model is introduced to improve the classification accuracy of NIDS by integrating the predictions from multiple classifiers. In [20], principal component analysis (PCA) and mutual information techniques are applied to reduce data dimensionality, and long short-term memory (LSTM) network is used to detect attack mechanisms. In [40], a discretisation method based on an inconsistency metric is proposed to handle continuous features in network traffic data. In [15], a bidirectional deep long short-term memory (BiDLSTM) method is introduced to implement NIDS for detecting user-to-root (U2R) and remote-to-local (R2L) attacks. In [39], a kernel-based fuzzy-rough feature selection method is proposed to extract significant features from raw network traffic data.

Deep metric learning (DML) [16] integrates a metric learning (ML) algorithm [5] into a deep learning (DL) network to enhance the discriminative ability of high-level features for accurate data classification. Based on our previous work, a DML-based approach, entitled a self-adaptive discriminative autoencoder (SADAE), is adopted to enhance the performance of NIDS. SADAE uses K local autoencoders (AEs) to capture diverse subspace features to model complex data distributions, and a global AE to oversee feature extraction across appropriate spatial scales. Central to SADAE is its an adaptive metric strategy, which automatically optimises classification boundaries to extract discriminative features. These features can help NIDS enhance the capability in network intrusion anomaly detection and provide a robust technical support for network security. The comparative studies are conducted on the NSL-KDD dataset [11] and a class-balanced dataset sampled from the CSE-CIC-IDS2018 dataset [28], with competitive results demonstrated. Compared to alternative DL and ML methods, SADAE can effectively detect the anomaly information of the network intrusion and further identify the type of the malicious network behaviours.

The remainder of the paper is presented as follows. Section 2 presents a brief literature review of the relevant background and technologies. Section 3 presents the SADAE algorithm proposed in this study. Section 4 presents comprehensive experimental results, and Section 5 concludes the paper with final remarks.

2 Background

In this section, the related works on DML and the application of DL in NIDS are briefly summarised.

2.1 Metric Learning

DML is able to effectively map raw features to an embedding space using a deep model, highlighting similarities or differences between data objects. In this embedding space, features of samples are effectively distinguished: objects belonging to the same class are close, while those belonging to different classes appear to be distant. DML research focuses on three main areas: sampling strategy selection, loss function design, and metric model enhancement.

In DML, sampling strategy refers to how a set of samples from a dataset is selected to train a DML model. A good sampling strategy allows the model to figure out a valid distance measure from challenging samples while avoiding overfitting or inefficient training. In [7], a deep credibility learning (DCML) method is proposed to avoid misleading noisy labels by adaptively mining credible samples for training. In [22], a graph sampling (GS) method for efficient small-batch sampling for large-scale DML is proposed, which samples information by constructing nearest neighbour graphs of all classes.

The network loss function directly reflects the goal of DML and guides the learning process of DML methods. An efficient deep loss function plays a crucial role in DML optimisation. In [24], a new loss criterion is proposed, which explicitly monitors the displacement direction of the samples and uses the rejection direction as another optimisation factor, which in turn allows for better separation of classes in the space. In [6], a multiscale deep nearest neighbour (MsDNN) loss function is proposed, which not only distinguishes between known classes, but also implicitly improves the clustering behaviour within known classes by minimising the upper bound of the classification error rate used in the leave-alone method in the latent space.

In DML models, a good network structure enables the model to learn high-level nonlinear features while maintaining computational efficiency and scalability. Deep local metric learning (DLML) [10] learns a number of fine-grained deep local metrics through several AE models. Deep relational metric learning (DRML) [41] is an end-to-end training method that discovers structural patterns in the feature set and uses these patterns to obtain relational embeddings.

2.2 Network Intrusion by Deep Learning

In the study of NID, DL provides an effective means for processing large-scale and complex network traffic data and adapting to changing intrusion behaviours. It provides a more intelligent and efficient solution for secure computer networks thanks to its effective feature learning and pattern recognition functionalities.

A hybrid convolutional recurrent neural network was proposed to detect network intrusion as reported in the work of [18]. In this work, the convolutional neural network is employed to implement convolution to identify and extract local features. In addition, a recurrent neural network is used to extract temporal features to better predict computer network intrusions and thus further improve the overall performance of the network intrusion detection system. The Q-learning based reinforcement learning approach is integrated into a deep neural network approach, leading to a deep Q-learning approach, which can provide continuous and automatic learning capabilities for networked environments.

Autoencoder [12], a widely used unsupervised DL approach, learns to match input to output by discovering optimal features. AE operates in an encoder-decoder structure and includes variants such as stacked AE, sparse AE, and variant AE [17]. In [36], a method using stacked sparse autoencoder (SSAE) is proposed to enhance NIDS performance by extracting discriminative features through dimensionality reduction, mapping input data to a more compact representation space. In [38], a supervised adversarial variational autoencoder (SAVA) based approach is proposed, where regularisation methods are integrated to improve the model's robustness and generalisation. A method combines an autoencoder and a triple network for deep metric learning, using the autoencoder to learn a low-dimensional data representation and adding a metric learning layer post-encoder to measure similarity between samples, as reported in [2]. In [3], using the concept of AE, a multilevel model is proposed, which mainly contains an ID convolutional layer, in addition to two stacked fully-connected layers. This approach efficiently extracts high-level feature representations from raw data through multi-channel deep feature learning. In [14], a stacked asymmetric deep autoencoder model is proposed for unsupervised feature learning.

3   The SADAE Algorithm for NIDS

This paper proposes a self-adaptive discriminative autoencoder (SADAE) model to expand the application of DML in NIDS. SADAE comprises K local AEs and a global AE shown in Fig. 1. After pretraining these autoencoders to identify data differences, the model employs a self-adaptive metric learning algorithm [30] to determine an optimal radius threshold, enhancing the sample class differentiation. This approach aims to minimise intra-class variations and boost inter-class distinctions, thereby enhancing classification performance based on these features.

3.1   Initialisation

SADAE generates discriminative features adaptively to distinguish between classes while minimising excessive inter-class differences. For the global autoencoder AE_0, given a dataset X, all the training samples are taken for initialisation and the network parameters are updated by computing the reconstruction loss.

Each AE_k, $k = 0, \ldots, K$, has M layers. Given a sample $x \in X_k$, let $O_k^{(0)}$ represent the input x. The output of the m-th layer of the k-th local AE is

$$O_k^{(m)} = f(W_k^{(m)} O_k^{(m-1)} + b_k^{(m)}), \; m = 1, \ldots, M. \tag{1}$$

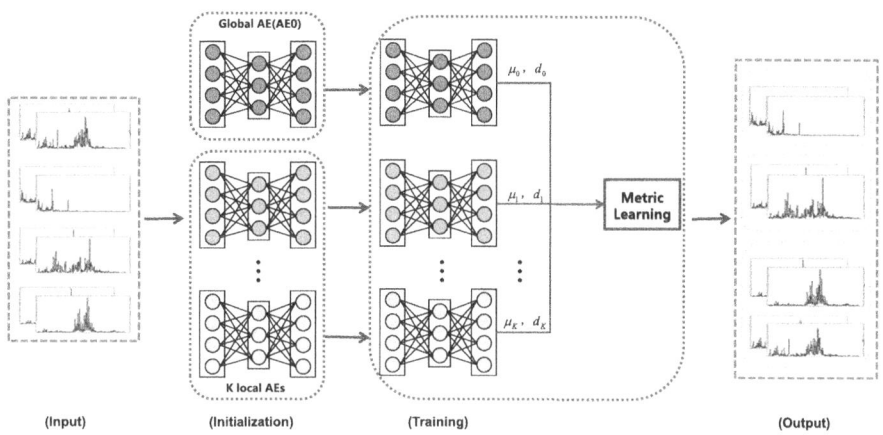

Fig. 1. Flowchart of SADAE

Here, $W_k^{(m)}$ and $b_k^{(m)}$ are the weights and bias connect the $(m-1)$-th layer and m-th layer, respectively. $f(\cdot)$ is an element-wise nonlinear activation function. The reconstruction loss of AE_k is defined by the Euclidean distance as

$$\Omega_k = ||O_k^{(M)} - x||_2^2. \tag{2}$$

There are two main steps in the training strategy for K local AEs (AE_k, $k = 1, \ldots, K$). Firstly, a sample $x \in X$ is clustered into a single local AE obtained in the subspace on line with the smallest reconstruction loss to x. Then, based on clustering results, AE_k is updated selectively for samples in X_k, which is the set of samples have the smallest Ω_k. These two steps iterate for expanding the inter-cluster distances.

3.2   Training SADAE

Assume a dataset X is given, $X = \{x_i\}_{i=1}^n$, the application of AE_k leads to the output of $\{O_{k,i}^{(M)}\}_{i=1}^n$, $k = 0, \ldots, K$. Therefore, the corresponding reconstruction loss of x_i regarding AE_k can be expressed as:

$$\Omega_{k,i} = ||O_{k,i}^{(M)} - x_i||_2^2. \tag{3}$$

The distance between each pair of features (x_i, x_j) for each individual AE_k, $k = 0, \ldots, K$, is computed as:

$$dis_k(x_i, x_j) = ||O_{k,i}^{(M)} - O_{k,j}^{(M)}||_2^2. \tag{4}$$

For each $dis_k(x_i, x_j)$, the associated weight is

$$\omega_k(x_i, x_j) = \frac{\tau(\Omega_{k,i}, \Omega_{k,j})}{\sum_{l=0}^K \tau(\Omega_{l,i}, \Omega_{l,j})}, \tag{5}$$

where

$$\tau(\Omega_{k,i}, \Omega_{k,j}) = \frac{1}{\Omega_{k,i} + \Omega_{k,j}}. \tag{6}$$

For all AE_k, the sample pairwise distance between x_i and x_j) with weights applied can be computed as:

$$D(x_i, x_j) = \sum_{k=0}^{K} \omega_k(x_i, x_j) dis_k(x_i, x_j). \tag{7}$$

Let $u_{ij} = 0$ represent that x_i and x_j are in the same class, otherwise $u_{ij} = 1$. Furthermore, denote the uniform radius of each sample's neighbourhood in X as R, the SADAE's main object rule can then be expressed:

$$\forall x_i, x_j \in X : \text{if } D(x_i, x_j) < R, \text{ then } u_{ij} = 0. \tag{8}$$

Consequently, the primary objective rule as expressed in Eq. (8) can be expressed as the following hinge loss function:

$$L_1(W, b, \rho) = \sum_{i,j} \frac{1}{\beta} \log(1 + \exp(\beta u_{ij}(R - D(x_i, x_j)))) \tag{9}$$

Two more regularisation terms, as follows, will be incorporated into L_1.

$$L_2(\rho) = -R. \tag{10}$$

$$L_3(W, b) = \sum_{k=0}^{K} \sum_{m=1}^{M} (\|W_k^{(m)}\|_F^2 + \|b_k^{(m)}\|_2^2). \tag{11}$$

As the summation of L_1, L_2 and L_3, the general loss function of SADAE is

$$L(W, b, R) = \lambda_1 L_1(W, b, R) + \lambda_2 L_2(R) + \frac{1}{2}\lambda_3 L_3(W, b) \tag{12}$$

In this paper, the parameters $W_k^{(m)}, b_k^{(m)}$ for $k = 0, \ldots, K$ and $m = 1, \ldots, M$, along with the radius ρ, are optimised via the SGD algorithm. Once the SADAE is fully trained, the resultant parameter values are utilised to generate the discriminative features that will represent the samples:

$$O_i = \sum_{k=0}^{K} \rho_{k,i} O_{k,i}^{(M)}, i = 1, \ldots, n. \tag{13}$$

$$\rho_{k,i} = \frac{\frac{1}{\theta_{k,i}}}{\sum_{k=0}^{K} \frac{1}{\theta_{k,i}}}, \tag{14}$$

where O_i represents the enhancement of x_i, which will be employed in network intrusion detection tasks as reported in the next section.

4 Experimental Evaluation

4.1 Used Datasets

This section reports comparative studies using the NSL-KDD dataset in addition to a class-balanced dataset sampled from the CSE-CIC-IDS2018 dataset. The detailed setup of theses two datasets are as follows. The information of the two used datasets is shown in Tables 1 and 2, respectively.

Table 1. The binary datasets of NSL-KDD dataset and CSE-CIC-IDS2018

Dataset	Type	Total	Training set	Testing set
NSL-KDD	Normal	77054	67343	9711
	Anomaly	71465	58630	12835
CSE-CIC-IDS2018	Benign	50000	40000	10000
	Attack	50000	40000	10000

Table 2. The multi-classification distribution of datasets NSL-KDD and the processed CSE-CIC-IDS2018

Dataset	Type	Total	Training set	Testing set
NSL-KDD	Normal	77054	67343	9711
	DoS	54879	47420	7459
	Probe	12584	10163	2421
	R2L	3880	995	2885
	U2R	119	52	67
CSE-CIC-IDS2018	Benign	50000	40000	10000
	DoS attacks (Hulk)	25000	20000	5000
	DoS attacks-Slow HTTP Test	25000	20000	5000

4.2 Local AEs:

This subsection investigates different K values and their effect on the NSL-KDD dataset. The respective K values obtained for the six SADAE frames are 0, 1, 2, 3, 4, and 5. A fully connection layer is used to classify the features extracted by these SADAE models.

The comparative results using different K values are summarised in Table 3 and Table 4. The classification accuracies of SADAE increase with higher values of K. However, a large K makes the training process time-consuming. Hence, selecting an appropriate K beforehand significantly enhances classification results. For our experiments, K is set to 4.

Table 3. Binary classification results of SADAE on the NSL-KDD dataset with various K values

K	Accuracy	Precision	Auc	Recall	F1-score
0	0.8537	0.8186	0.8422	0.7256	0.8021
1	0.8749	0.8321	0.8601	0.7510	0.8291
2	0.8805	0.8397	0.8763	0.7586	0.8408
3	0.8873	0.8455	0.8784	0.7750	0.8469
4	**0.9031**	**0.8589**	**0.8839**	**0.7831**	**0.8625**
5	**0.9088**	**0.8601**	**0.8954**	**0.7920**	**0.8698**

Table 4. Multi-classification results of SADAE on the NSL-KDD dataset with various K values

K	Accuracy	Precision	Auc	Recall	F1-score
0	0.8099	0.7638	0.7728	0.7481	0.7357
1	0.8325	0.7844	0.8049	0.7626	0.7531
2	0.8549	0.8071	0.8288	0.7751	0.7835
3	0.8620	0.8231	0.8433	0.7959	0.7866
4	**0.8642**	**0.8315**	**0.8532**	**0.8031**	**0.7956**
5	**0.8756**	**0.8434**	**0.8548**	**0.8059**	**0.8131**

4.3 Binary and Multi-Class Network Intrusion Detection

In this experiment, SADAE is compared against three popular classification methods (SVM, KNN and random forest (RF)), three deep learning methods (DNN [31], CNN [4] and Autoencoder [12]), and three metric learning algorithms (ITML [26], LSML [35] and NCA [8]).

The SADAE framework includes four local AEs and one global AE. Each AE consists of seven layers with varying model parameters. In Algorithm 3, the values of parameters λ_1, λ_2, and λ_3 are determined as 0.1, 0.9, and 0.0005, respectively. In addition, the learning rate is est as 0.001, and the original radius threshold is set as 3.0.

Based on the experimentation on the NSL-KDD dataset, the precision, accuracy, AUC, recall, as well as f1-score results for binary and multi-class NID are recorded in Tables 5 and 6, respectively. Also, those for the sampled CSE-CIC-IDS2018 dataset are recorded in Tables 7 and 8, respectively.

Based on the comparison results, SADAE performs the best in reference to all of the referenced approaches in terms of all evaluation metrics. This indicates that the proposed SADAE approach can effectively handle NID tasks with competitive performance demonstrated. The excellent results are resulted from both the AEs which reveal the local nonlinearity entailed in the datasets and the self-adaptive deep ML which well detects the marginal differences between various

Table 5. Binary results (NSL-KDD)

Method	Precision	Accuracy	AUC	Recall	F1-score
SVM	0.8226	0.7638	0.8034	0.7267	0.7128
KNN	0.8118	0.7879	0.8163	0.7150	0.7601
RF	0.8121	0.7747	0.8309	0.7183	0.7522
DNN	0.8649	0.8233	0.8764	0.7801	0.8421
CNN	0.8562	0.8113	0.8519	0.7725	0.8146
Autoencoder	0.8508	0.8209	0.8365	0.7612	0.8357
ITML	0.8634	0.8326	0.8532	0.7521	0.8244
LSML	0.8521	0.8259	0.8627	0.7638	0.8051
NCA	0.8369	0.8037	0.8461	0.7532	0.7937
SADAE	**0.9031**	**0.8589**	**0.8839**	**0.7831**	**0.8625**

Table 6. Multi-classification results (NSL-KDD)

Method	Accuracy	Precision	AUC	Recall	F1-score
SVM	0.8137	0.7666	0.7445	0.7366	0.6966
KNN	0.8107	0.7715	0.7591	0.7703	0.7353
RF	0.8243	0.7853	0.7787	0.7569	0.7477
DNN	0.8369	0.8256	0.8369	0.7725	0.7576
CNN	0.8428	0.8185	0.7912	0.7636	0.7549
Autoencoder	0.8108	0.8019	0.8068	0.7448	0.7359
ITML	0.8219	0.8053	0.7875	0.7629	0.7913
LSML	0.8424	0.8237	0.7921	0.7738	0.7613
NCA	0.8227	0.8133	0.8160	0.7835	0.7721
SADAE	**0.8642**	**0.8315**	**0.8532**	**0.8031**	**0.7956**

Table 7. Binary results (CSE-CIC-IDS2018)

Method	Precision	Accuracy	AUC	Recall	F1-score
SVM	0.9531	0.9429	0.9537	0.8726	0.9158
KNN	0.9499	0.9314	0.9653	0.8657	0.9271
RF	0.9588	0.9425	0.9704	0.8865	0.9233
DNN	0.9805	0.9659	0.9825	0.9359	0.9646
CNN	0.9764	0.9617	0.9816	0.9428	0.9583
Autoencoder	0.9692	0.9536	0.9759	0.9237	0.9337
ITML	0.9751	0.9596	0.9812	0.9433	0.9631
LSML	0.9727	0.9534	0.9860	0.9389	0.9782
NCA	0.9649	0.9388	0.9735	0.9105	0.9565
SADAE	**0.9973**	**0.9982**	**0.9931**	**0.9798**	**0.9957**

Table 8. Multi-classification outcomes (CSE-CIC-IDS2018)

Method	Precision	Accuracy	AUC	Recall	F1-score
SVM	0.9655	0.9521	0.9736	0.9351	0.9566
KNN	0.9434	0.9315	0.9659	0.9103	0.9264
RF	0.9572	0.9459	0.9683	0.9156	0.9329
DNN	0.9846	0.9717	0.9894	0.9533	0.9617
CNN	0.9801	0.9691	0.9851	0.9460	0.9526
Autoencoder	0.9638	0.9432	0.9773	0.9302	0.9514
ITML	0.9742	0.9554	0.9852	0.9315	0.9452
LSML	0.9685	0.9526	0.9746	0.9322	0.9385
NCA	0.9533	0.9373	0.9640	0.9244	0.9199
SADAE	**0.9970**	**0.9982**	**0.9990**	**0.9988**	**0.9847**

network attacks, and thus significantly enhance the separability of instances in different classes.

5 Conclusion

This paper employs a DML method and develops SADAE for the detection of network intrusions. SADAE integrates several local and global AEs, where each local AE is responsible for mining the local nonlinear features of the data whilst the global AE controls the spatial extent of the image features. By utilising the adaptive metric learning technique, the SADAE is able to automatically identify and delineate the boundaries of different categories, thus enhancing the differentiation of heterogeneous data. The outcome of the experiments show that SADAE performs better than multiple state-of-the-art intrusion detection approaches based on NSL-KDD and the sampled CSE-CIC-IDS2018. This result signals that SADAE has great potential in practical applications and deserves further research for NIDS.

In the future, this paper will develop and test the performance of SADAE on other publicly available network intrusion detection datasets, such as UNSW-NB15, CTU-13, etc., to validate its generalisation capability. In addition, this paper will optimise the training process of SADAE to reduce the computing cost, increase the processing speed, and optimise the model performance in combination with other deep learning methods.

References

1. Ahmad, Z., Shahid Khan, A., Wai Shiang, C., Abdullah, J., Ahmad, F.: Network intrusion detection system: a systematic study of machine learning and deep learning approaches. Trans. Emerg. Telecommun. Technol. **32**(1), e4150 (2021)
2. Andresini, G., Appice, A., Malerba, D.: Autoencoder-based deep metric learning for network intrusion detection. Inf. Sci. **569**, 706–727 (2021)
3. Andresini, G., Appice, A., Mauro, N.D., Loglisci, C., Malerba, D.: Multi-channel deep feature learning for intrusion detection. IEEE Access **8**, 53346–53359 (2020)
4. Ashiku, L., Dagli, C.: Network intrusion detection system using deep learning. Procedia Comput. Sci. **185**, 239–247 (2021)
5. Bellet, A., Habrard, A., Sebban, M.: Metric Learning. Springer (2022)
6. Chauhan, A., Davoudi, O., Komeili, M.: Multi-scale deep nearest neighbors. In: 2021 International Joint Conference on Neural Networks (IJCNN), pp. 1–8 (2021)
7. Chen, G., Lu, Y., Lu, J., Zhou, J.: Deep credible metric learning for unsupervised domain adaptation person re-identification. In: Vedaldi, A., Bischof, H., Brox, T., Frahm, J.-M. (eds.) ECCV 2020. LNCS, vol. 12353, pp. 643–659. Springer, Cham (2020). https://doi.org/10.1007/978-3-030-58598-3_38
8. Daanouni, O., Cherradi, B., Tmiri, A.: Diabetes diseases prediction using supervised machine learning and neighbourhood components analysis. In: Proceedings of the 3rd International Conference on Networking, Information Systems & Security. NISS '20, Association for Computing Machinery, New York, NY, USA (2020)
9. Deng, C., Qiao, H.: Network security intrusion detection system based on incremental improved convolutional neural network model. In: 2016 International Conference on Communication and Electronics Systems (ICCES), pp. 1–5 (2016)
10. Duan, Y., Lu, J., Feng, J., Zhou, J.: Deep localized metric learning. IEEE Trans. Cir. Syst. Video Technol. **28**(10), 2644–2656 (2018)
11. Engen, V., Vincent, J., Phalp, K.: Exploring discrepancies in findings obtained with the KDD cup '99 data set. Intell. Data Anal. **15**(251–276), 2 (2011)
12. Farahnakian, F., Heikkonen, J.: A deep auto-encoder based approach for intrusion detection system. In: 2018 20th International Conference on Advanced Communication Technology (ICACT), pp. 178–183 (2018)
13. Ghanem, K., Aparicio-Navarro, F.J., Kyriakopoulos, K.G., Lambotharan, S., Chambers, J.A.: Support vector machine for network intrusion and cyber-attack detection. In: 2017 Sensor Signal Processing for Defence Conference (SSPD), pp. 1–5 (2017)
14. Imran, M., Haider, N., Shoaib, M., Razzak, I.: An intelligent and efficient network intrusion detection system using deep learning. Comput. Electr. Eng. **99**, 107764 (2022)
15. Imrana, Y., Xiang, Y., Ali, L., Abdul-Rauf, Z.: A bidirectional LSTM deep learning approach for intrusion detection. Expert Syst. Appl. **185**, 115524 (2021)
16. Kaya, M., Bilge, H.S.: Deep metric learning: a survey. Symmetry **11**(9), 1066 (2019)
17. Kelleher, J.D.: Deep Learning. MIT Press (2019)
18. Khan, M.A.: HCRNNIDS: hybrid convolutional recurrent neural network-based network intrusion detection system. Processes **9**(5), 834 (2021)
19. Kim, J., Kim, J., Kim, H., Shim, M., Choi, E.: CNN-based network intrusion detection against denial-of-service attacks. Electronics **9**(6), 916 (2020)
20. Laghrissi, F., Douzi, S., Douzi, K., Hssina, B.: Intrusion detection systems using long short-term memory (LSTM). J. Big Data **8**(1), 65 (2021)

21. Li, J., Qu, Y., Chao, F., Shum, H.P.H., Ho, E.S.L., Yang, L.: Machine learning algorithms for network intrusion detection, pp. 151–179. Springer, Cham (2019)
22. Liao, S., Shao, L.: Graph sampling based deep metric learning for generalizable person re-identification. In: Proceedings of the IEEE/CVF Conference on Computer Vision and Pattern Recognition (CVPR), pp. 7359–7368 (2022)
23. Lin, W.H., Lin, H.C., Wang, P., Wu, B.H., Tsai, J.Y.: Using convolutional neural networks to network intrusion detection for cyber threats. In: 2018 IEEE International Conference on Applied System Invention (ICASI), pp. 1107–1110 (2018)
24. Mohan, D.D., Sankaran, N., Fedorishin, D., Setlur, S., Govindaraju, V.: Moving in the right direction: a regularization for deep metric learning. In: Proceedings of the IEEE/CVF Conference on Computer Vision and Pattern Recognition (CVPR) (2020)
25. Pimsarn, C., Boongoen, T., Iam-On, N., Naik, N., Yang, L.: Strengthening intrusion detection system for adversarial attacks: improved handling of imbalance classification problem. Complex Intell. Syst. **8**(6), 4863–4880 (2022)
26. Qingjun, T., Jianzhong, H.: Bearing performance degradation assessment based on information-theoretic metric learning and fuzzy c-means clustering. Measur. Sci. Technol. **31**(7), 075001 (2020)
27. Roopa Devi, E., Suganthe, R.: Enhanced transductive support vector machine classification with grey wolf optimizer cuckoo search optimization for intrusion detection system. Concurrency Comput. Pract. Exp. **32**(4), e4999 (2020)
28. Sharafaldin, I., Lashkari, A.H., Ghorbani, A.A., et al.: Toward generating a new intrusion detection dataset and intrusion traffic characterization. ICISSp **1**, 108–116 (2018)
29. Sommer, R., Paxson, V.: Outside the closed world: on using machine learning for network intrusion detection. In: 2010 IEEE Symposium on Security and Privacy, pp. 305–316 (2010)
30. Taheri, M., Moslehi, Z., Mirzaei, A., Safayani, M.: A self-adaptive local metric learning method for classification. Pattern Recogn. **96**, 106994 (2019)
31. Tang, C., Luktarhan, N., Zhao, Y.: SAAE-DNN: deep learning method on intrusion detection. Symmetry **12**(10), 1695 (2020)
32. Tang, Y., Gu, L., Wang, L.: Deep stacking network for intrusion detection. Sensors **22**(1), 25 (2022)
33. Wang, W., Zhu, M., Wang, J., Zeng, X., Yang, Z.: End-to-end encrypted traffic classification with one-dimensional convolution neural networks. In: 2017 IEEE International Conference on Intelligence and Security Informatics (ISI), pp. 43–48 (2017)
34. Wang, Z., et al.: Honeynet construction based on intrusion detection. In: Proceedings of the 3rd International Conference on Computer Science and Application Engineering. CSAE '19, Association for Computing Machinery, New York, NY, USA (2019). https://doi.org/10.1145/3331453.3360983
35. Wei, Z., Zhang, B., Wu, Y.: Accurate wide angle SAR imaging based on LS-CS-residual. Sensors **19**(3), 490 (2019)
36. Yan, B., Han, G.: Effective feature extraction via stacked sparse autoencoder to improve intrusion detection system. IEEE Access **6**, 41238–41248 (2018)
37. Yang, L., Li, J., Fehringer, G., Barraclough, P., Sexton, G., Cao, Y.: Intrusion detection system by fuzzy interpolation. In: 2017 IEEE International Conference on Fuzzy Systems (FUZZ-IEEE), pp. 1–6 (2017)
38. Yang, Y., Zheng, K., Wu, B., Yang, Y., Wang, X.: Network intrusion detection based on supervised adversarial variational auto-encoder with regularization. IEEE Access **8**, 42169–42184 (2020)

39. Zhang, Q., Qu, Y., Deng, A.: Network intrusion detection using kernel-based fuzzy-rough feature selection. In: 2018 IEEE International Conference on Fuzzy Systems (FUZZ-IEEE), pp. 1–6 (2018)
40. Zhao, R., Qu, Y., Deng, A., Zwiggelaar, R.: Inconsistency measure associated discretization methods to network-based intrusion detection. In: 2018 IEEE International Conference on Fuzzy Systems (FUZZ-IEEE), pp. 1–6 (2018)
41. Zheng, W., Zhang, B., Lu, J., Zhou, J.: Deep relational metric learning. In: Proceedings of the IEEE/CVF International Conference on Computer Vision (ICCV), pp. 12065–12074 (2021)

AI and Forensics Security with Cloud, Networks Impact on Education

Xiaohua Feng[✉]

University of Bedfordshire, Luton 1 3JU, UK
`Xiaohua.Feng@beds.ac.uk`

Abstract. The generative Artificial Intelligence (AI) innovation to cloud-edge computing and wireless networks has impact on forensics sciences education and pedagogy. A research has been carried out, concentrating on the influence on recent generative AI innovations affected the cloud-edge computing. Case studies in digital forensics were investigated, currently. Research has been conducted in information communications technology data, and so on relevant field. It should be significant to let the forensics sciences educators aware the challenges they face, and mitigation would be helpful for teaching and learning. The outcome of this research is to update the curriculum strategy, in order to mitigate AI impact to forensics sciences using computer laws.

Keywords: Wireless Networks · Cloud–Edge Computing · Artificial Intelligence and Education Impact · Forensics Sciences and Security · Computer Law

1 Introduction

Nowadays, generative Artificial Intelligence (AI) innovation has created more unlawful challenges for cloud-edge computing; such as model stealing and data poisoning, particularly on digital forensics.

Generative AI could cause some misleading knowledge, in particular, legal knowledge, especially for digital forensics education on the cloud. In this article, we investigated some case studies and discussed the mitigation impact on curriculum development, particularly regarding digital forensics education curriculum policy, with a number of collaboration experts worldwide. Some states had published codes to co-operate these trends. The following sections introduced cloud-edge computing, the forensic science serving them, the legal importance, and AI impact, especially the impact on education. Further development actions with collaboration experts worldwide are suggested [2–7].

2 Background

An investigation on teaching and learning of the cloud-edge computing and with wireless networks digital forensics threat [7–10] resulted from generative AI innovation impact, had been carried out at the University of Bedfordshire and some of UK HEIs (Higher

X. Feng et al. (Eds.): CloudComp 2024, LNICST 617, pp. 118–130, 2026.
https://doi.org/10.1007/978-3-031-92517-7_9

Education Institution) [11–15]. Investigation focused on the education data and law data; in particular, forensics science education information and the related T and L (Teaching and Learning) data information.

Presently, wireless networks have been got into everybody's daily life, it affects the whole world. Through smart phone, iPad, GPS (Global Positioning System), E-business, E-government, E-banking, E-voting, E-healthcare, social media online service and so on, computing is everywhere at every-time, for human being.

Wireless computing network is one of the fast evolved area, rapidly change all the time; which made computing education and pedagogic research developing all the time. Cyber criminal is taking advantage of rapid technologies development, Forensics science and security technologies could ensure safety and reliability communications and so on.

With wireless computing networks increasing, the cloud-edge computing, robust security setting guaranteed digital forensics sciences and cybersecurity for cloud users' activities; especially at smart cities [15]. While edge computing process data information locally. Reduce timing latency issues. Not only there is no transmission bandwidth problem, but also escaped traffic jam, network congestions. As well as, avoid privacy of sensitive data protection issues.

Education of wireless networking needs keep pace with the times, and teaching each students in accordance with their aptitude. To academic staff, there are huge demands around student-centred computing education, in particular, the innovation impact leads many challenges to us (Fig. 1).

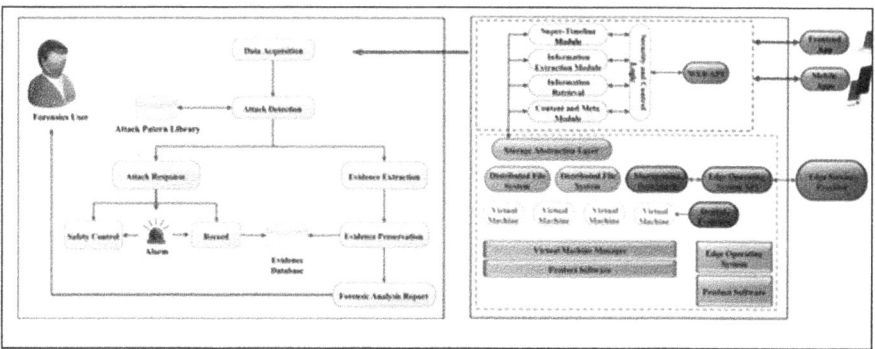

Fig. 1. Forensics Attack-resisting Framework [15]

2.1 Generative AI Innovation Impact

This investigation approach crossed subject areas and involved PG (post-graduate) and UG (under-graduate) students at CSEE of HEIs (Higher Education Institution), including Copilot, ChatGPT, and other Large Language Models (LLMs). When LLMs (Large Language Models) generative AI tools were developed, training is naturally required, needing plenty of data to feed into the models. The process may store sensitive information data, even PII (Personally Identifiable Information) confidential data, and leak it under the inducement of some deliberate questions.

For instance, the CEO (Chief Executive Officer) of OpenAI, Sam Altman, was accused of deceptive misleading information, which threatened public trust as never before. When the public received untrustworthy information data, the credibility of society as a whole might be damaged. For example, in 2023, the New York Times sued OpenAI and Microsoft, accusing these two companies of using millions of articles published by the New York Times to train artificial intelligence models, which could lead to integrity risks and sensitive information challenges. Similarly, training Copilot could lead to copyright issues threatening coding T and L (teaching and learning) in ICT (Information Communication Technology) education. Such examples emerged frequently [11–15].

2.2 The Cloud-Edge Computing and Forensics Concept

A literature review has been carried out recently. The NIST (National Institute of Standards and Technology) defined cloud computing as: "A computing storage system that provides on-demand network access for multiple users and can allocate storage to users to keep up with changes in their needs." [16-22] Historically, the idea of cloud computing came from several people. [7-12]

The cloud has three service levels: Software as a service (SaaS) - applications are delivered via the Internet. Platform as a service (PaaS) - a new Operating System has been installed on a cloud server. Infrastructure as a service (IaaS) - customers could rent hardware and install whatever Operating Systems and applications they demanded. Deployment methods for the cloud were:

Public - accessible to anyone.

Private - could be accessed only by people who have the necessary credentials, and Hybrid." [23].

"The cloud itself has advantages in storage capacity, considerable computational power, robust security, and so on. Nevertheless, cloud forensics investigations face unique challenges – standard and ICT laws for cloud-edge computing are still in demand." [11].

2.3 Regarding the Cloud-Edge in Forensics Science

"Cloud forensics is considered a subset of network forensics in the forensic sciences subject area, which is a cross-subject area between Law and Science and technologies. Cloud forensics could have three dimensions: Organisational - addresses the structure of the cloud; Legal - covers service agreements and other jurisdictional matters; and Technical - deals with procedures and specialised applications designed to perform forensic recovery and analysis in cloud-edge computing."

"Cloud forensics investigations face unique challenges. Forensic tool capabilities are needed to handle acquiring data from the cloud. Evidence segregation, etc., are technical challenges." [23] "AccessData, PhoneLogs, and F-Response, etc., are all cloud integration tools to select. So did Forensic Open Stack tool (FROST)." When LLMs launched, challenges emerged in Cloud and networks forensics education [1].

"Edge Computing is the current developing trend. Edge Computing Forensics applications running on edge computing must be capable of supporting taking legal action against invaders for malicious damage or information theft." [25] "There were no network configuration, transmission jam, bandwidth, network congestion, latency, information sniff and reveal, and so on threat." [1] Alexakos published their work in this subject area, suggesting development. [2] "Edge computing could provide better rates at the edge. However, recent AI innovations have increased legal challenges. Secure edge computing methodology is applied in both open and heterogeneous networked systems to protect them. [10] from many potential security threats and risks.". [11] The Fig. 2 below demonstrates a forensics framework example as follows.

2.4 Computer Law Challenge

In legal issues, some problems have been revealed. In forensic science, the key is evidence accuracy and integrity. Evidence preservation is necessary. If evidence is not original, the evidence is not valid and cannot be used in legal matters. Any modifications to evidence, including any generative AI LLMs did, have to be dealt with and legal actions taken.

2.4.1 Limitations

The LLMs training data could have word text, log files, records, graphs, photos, images, audio, video, copyright protection cover. Also, LLMs might store these data and be revealed in transfer situations by malicious sniffing in cyberspace. For instance, in 2023, the CEO of OpenAI company Mr. Sam Altman publicly admitted that a mistake had happened in the open-source repository, leading to a few chat histories of customers with ChatGPT being leaked [7]. And after Samsung Ltd. allowed the use of ChatGPT, the company was exposed to data breaches that led to the leakage of sensitive and confidential information in internal meetings [13]. The security threat shown.

2.4.2 Data Governance Under GDPR

The 2018 enforced GDPR offered stronger legal protection for more sensitive information, like race, ethnic background, political opinions, religious beliefs, trade union membership, genetics, biometrics, EDI (Equality, diversity and inclusion) information etc., to serve European residents, European organisations, European business partners, and whoever provides service to Europeans. Offering robust security to protect their sensitive information, PII data, and so on [10].

2.4.3 Generative AI Impact

Currently, ML (Machine Learning) and DL (Deep Learning) generative AI techniques are very popular. Their applications are spread over many areas, not only in the ICT field but also in other subject areas. However, ML and DL all need much training before performing service. These training data served for AI could expose CIAA (Confidentiality, Integrity, Availability and Audit). Forensic science could discover the revealed impact on original data then act accordingly.

2.4.4   Digital Forensics Generative AI Case Example

The famous media Reuters reported, [21] "New York lawyers sanctioned for using fake ChatGPT cases in legal brief." We have investigated that sensitive data had been carried out in cases. This kind of approach had crossed subject areas, involving PG (postgraduate) and UG (undergraduate) students at CSEE (Computer Sciences and Electrical Engineering) of HEI, further education colleges, schools, and online professional training by the cloud, including Copilot, ChatGPT, DeepSeek and AI education tools such as teacher matic, CoPilot sidebar etc.

Although current performance testing innovations such as Apache JMeter, BlazeMeter, and Gatling had given useful capabilities and features, there was one common gap: dynamic load testing. These technologies were not capable of dynamically applying loads to web applications based on the response rates expected, including in the cloud.

3   Proposed System

Qualitative method were applied in the explorations. In the case study, Idris [15] had proposed a framework for LLMs in the cloud and networks as Fig. 2 shown from the qualitative research. After collaborating with legal experts, forensics science education about systemed networks, especially vulnerable wireless networks architecture cyber security defence as well as the cloud-edging architecture cyber security consideration should include law impact, when deploying security education methods for a cloud education, including making use of wireless networks to carry out remote education [15].

This framework could help to be used in cloud or wireless networks environments, both for public, private, and hybrid cloud or wireless networks applications with networks technology by LLMs assistance. Furthermore, to be reflected in curriculum design strategies would benefit the cloud-edging networks forensics applications in HEI, schools, professional training, and all the education organisations about forensic science in societies worldwide [11]. Idris [15] had also discussed the weight of generative AI LLMs impact on T & L data. The basic concept is shown in Table 1 as follows.

Thinking about the education philosophy should be teaching each individual student according to their aptitude. That could be as one of the HEI principles. In order to ascend another storey to see a thousand miles further. Keep pace with the times; to densify the higher education students' progress. To make an efficient use of the opportunities, to take a ride in the current time development of generative AI challenges. Figure 2 had shown a wireless networking course at a hybrid-Learning environment through generative AI-Driven LLMs Framework Example [15]. It is also could available to Wireless Networks or the hybrid cloud edging computing circumstances.

Based on the above, generative AI case study analytics of impact challenges were facing had been carried out. Idris did some investigation [15]. Output a suggested resource data allocation could be prioritized to: Skills and staff development (25%), information management and ethics (20%), Curriculum UCIF (unit and course information forms) Design (30%), Pedagogy and innovation (10%), with Infrastructure and Inter-operability receiving (10%); as a further research reference. A summarized as Table 1 shown.

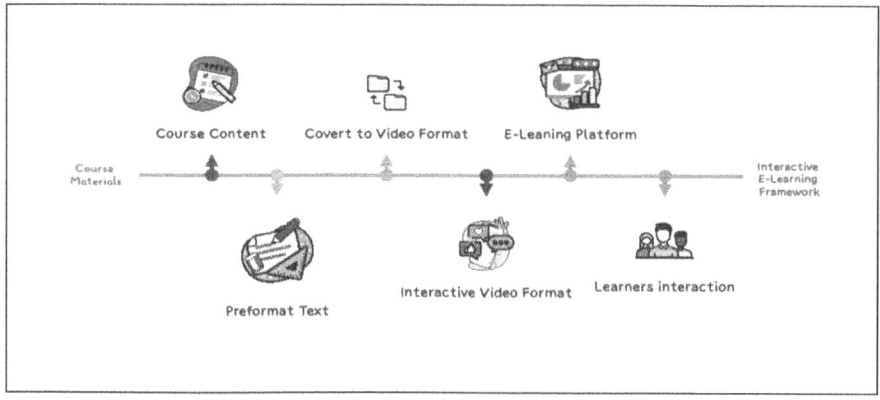

Fig. 2. A Hybrid T & L through Generative AI-Driven LLMs Framework Example [15]

Table 1. The Data Resource in the Case Study

Data source	Allocated percentage	Note
Skill and staff development	25%	
Management and Ethics	25%	
UCIF design	30%	
Infrastructure & Interoperability	10%	
Pedagogics and innovation	10%	

The above table shown the workforce and their load in our case study investigation. It provide a research planning potential comparisons. From the survey shown, curriculum design took an important role. Therefore future work could consider the curriculum design strategy priorities. Especially in this technology innovation exploration period. Generative AI in forensics sciences education taking an considerable role, particularly for HEIs.

In the later section, the impact of generative AI to law will be discussed in details. The consequence of law in forensics sciences education position will be demonstrated.

In our exploration project, another analysis focused on generative AI impact influence were also being carried out. Table 2 demonstrated this work.

In this way, the Table 2 about LLMs impact on data analysis shown the potential of consequence of generative AI, therefore priority of response required with the society could be predicted and planned.

Because of forensics sciences heavily rely on evidence for case decisions; legal matter is quite important for forensics. Particularly digital forensics is easily affected by generative AI impact for digital forensics evidence, all of these potentially produce consequence for forensics sciences education and pedagogic researches. Nowadays, the release of the ChatGPT developed by OpenAI swiftly triggered an extensive interest in the field of generative AI in the world. Generative AI is applied in a wider range of

Table 2. LLMs Impact on Data Analysis

Number	Evidence Data Item	Impact	Notes
1	Data Management and Ethics	90%	By qualitative pedagogic research
2	Information Governance	80%	
3	Structure /Inter-operation	60%	
4	Skills and Training	70%	
5	Computer Law	50%	
6	Education Curriculum Strategy	100%	By T & L result
7	Research and Innovation	60%	

scenarios while efficiently contributed to the development of technology, economy and society. The innovation results have prompted a new era of worldwide; in particular, a number of education subjects facing challenges. People had to admit, generative AI had brought many positive effect for human beings' daily life. Meanwhile, mitigation on the non-positive side is in urgent demand. However, generative AI had brought technological impact to legislation multi-faceted challenges. Considering the widespread use of generative AI, legislators, scholars and the legal industry still have a long way to go in risk mitigation for the evolving AI technology. The trustworthy AI regulatory philosophy is worth further perception or insight by academics and legislation. The Internet and cloud service providers should take corporate social responsibilities for our society. Cross subject collaboration could be necessary for forensics sciences education and research. While forensics sciences unlike Blockchain technology, would be affected by the generative AI. In the case study of digital forensics, it was shown to this kind of situations, digital forensics could have the similar impact which will be discussed in the next section.

4   The Investigation Output About Date

Have been focused on the recent generative AI impact on UK HEI Education and Pedagogic Research, further development will include analysis and updated results in the next publication. Furthermore, we suggest a curriculum development for student-centered Teaching & Learning strategy and recommendations to serve non-HEI users in society in the world.

Through a literature review and interviews with experts, plus analysis of existing LLMs, results were summarized. Generative AI tools could distort evidence or provide misleading legal case evidence to law enforcement professionals [15]. Mohamed Idris et al. [15] pointed out that AI LLM models require training to be powerful and functional. Training material could be sensitive or confidential and might be leaked unconsciously by generative AI developers, resulting in invalid evidence and damage to forensic science. In the case study, several law companies or agencies were investigated regarding AI impact, particularly the effect of LLMs on them, as shown in the following Table 3. A few experts suggested that before training, the training corpus should be carefully checked by competent human staff, to ensure generative AI innovation still keep forensics evidence integrity to case.

In the case study, a number of Law companies or agencies were investigated on AI impact; in particular, LLMs effect to them; as following Table 3 shown.

Table 3. Computer Law *Company*/Agency Examples in the Case Study

Name	Function
Allen & Overy	legal advice on *build a commercial practice*
Bryan Cave Leighton Paisner	deliver legal solutions to Real Estate, Corporate and Finance Transactions, and Litigation & Investigations
Clifford Chance	corporate reorganisations, distressed situations and bankruptcy and insolvency proceedings
DWF	integrated legal and business services
Fagougou	search engine for sentence prediction for criminal cases
FaXin	legal information platform
Gowling WLG	Intellectual property, construction, commercial litigation and international disputes fraud, asset tracing, contentious trusts and insurance or reinsurance
Mecheck	A legal search platform provider
MetaLaw	An AI-powered legal tool service
Pecoepic	Intellectual property investigation (evidence acquisition)
Taylor Wessing	On business growth and protection
Wolters Kluwer	Legitimate Recommendation to Case Legal document provider

4.1 Generative AI Impact in Laws

From investigation about forensics sciences education, the research output shown, generative AI impact in Laws are mainly in the aspect of Sect. 4.1 discussed and the evidence from the case study are in the next section.

Research shown that, generative AI impact in laws were mainly in the aspects of the follows:

In data security, Large Language Models (LLMs) could unintendedly release information from training data, including private or sensitive data or material covered by copyright protection. From above analysis, LLMs might unintendedly release information from training data, including private or sensitive data or material covered by copyright protection. Although generative AI saved time and cost for human beings, the training corpus data checking before training do affect the cost effective rate in many ways [16].

For instance, some incident happened globally. On 23 March 2023, Open AI's CEO Sam Altman publicly admitted that an error in the open-source repository led to some users' information with ChatGPT leaked. Samsung was also exposed to data breaches that led to the leakage of sensitive and confidential information in internal meetings. As well as, the Italian Data Protection Authority (DPA) had banned the use of ChatGPT starting from March 31, 2023. All of the non-positive impact increased demanding for forensics sciences education curriculum strategy making.

Risk of generating incorrect or misleading information is also possible one of generative AI issues. In the areas of specialization that require high levels of information accuracy, particularly in the legal industry and forensics sciences education fields. Generative AI heavily rely on information generated by large models without verifying it could result in considerable damage. For instance, two lawyers in the US state of New York cited six cases collected by ChatGPT in legal papers submitted to the court. Another one, deepfake can also duplicate the facial, voice, and even behavioral patterns of one person to another, creating fictional content that appears to be authentic such as Law enforcement with facial recognition systems and bio-matrix information.

Integrity Issue in generative AI and cyber security would also to be think of. Generative AI LLMs to be built on the results of pre-existing human artistic creations have led creators to worry about the repercussions of copyright ownership of their works, like Open AI's Sora leads the Hollywood screenwriters' strike. In addition, the New York Times sued Open AI and Microsoft case Telecommunication fraud detection and administration of justice are all possible facing generative AI impact in laws.

There were also ethical challenges on AI recruitment and information cocoon assessment and so on.

4.2 Generative AI Impact on Forensics Sciences Evidence

Generative AI Impact on Forensics Sciences Evidence are as following.

Forensics sciences' evidence will submit to Crown court for Judge's decision. So they have to be original, accurate and keep integrity. Generative AI could autonomously generate content such as text, images, audio, video, and so on. Therefore not easy to assess the evidence is validate. There is a risk of generative AI could generate incorrect or misleading data (pseudo-normal evidence).

Also, generative AI not only could impact attribution and integrity; but also a doubt on trustworthy AI regulatory model. Provider obligation artificial intelligence is always driven by human beings, and the operation of generative AI requires human participation and control have to be trustworthy. For instance, Cloud forensics heavily rely on the CSP's (Cloud Service Provider) consent. The evidence accuracy have to be trustworthy in legal matters. Furthermore, information transportation, which verifies the discretion of law enforcement in which the application of generative AI to fix evidence has become the methodology of investigation.

Trustworthy issue, generative AI regulatory model issue lie in transparency and interpretability requirements for the design of generative AI systems. The decision-making process must be transparent in order to make users and regulators can understand the principle of the training model and the basis for decisions. Nevertheless, the trustworthy human-centred model seems to be a more compatible way of generative AI regulation. That is another challenge to forensics sciences education.

Another consideration is ISP (Internet service provider) obligation. Since the binding party of the contract, it shall obtain consent from the individual at the first step, especially in cloud forensics case to acquire cloud forensics evidence; and then with the collective data, it shall bear the responsibility of not infringing on the personal rights and privacy by users etc. human beings. Internet service provider shall have the obligation to take measures such as ML (Machine Learning) and DL (Deep Learning) as well as model optimization and training for rectification and to report to the relevant competent authorities.

5 Evaluation

Because AI innovation is relatively new, there are not many solutions in the market for detailed comparison and testing. Since these are still in the early stages, concept achievements could be reported. However, quantitative comparisons will be available in the near future. As more researchers realize the importance and participate in the trends, there will be more results with precise values to demonstrate the significance of the challenge.

5.1 Discussion

The core technology in forensic science is to provide precisely accurate evidence, which is legally responsible. Nevertheless, these AI innovations make maintaining evidence integrity very difficult. Evidence preservation heavily relies on forensic tools' support. These should be reflected in the curriculum strategy for forensic sciences education.

To avoid any misleading and distortion, the evidence impacting the significance of the case's judgment is the top priority. Hopefully, through worldwide collaboration, proper, efficient, and successful performance testing analysis will be accepted and pursued in high demand by relevant societies globally. At present, it is primary to cooperate the generative AI impact to forensics sciences. However, to education, it is in urgent demand, actions need to asap.

5.2 Challenges Emerging

AI technology has developed rapidly. To consistently follow cutting-edge technology updates, a consistent demand would be upon forensic teachers, students, professionals, particularly wireless networking and cloud-edging computing engineers and management staff.

Nevertheless, the effort to maintain the validity and truthfulness of legal evidence data and PII (Personally identifiable information) data [11] evidence is extremely important for societies. Idris et al. [17] has developed an algorithm, based on the experiment. Although pros and cons analysed, there are more challenges emerging in the applications.

6 Conclusions

Finally, to reach a conclusion. Overall, the following have been achieved. Working on curriculum strategies for forensic science education is necessary. A case study on digital forensics has been investigated. Computer laws are affected by recent AI innovations, as is digital forensics. Further work is in demand for forensic sciences worldwide.

6.1 Summary

In this article, a demonstration of students' investigation output was shown. AI technology has facilitated digital transformation, lightening the legal document paperwork burden of legislative, judicial, law enforcement, and clerical activities. However, technological advances have also created challenges.

Furthermore, CSP service providers should also take corporate social responsibilities. They ought to take countermeasures to protect confidential sensitive data and personal privacy (PII) of the customer's data governance. Not only focus mainly on liability avoidance, particularly for digital forensics on cloud-edge computing cases. Moreover, given the cross-border nature of AI technology, we look forward to collaborative efforts among the global community for the well-being of humankind. AI technology has facilitated the digital transformation of burdensome paperwork of legislative, judicial, and legal enforcement activities. Bear in mind, technological advances have created challenges at the same time. The recent technical development has demonstrated a vital impact on education and pedagogic research, which needs to be reflected in student-centered teaching strategies.

To protect PII security, relying on cyber law is limited, which is the lowest bottom line. Proactively preventing attack risk and protecting privacy information is needed.

6.2 Further Development

Future work on improving AI control and recognition in cloud education curriculum design should be in great demand. Moreover, because forensic sciences are a cross-border subject area, regarding AI technology-related issues, collaborative efforts between international education and pedagogic research professional societies are needed to work together for the citizens of the world. To protect PII security, relying on cyber law alone has limitations, which might affect the lowest bottom line. Proactively preventing threats or risks and protecting privacy information is needed. Although primary quantitative analytics have been implemented in a test manner, further quantitative implementation should be deployed in forensic science teaching and learning, particularly with global higher education institutes. More collected data with analytics reports will be submitted to the SWC 2025 conference for more insightful views.

References

1. Razaque, A., Aloqaily, M., Almiani, M., Jararweh, Y., Srivastava, G.: Efficient and reliable forensics using intelligent edge computing. ScienceDirect Future Generation Computer Systems serials, vol. 118, pp. 230–239 (2021). https://www.sciencedirect.com/science/article/pii/S0167739X21000224. Accessed 8 May 2024

2. Alexakos, C., Katsini, C., Votis, K., Lalas, A., Tzovaras, D., Serpanos, D.: Enabling digital forensics readiness for internet of vehicles 23rd EURO workgroup on transportation meeting, EWGT 2020, Paphos, Cyprus, ScienceDirect. Transport. Res. Procedia **52**, 339–346 (2020)
3. Shalaginov, A., Johann, A.I.: IoT digital forensics readiness in the edge. Springer (2020). https://link.springer.com/chapter/10.1007/978-3-030-59824-2_1. Accessed 7 May 2024
4. BCS: A manager's guide to IT law, 2nd Edition, BCS. ISBN 978-1906124755 (2011)
5. Carrier Brain: File system forensic analysis. Addison Wesley. ISBN-978-0-321-26817-4 (2012)
6. McCarthy, H. V., Podolskiy, M.G, Patros, P.: Consistent resource utilization for cross-platform and replicable load-testing: a position paper. In: 2021 ACM/IEEE International Conference on Model Driven Engineering Languages and Systems Companion (MODELS-C), pp. 203–209. Fukuoka, Japan (2021). https://doi.org/10.1109/MODELSC53483.2021.00035
7. Derico, B.: ChatGPT bug leaked users' conversation histories. BBCNews 2023. https://www.bbc.com/news/technology-65047304. Accessed 9 May 2024
8. Elastic Cloud: Explore Elastic Cloud. elastic.co (2020). https://www.elastic.co/elastic/cloud. Accessed 15 May 2024
9. Feng, X., Dawam, E., Amin, S.: A new digital forensics model of smart city automated vehicles. In: 2017 IEEE International Conference on Internet of Things (iThings), UK (2017). https://doi.org/10.1109/iThings-GreenCom-CPSCom-SmartData.2017.47.
10. Feng, X.: Computer laws consideration on data planning. In: IEEE International workshop ACE2019, UK
11. Feng, X.: Smartcity data analysis and data governance. In: Emrouznejad, A. (eds.) Proceedings of the 5th International Conference on Computer Science and Application Engineering (CSAE 2021). Association for Computing Machinery, New York, NY, USA, Article 37 (2021a). https://doi.org/10.1145/3487075.3487112
12. Goldman David, C.D.: The New York Times sues OpenAI and Microsoft for copyright infringement, CNN (2023). https://edition.cnn.com/2023/12/27/tech/new-york-times-sues-openai-microsoft/index.html. Accessed 5 May 2024
13. Gurman, M.: Samsung bans staff's AI use after spotting ChatGPT data leak" Bloomberg law (2023). https://news.bloomberglaw.com/tech-and-telecom-law/samsung-bans-staffs-ai-use-after-spotting-chatgpt-data-leak-2. Accessed 1 May 2024
14. Hashishi, M., Feng, X.: A collective study of the challenges with cloud computing forensics for a sufficient cloud-based investigations reference model. In: The IEEE Conference in Security Telecoms and Networking (STAN 2011), 2011 Best Paper Award
15. Idris, M.: Transforming E-learning through AI-driven interactive video generation: a framework for personalized learning experiences. Internal report, University of Bedfordshire (2024a)
16. Idris, M., Feng, X., Dyo, V.: Revolutionizing higher education: unleashing the potential of LLMs for strategic transformation. IEEE Access **12**, 67738–67757 (2024). https://doi.org/10.1109/ACCESS.2024.3400164
17. Idris, M.: Progress Report. University of Bedfordshire, UK (2025). https://www.beds.ac.uk
18. IoT Digital Forensics. Readiness in the edge: a roadmap for acquiring digital evidences from intelligent smart applications. In: International Conference on Edge Computing. Springer, pp. 1–17. https://link.springer.com/chapter/10.1007/978-3-030-59824-2_1. Accessed 11 May 2024
19. Legislation.: Regulation of Investigatory Powers Act 2000. Legislation.gov.uk (2000). https://www.legislation.gov.uk/ukpga/2000/23/contents. Accessed 11 May 2024
20. Li, F., Li, W., Tu, J.: Media-based Inter-Industry Network and Information Transmission. Singapore Management University (SMU) (2019)

21. Kelly, S.M.: TV and film writers are fighting to save their jobs from AI. They won't be the last. CNN (2024). https://edition.cnn.com/2023/05/04/tech/writers-strike-ai/index.html. Accessed 11 May 2024

22. Merken, S.: New York lawyers sanctioned for using fake ChatGPT cases in legal brief. New York Times, Reuters (2023). https://www.reuters.com/legal/new-york-lawyers-sanctioned-using-fake-chatgpt-cases-legal-brief-2023-06-22/. Accessed 10 March 2024

23. Trabelsi, M., Chen, Z., Davison Brian, D., Jeff, H.: A deep look into neural ranking models for information retrieval (2021), arxiv.org IEEE Xplore. https://ieeexplore.ieee.org/document/9585025

24. Bill, N.: Guide to computer forensics and investigations. 5th edn. ISBN 9781337568944, 1337568945 Cengage Learning (2021)

25. NIST: Cybersecurity Framework. National Institute of Standards and Technology (2018). http://www.nist.gov

26. Razaque, A.: Avoidance of Cybersecurity Threats with the Deployment of a Web-Based BlockchainEnabled Cybersecurity Awareness System. Semantic Scholar (2021). https://doi.org/10.3390/app11177880Corpus ID: 235805630. https://www.semanticscholar.org/paper/Avoidance-of-Cybersecurity. Accessed 15 May 2024

27. Shalaginov: The Evolving Pathogenesis of Alopecia Areata: Major WEB1. ScienceDirect (2020). https://www.sciencedirect.com/science/article/pii/S1087002420300022. Accessed 15 May 2024

28. Somers, M.: Deepfakes, explained, MIT Sloan (2024). https://mitsloan.mit.edu/ideas-made-to-matter/deepfakesexplained. Accessed 15 May 2024

29. Zhao, R.: Insights and reflections of the impact of ChatGPT on intelligent knowledge services in libraries in journal of library and information. Sci. Agric. **35**(1), 29–38 (2023). https://doi.org/10.13998/j.cnki.issn1002-1248.23-0116.(2023)

Lightweight CSI Feedback with Global Context Attention for RIS-Assisted Communications

Hao Feng[1,2,3], Yuting Xu[1,2,3], and Yuping Zhao[3(✉)]

[1] Peking University Shenzhen Graduate School, Peking University, Shenzhen 518066, China
`hfeng@pku.edu.cn, yutingxu@stu.pku.edu.cn`
[2] Pengcheng Laboratory,Shenzhen 518066, China
[3] School of Electronics, Peking University,Beijing 100871, China
`yuping.zhao@pku.edu.cn`

Abstract. In future wireless communication systems, reconfigurable intelligent surfaces (RIS) present a promising technology. However, in RIS-assisted communication systems, feedback of downlink channel state information (CSI) poses significant challenges, particularly with a large number of base station (BS) antennas and RIS unit cells. Traditional CSI feedback methods based on compressed sensing assume channel sparsity and require extensive computation and storage operations by both the user equipment (UE) and the BS, thereby increasing the burden on the UE. This paper proposes a lightweight CSI feedback mechanism based on global context attention network (GCANet). This method uses a lightweight autoencoder at the UE for CSI encoding, reducing the computational and storage burden on the UE, while deploying the decoder at the BS to leverage its powerful computational capabilities for complex decoding tasks. Simulation results demonstrate that this method significantly reduces feedback overhead and enhances system performance, with the UE's encoder model parameters and computational load being substantially reduced compared to baseline methods.

Keywords: RIS · Deep Learning · CSI Feedback · Lightweight

1 Introduction

With the large-scale commercialization of fifth-generation (5G) mobile communications, the upcoming sixth-generation (6G) cellular networks are expected to support a broader range of applications and services compared to 5G wireless networks [1–3]. Applications such as high-resolution streaming, video calls, virtual reality, and augmented reality are driving the demand for increased network capacity, resulting in a significant surge in data rates [4–6]. Consequently,

This work was supported by the National Key Research and Development Program under Grant 2024YFB29NL00100 and Grant 2020YFB1806405.

X. Feng et al. (Eds.): CloudComp 2024, LNICST 617, pp. 131–142, 2026.
https://doi.org/10.1007/978-3-031-92517-7_10

researchers are exploring new network architectures and transmission technologies to meet the critical requirements of 6G in terms of data rates, connectivity, and reliability.

Reconfigurable intelligent surface (RIS) is a promising technology for future wireless communication systems. It utilizes numerous low-cost passive devices to intelligently control the reflection phase of incident electromagnetic waves, thereby improving the quality of transmission links as well as spectrum and energy efficiency [7–10]. When the line-of-sight link between user equipment (UE) and the base station (BS) is blocked, RIS can enhance the coverage of wireless communication systems by appropriately configuring the RIS position and adjusting the phase shifts of its unit cells [11]. In RIS-assisted communication systems, downlink channel state information (CSI) is crucial for BS and RIS beamforming. In a time-division duplex system, considering channel reciprocity, the BS can directly estimate the downlink CSI through the uplink channel. In frequency-division duplex systems, where channel reciprocity does not hold, the UE needs to feedback the downlink CSI through an additional uplink channel. However, in RIS-assisted communication systems, efficient CSI feedback faces significant challenges, especially when the BS has a large number of antennas and the RIS has numerous unit cells, resulting in a vast amount of CSI feedback data.

Traditional compressed sensing (CS) methods typically assume that the channel is sparse [12,13], but the CSI may not be sparse in reality, making CS methods unable to fully extract channel characteristics. Additionally, CS methods require substantial computation and storage operations from the UE and BS, posing a significant burden on resource-limited UEs.

In recent years, researchers have used deep learning-based methods to improve feedback accuracy and overcome the sparsity assumption of compressed sensing. Reference [14] first proposed a channel feedback framework based on a convolutional autoencoder called CsiNet. In [15], feedback accuracy was further improved by utilizing long short-term memory layers and convolutional neural networks to learn the temporal correlation of channels. In [16], an attention mechanism was applied to the CLNet network to achieve information fusion between different channels. In [17], CRNet enhanced CSI reconstruction performance by extracting multi-resolution features of the CSI matrix. Despite the good results achieved by these deep learning-based methods in CSI feedback accuracy, they generally have complex model structures and significant model parameters, increasing the computational and storage burden on UEs in practical applications.

To alleviate the computational and storage burden on UE and optimize system performance, this paper proposes a CSI feedback mechanism based on a global context attention-enhanced autoencoder (GCANet). An autoencoder, as an effective dimensionality reduction and compression tool, can significantly reduce the size of CSI feedback. However, traditional autoencoders require substantial computational resources at both the UE and BS ends, conflicting with the resource limitations of UEs. To address this issue, we shift the complex decoding tasks to the BS, leveraging its powerful computational and storage capabilities to optimize resource allocation and task scheduling through centralized processing. Specifically, we design a lightweight autoencoder model for CSI encoding at the UE end, minimizing the computational and storage burden on UEs. Simultaneously, the decoder is deployed at the BS end, utilizing the BS's strong computational capabilities to perform complex decoding tasks, thereby achieving efficient CSI feedback.

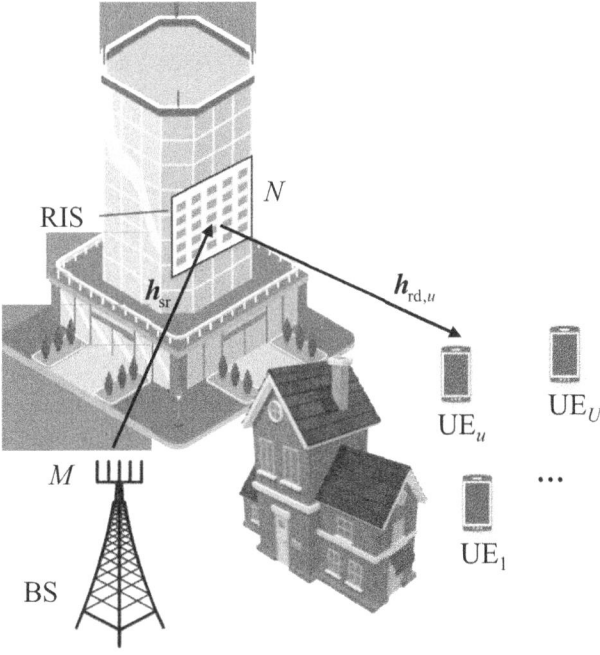

Fig. 1. Downlink RIS-assisted communication system.

The main innovations and contributions of this paper are as follows:

1) A CSI feedback mechanism based on an autoencoder is proposed, significantly reducing the computational and storage requirements at the UE end.

2) The global context attention mechanism enhances the network's CSI reconstruction performance by capturing global information to compute attention weights.

3) Simulations and experiments validate the effectiveness of this method in improving system performance, with the encoder model parameters and computational load at the UE end significantly reduced compared to benchmark methods.

The remainder of this paper is organized as follows. Section II briefly introduces the system model. Section III describes the proposed autoencoder model in detail. Section IV presents the simulation settings and experimental results. Section V summarizes the main contributions of this paper and points out future research directions.

2 System Model

Let's consider a downlink multi-user communication system with U UEs, as shown in Fig. 1. The BS is equipped with M uniform linear array antennas, each UE has one antenna, and the RIS consists of a uniform planar array with N passive reflecting unit cells. The direct path from the UE to the BS is obstructed by obstacles, so the direct path is not considered here.

2.1 Channel Model

Assuming the user is stationary or moving slowly, the channel changes relatively slowly. The channel adopts a quasi-static block fading model, where the characteristics within each block can be considered approximately constant. As shown in Fig. 1, $h_{\mathrm{sr}} \in \mathbb{C}^{N \times M}$ represents the channel vector from the BS to the RIS, $h_{\mathrm{rd},u} \in \mathbb{C}^{N \times 1}$ represents the channel vector from the RIS to the u-th UE, and $\Omega = \mathrm{diag}\{\phi_1, \phi_2, \ldots, \phi_N\} \in \mathbb{C}^{N \times N}$ represents the reflection coefficient matrix of the RIS, where $\phi_i = \alpha e^{j\theta_i}$, $i \in \{1, \ldots, N\} \triangleq \mathcal{N}$, and $\alpha \in (0, 1]$ are the magnitudes of the reflection coefficients, and $\theta_i \in [0, 2\pi)$ is the reflection phase shift. For simplicity, assume the reflection coefficient magnitude $\alpha = 1$ of the RIS in this paper.

2.2 Signal Model

In the downlink channel, the signal received by the u-th UE can be expressed as:

$$
\begin{aligned}
y &= h_{\mathrm{rd},u}^T \Omega h_{\mathrm{sr}} s + z \\
&= \phi^T \mathrm{diag}\left(h_{\mathrm{rd},u}^T\right) h_{\mathrm{sr}} s + z
\end{aligned}
\tag{1}
$$

where $\phi \triangleq \left[e^{j\theta_1}, \ldots, e^{j\theta_N}\right]^T$ is the phase shift vector of the RIS, s is the signal transmitted by the BS, and z is additive white noise. The cascaded CSI at the u-th UE can be depicted as:

$$
H_u^T \triangleq \mathrm{diag}\left(h_{\mathrm{rd},u}^T\right) h_{\mathrm{sr}}
\tag{2}
$$

The UE needs to feedback the downlink CSI to the BS. However, since the number of BS antennas M and the number of RIS unit cells N are usually large, and each element of the CSI matrix has high quantization precision, the amount of feedback data is enormous, occupying a significant amount of spectral resources. Therefore, reducing the amount of data in CSI feedback is a pressing issue. Without loss of generality, we assume the CSI feedback for the u-th UE and denote it as $H \triangleq H_u^T$, and this assumption can be extrapolated to other UEs.

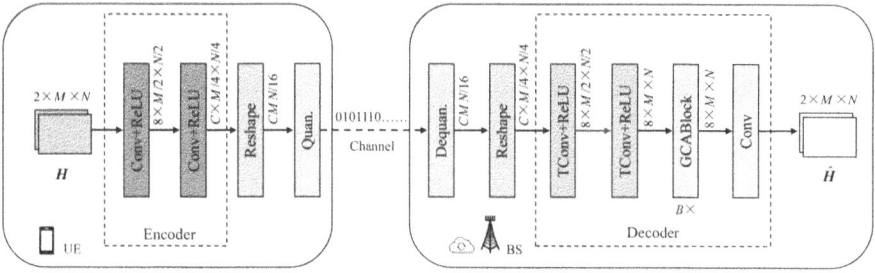

Fig. 2. CSI feedback flowchart based on GCANet.

3   GCANet-Based CSI Feedback Scheme

This section introduces the proposed GCANet-based CSI feedback process, followed by the network architecture and training details.

3.1   GCANet-Based CSI Feedback Process

Figure 2 illustrates the CSI feedback process based on GCANet. First, the encoder compresses and flattens the CSI matrix to obtain multiple feature vectors. These feature vectors are then converted into bitstreams for transmission to the BS. Upon receiving the bitstreams, the BS performs dequantization and reshapes them into matrix form, which is then input into the decoder to reconstruct the CSI matrix.

Specifically, the CSI feedback process based on GCANet can be divided into two stages.

1) UE Encoder for CSI Compression: First, the UE's encoder compresses the CSI to obtain a floating-point feature vector $\boldsymbol{v}$:

$$\boldsymbol{v} = \text{Flatten}\left(f_{\text{encode}}\left(\boldsymbol{H}\right)\right) \tag{3}$$

where $f_{\text{encode}}\left(\cdot\right)$ and $\text{Flatten}\left(\cdot\right)$ represent the compression and flattening operations, respectively. Next, $\boldsymbol{v}$ is uniformly quantized to form the bit stream for transmission to the BS,

$$\boldsymbol{v}_{\text{bit}} = \text{bit}\left(\mu\left\lfloor\frac{\boldsymbol{v}}{\mu}\right\rfloor\right) \tag{4}$$

where $\text{bit}\left(\cdot\right)$ denotes the conversion to bits operation, $\lfloor\cdot\rfloor$ denotes the floor operation, $\mu = \frac{Z}{2^q}$ is the quantization interval, q is the number of quantization bits, and Z is the range of $\boldsymbol{v}$.

2) BS Decoder for CSI Reconstruction: Assuming an ideal feedback channel, the bit stream $\boldsymbol{v}_{\text{bit}}$ sent by the UE is correctly received by the BS. The BS decoder reconstructs the complete CSI matrix:

$$\hat{\boldsymbol{H}} = f_{\text{decode}}\left(\text{Reshape}\left(\boldsymbol{v}_{\text{bit}}\right)\right) \tag{5}$$

where $f_{\text{decode}}(\cdot)$ and $\text{Reshape}(\cdot)$ represent the decompression and reshaping operations, respectively.

Finally, from the dimensions of matrix $\boldsymbol{H}$, it can be seen that originally $2MN$ elements (real and imaginary parts) needed to be transmitted. Now, the encoder's output is $CMN/16$ elements, so the compression rate can be stated as:

$$\gamma = \frac{CMN/16}{2MN} = \frac{C}{32} \tag{6}$$

where C equals the number of convolutional channels in the encoder output.

3.2   Network Architecture

The network structure includes two parts: the encoder and the decoder.

Encoder: The real and imaginary parts of $\boldsymbol{H}$ are separated into two channels and normalized as input to the encoder. Each part passes through two convolution and ReLU layers, with convolution channels of 8 and C, kernel size of 4 $\times$ 4, a stride of 2, and padding of 1. The fully convolutional module extracts and compresses high-dimensional features of the CSI matrix. After flattening, the output is a feature vector of size $CMN/16$.

Decoder: The BS decodes and reshapes the bitstream sent by the UE, recovering it into C matrices of size $M/4 \times N/4$. It then uses two transposed convolution (TConv) and ReLU layers to upsample the matrix to the original CSI matrix size, with a kernel size of 4 $\times$ 4, stride of 2, and padding of 1. Then, through B GCABlocks as shown in Fig. 3, it further extracts the features of the channel matrix [18], followed by a 3 $\times$ 3 convolution layer to reconstruct the complete channel estimation matrix $\hat{\boldsymbol{H}}$.

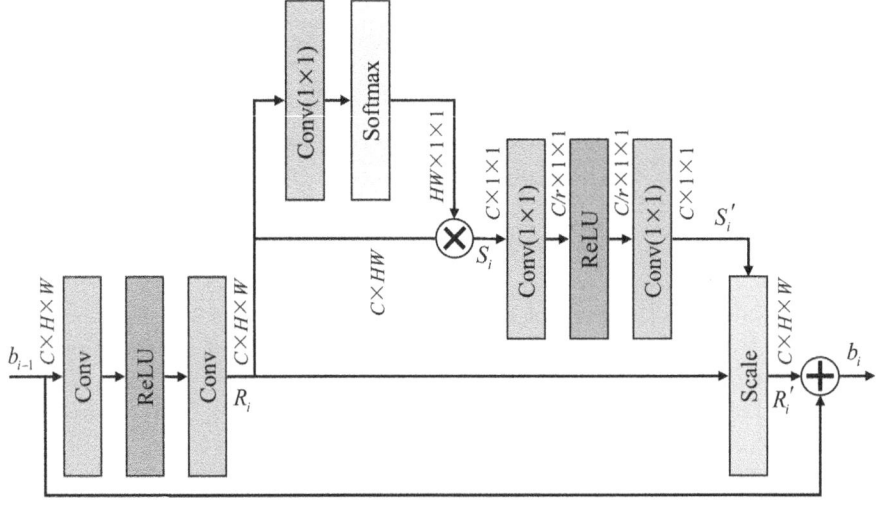

Fig. 3. The i-th GCABlock.

The GCABlock consists of a global context attention mechanism and local residual learning. The GCABlock is a dual-branch network where the global context attention mechanism captures global information, calculating attention weights for each channel to learn broader image features. The network also introduces a residual connection from the input to the output of the GCABlock, greatly reducing computational complexity and improving performance. Specifically:

Global Context Attention Mechanism: The module input passes through a 3×3 convolution layer, ReLU, and another 3×3 convolution layer, outputting R_i. The dimension of R_i is $H \times W \times C$, where H is height, W is width, and C is the number of convolution channels. R_i is divided into two paths: one undergoes reshaping to $C \times HW$, and the other undergoes a 1×1 convolution and Softmax to obtain attention weights $HW \times 1 \times 1$. Multiplying these with gives the global context information S_i. After global pooling, the output dimension is $C/r \times 1 \times 1$, where r is the global scaling factor, then it passes through a 1×1 convolution, ReLU to restore the original dimension $C \times 1 \times 1$. The output, labeled S_i, multiplies with corresponding channels of R_i, outputting $R_i{'}$.

Local Residual Learning: To ensure stable training, residual learning is introduced. The output from feature fusion, $R_i{'}$, is added to the input b_{i-1} to obtain the GCABlock output b_i

$$b_i = \mathrm{R}' + b_{i-1} \tag{7}$$

3.3   Network Training

Recent studies have developed channel models for CSI that accurately describe real channels from a statistical perspective, allowing training data generation via simulation. Based on the channel model in [19], we generated 44,000 channel realizations, with 40,000 for training, 2,000 for testing, and 2,000 for validation. The training learning rate is set to 0.005, batch size to 16, and total epochs to 100. We use the MSE function as the loss function:

$$Loss\left(\hat{\boldsymbol{H}}, \boldsymbol{H}\right) = \left\|\hat{\boldsymbol{H}} - \boldsymbol{H}\right\|_2^2 \tag{8}$$

where $\hat{\boldsymbol{H}}$ is the reconstructed CSI matrix, and $\boldsymbol{H}$ is the original CSI matrix. The network optimizer is Adam with default parameters. To adjust the learning rate, we adopt a cosine annealing strategy with warm-up [20]:

$$\eta_t = \eta_{\min} + \frac{1}{2}\left(\eta_{\max} - \eta_{\min}\right)\left(1 + \cos\left(\frac{t - T_w}{T - T_w}\pi\right)\right) \tag{9}$$

where η_t is the current learning rate, $\eta_{\min}$ is the minimum learning rate (5e-5), $\eta_{\max}$ is the maximum learning rate (2e-3), t is the current epoch, T_w is the warm-up epochs (30), and T is the maximum adjustment epochs (200).

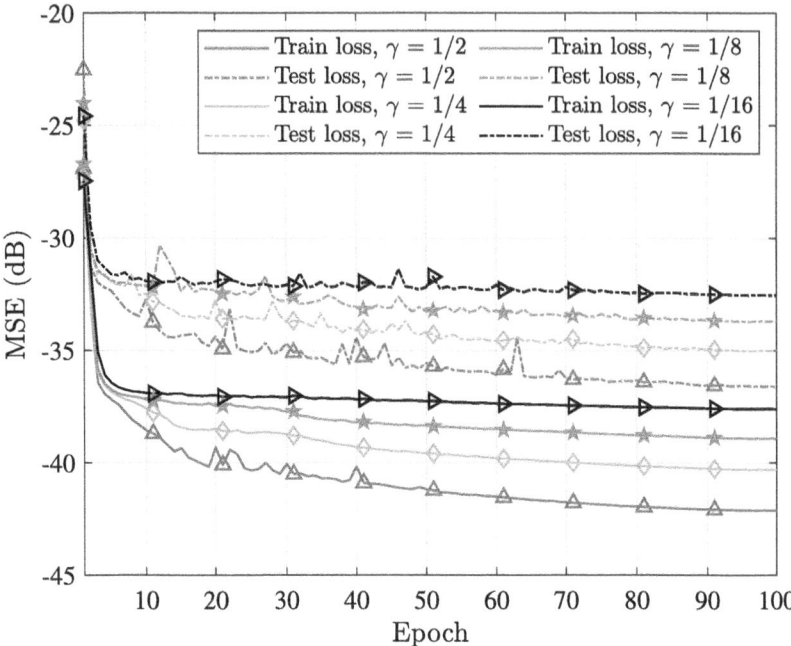

Fig. 4. Convergence results of proposed GCANet network under different compression rates.

4 Simulation Results

In this section, to validate the performance of our proposed GCANet-based CSI feedback scheme, we use the NMSE between the reconstructed CSI matrix $\hat{H}$ and the encoder input CSI matrix H as the performance metric:

$$\text{NMSE} = \frac{\mathbb{E}\left[\left\|\hat{H} - H\right\|_2^2\right]}{\mathbb{E}\left[\|H\|_2^2\right]} \tag{10}$$

The simulation parameters are set as follows: $M = 16$ for the number of BS antennas, $N = 64$ for the number of RIS unit cells, and $B = 2$ for the number of GCABlocks. All models are implemented in the Pytorch 1.11 framework and trained using an Nvidia A6000 GPU.

Figure 4 shows the convergence results of the proposed GCANet network under different compression rates. The solid lines represent the loss during training, and the dashed lines represent the loss during testing. As can be seen from Fig. 4, with the increase in training epochs, both training and testing losses significantly decrease and eventually stabilize under various compression rates.

Figure 5 illustrates the NMSE performance of the proposed GCANet under different compression rates. From Fig. 5, it can be seen that as the number of quantization bits increases, the NMSE value decreases significantly under all compression rates, indicating improved CSI reconstruction accuracy. Specifically, when the number of quantization bits is 2, the NMSE is relatively high, but as the number of quantization bits increases to 8, the NMSE value decreases substantially. This indicates that increasing the number of quantization bits effectively enhances network performance. At the same quantization bit rate, higher compression rates (i.e., smaller γ values) result in higher NMSE values, indicating that higher compression rates affect the network's recovery performance.

Table 1. Comparison of NMSE (dB) between our proposed GCANet and existing CsiNet and CLNet at different compression rates.

Model	$\gamma = 1/2$	$\gamma = 1/4$	$\gamma = 1/8$	$\gamma = 1/16$
Proposed GCANet	**−34.263**	**−32.274**	**−30.891**	−29.614
CLNet	−31.984	−31.335	−30.790	**−29.842**
CsiNet	−28.958	−28.587	−27.964	−27.499

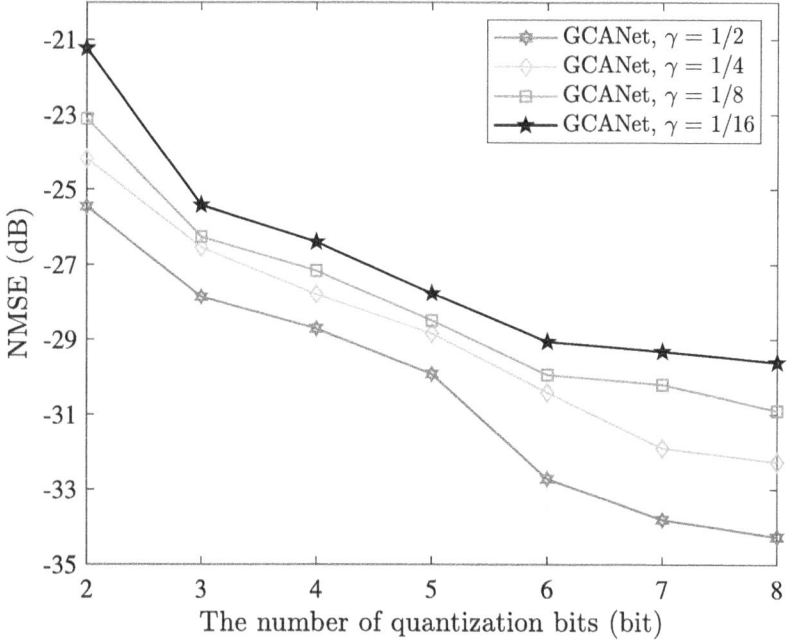

Fig. 5. NMSE performance of proposed GCANet network under different compression rates.

Table 1 compares the NMSE performance of the proposed GCANet and benchmark methods under different compression rates, with the number of quantization bits set to 8. From Table 1, it can be seen that GCANet achieves better NMSE values than CsiNet at all compression rates, and its NMSE is only slightly higher than CLNet at a compression rate of 1/16, indicating that GCANet can more effectively recover CSI information under various compression rates. Specifically, when $\gamma = 1/2$, GCANet's NMSE is -34.263 dB, significantly outperforming CLNet's -31.984 dB and CsiNet's -28.958 dB. As the compression rate increases (γ from 1/2 to 1/16), the NMSE values of all three models increase, but GCANet still maintains better performance.

Table 2. FLOPs and model size comparison between our proposed GCANet and existing CsiNet and CLNet under different compression rates.

γ	Model	Total FLOPs (M)	Total model size (M)	Encoder FLOPs of UE (M)	Encoder model size of UE (M)	Decoder FLOPs of BS (M)	Decoder model size of BS (M)
1/2	GCANet	**3.958**	**0.0093**	**0.909**	**0.0041**	**3.048**	**0.0052**
	CLNet	7.799	4.201	2.521	2.099	5.278	2.102
	CsiNet	7.741	4.199	2.142	2.098	5.599	2.101
1/4	GCANet	**3.801**	**0.0050**	**0.098**	**0.00078**	**3.703**	**0.0042**
	CLNet	5.702	2.103	1.473	1.049	4.229	1.054
	CsiNet	5.644	2.101	1.094	1.049	4.551	1.052
1/8	GCANet	**3.719**	**0.0045**	**0.0819**	**0.00052**	**3.637**	**0.0039**
	CLNet	4.653	1.054	0.948	0.525	3.705	0.529
	CsiNet	4.596	1.053	0.569	0.525	4.026	0.528
1/16	GCANet	**3.678**	**0.0042**	**0.074**	**0.00039**	**3.605**	**0.0038**
	CLNet	4.129	0.530	0.686	0.263	3.443	0.267
	CsiNet	4.071	0.528	0.307	0.262	3.764	0.266

Table 2 compares the floating-point operations (FLOPs) and model sizes of the proposed GCANet and benchmark methods under different compression rates. From Table 2, it can be seen that GCANet has significantly lower FLOPs and model size than CLNet and CsiNet under all compression rates, especially at the UE end. Specifically, at a compression rate of $\gamma = 1/2$, GCANet's UE-side encoder FLOPs is 0.909 M, while CLNet and CsiNet are 2.521 M and 2.142 M, respectively, reducing by 63.9% and 57.6%. Additionally, GCANet's UE-side encoder model size is 0.0041 M, while CLNet and CsiNet are 2.099 M and 2.098 M, respectively, reducing by 99.8%. Combined with the NMSE performance results in Table 1, GCANet not only has smaller computational load and model size but also significantly better NMSE performance than CsiNet and CLNet, demonstrating higher efficiency and practicality.

5   Conclusions

This paper proposes a lightweight autoencoder model based on global context attention (GCANet) to address the downlink CSI feedback issue in RIS-assisted communication systems. By designing a lightweight encoder and deploying complex decoding tasks at the BS end, this method significantly reduces the computational and storage burden on the UE. Simulation results show that, compared to traditional methods, GCANet excels in enhancing system performance, achieving high reconstruction accuracy while markedly decreasing the computational and storage demands on the UE. Future research can further optimize the model structure to improve its robustness in various environments and explore applying this method to other communication systems.

References

1. Tataria, H., Shafi, M., Molisch, A.F., Dohler, M., Sjöland, H., Tufvesson, F.: 6G wireless systems: vision, requirements, challenges, insights, and opportunities. Proc. IEEE **109**, 1166–1199 (2021)
2. Guo, F., Yu, F.R., Zhang, H., Li, X., Ji, H., Leung, V.: Enabling massive IoT toward 6G: a comprehensive survey. IEEE Internet Things J. **8**, 11891–11915 (2021)
3. Letaief, K.B., Chen, W., Shi, Y., Zhang, J., Zhang, Y.-J.A.: The roadmap to 6G: AI empowered wireless networks. IEEE Commun. Mag. **57**, 84–90 (2019)
4. Zheng, J., et al.: Mobile cell-free massive MIMO: challenges, solutions, and future directions. IEEE Wirel. Commun. **31**, 140–147 (2024)
5. Zhang, J., Björnson, E., Matthaiou, M., Ng, D., Yang, H., Love, D.J.: Prospective multiple antenna technologies for beyond 5G. IEEE J. Sel. Areas Commun. **38**, 1637–1660 (2020)
6. Zhang, Z., et al.: 6G wireless networks: vision, requirements, architecture, and key technologies. IEEE Veh. Technol. Mag. **14**, 28–41 (2019)
7. Wu, Q., Zhang, R.: Towards smart and reconfigurable environment: intelligent reflecting surface aided wireless network. IEEE Commun. Mag. **58**, 106–112 (2020)
8. Di Renzo, M., et al.: Smart radio environments empowered by reconfigurable intelligent surfaces: how it works, state of research, and the road ahead. IEEE J. Sel. Areas Commun. **38**, 2450–2525 (2020)
9. Liu, Y., et al.: Reconfigurable intelligent surfaces: principles and opportunities. IEEE Commun. Surv. Tutor. **23**, 1546–1577 (2021)
10. Basar, E., Di Renzo, M., De Rosny, J., Debbah, M., Alouini, M.-S., Zhang, R.: Wireless communications through reconfigurable intelligent surfaces. IEEE Access **7**, 116753–116773 (2019)
11. Wu, Q., Zhang, R.: Intelligent reflecting surface enhanced wireless network via joint active and passive beamforming. IEEE Trans. Wirel. Commun. **18**, 5394–5409 (2019)
12. Kuo, P.-H., Kung, H.T., Ting, P.-A.: Compressive sensing based channel feedback protocols for spatially-correlated massive antenna arrays. In: 2012 IEEE Wireless Communications and Networking Conference (WCNC), pp. 492–497 (2012)
13. Rao, X., Lau, V.: Distributed compressive CSIT estimation and feedback for FDD multi-user massive MIMO systems. IEEE Trans. Signal Process. **62**, 3261–3271 (2014)

14. Wen, C.-K., Shih, W.-T., Jin, S.: Deep learning for massive MIMO CSI feedback. IEEE Wirel. Commun. Lett. **7**, 748–751 (2018)
15. Wang, T., Wen, C.-K., Jin, S., Li, G.Y.: Deep learning-based CSI feedback approach for time-varying massive MIMO channels. IEEE Wirel. Commun. Lett. **8**, 416–419 (2019)
16. Ji, S., Li, M.: CLNet: complex input lightweight neural network designed for massive MIMO CSI feedback. IEEE Wirel. Commun. Lett. **10**, 2318–2322 (2021)
17. Lu, Z., Wang, J., Song, J.: Multi-resolution CSI feedback with deep learning in massive MIMO system. In: ICC 2020—2020 IEEE International Conference on Communications (ICC), pp. 1–6 (2020)
18. Cao, Y., Xu, J., Lin, S., Wei, F., Hu, H.: GCNet: non-local networks meet squeeze-excitation networks and beyond. In: the Proceedings of the IEEE/CVF International Conference on Computer Vision Workshops (2019)
19. Basar, E., Yildirim, I.: Reconfigurable intelligent surfaces for future wireless networks: a channel modeling perspective. IEEE Wirel. Commun. **28**, 108–114 (2021)
20. Loshchilov, I., Hutter, F.: SGDR: stochastic gradient descent with warm restarts. arXiv preprint arXiv:1608.03983 (2016)

Discriminative Features Learning Based Approach for Object Detection Enhancement

Tanvir Ahmad[1]([⊠]), Asad Ullah[2], Bian GenQing[1], Fan Zhang[1], and Belal Ahmad[3]

[1] School of Information and Control Engineering, Xi'an University of Architecture and Technology,Xi'an, Shaanxi, China
{tanvir,biangen,fanzhang}@xauat.edu.cn
[2] University of Bedfordshire,Bedfordshire, UK
asad.ullah@beds.ac.uk
[3] School of Computer Science and Technology, Huazhong University of Science and Technology,Wuhan, China

Abstract. Object detection algorithms aim to classify and detect object class instances in images or videos. The effectiveness of these object detectors is due to substantial improvement in the deep convolutions neural networks. However, very few attempts have been made to explore the positive and negative object regions and to differentiate between similar objects with a distracting background in challenging scenarios. To achieve optimum training and completely leverage the capacity of model architectures, it is important to mitigate inter-class and intra-class variations during the training of the classifier to improve accuracy. To improve the accuracy, we proposed a new framework, using InceptionResNet-V2 and Resnet101 models as a backbone with a triplet loss function. The proposed framework learns the mapping from images to compact Euclidean distance, where the distance directly corresponds to a measure of object similarity. This new framework backbone trained with triplet loss function can be plugged into any detector. In our case, we selected SSD and replaced the original backbone network VGG-16 of SSD. The triplet loss function improves the classification performance and improves accuracy which leads to efficient object detection. Moreover, extensive experiments on the PASCAL VOC 2007 and PASCAL VOC 2012 datasets show the efficacy and enhancement of the proposed method, by comparing it with other states of the art methods.

Keywords: Object detection · Triplet loss · Positive and negative object regions · Euclidean distance · Similarity distance learning

1 Introduction

Detection of an object can be described as the combination of localization of the object (i.e. the object location, that where the object is present) and recognition of that object (i.e. appearance of the object) as a long-standing, fundamental,

X. Feng et al. (Eds.): CloudComp 2024, LNICST 617, pp. 143–156, 2026.
https://doi.org/10.1007/978-3-031-92517-7_11

and challenging computer vision task, object recognition, and object detection, based on deep convolutional neural networks (CNN's) [1,2], has witnessed breakthroughs in a wide range of applications, such as object detection [3], person re-identification [4] pedestrian detection [5], object tracking [6,7], face detection [8], etc. The recent object detectors [5,9] pipeline, based on deep CNN can be divided into three main steps: In the first step regional proposals are selected from a given image as object contestant. The early-stage Cascade detectors [8], Edge Boxes [10], and Selective Search [11], are among the common regional proposal methods. Secondly, for categorization and recognition, these extracted features are fed into deep CNN. In the final step, the bounding box regression method is used for refining the rough proposals into more precise object bounds. These algorithms provide good efficiency performance and effective localization. However, their region proposals have low-level features that are sensitive to local appearance changes and are very likely to fail in partial occlusion. Contrarily, most of these typical methods focus on dense sliding windows [10] or image over-segmentation, which are hard to deploy in the real world due to their high computational cost.

More advanced deep CNNs are developed to overcome these disadvantages for the generation of object proposals to strengthen the capability of distinguishing positive regions and negative regions. In [12] an area proposal network (RPN) is trained to predict the bounding boxes of object candidates from anchor boxes i.e., the thresholds for determining foreground (Positive sample) and background (Negative samples). Since the aspect ratio and scales of these negative and positive samples are fixed and pre-designed, therefore, the RPN faced difficulties in managing the objects having large variations.

To improve the region of interest features, [13] used long short-term memory (LSTM) cells for capturing the proposal box's local context information and the global context information of whole images to learn object categories. Similarly, in [14], the authors used multiple subnetworks for large-scale changes. Furthermore, for performance improvement, some techniques utilized bootstrapping (also called hard negative mining). This technique was first introduced by Sung and Poggio [15] to train face detection models, which was widely adopted to train SVM in object detection tasks [9,11,16].

Since the recently advanced object detectors do not use SVM, so this method falls out of fashion. To overcome this issue an alternative method is proposed in [17], which suggests picking hard negative regions of interest (RoI's) online, and then the features of such RoI are forwarded again for better learning, as per RoI's classification and localization loss in the network forward stage. Various techniques are developed to implement the negative and positive hard mining ideas. One110 of the prominent methods is online hard example mining (OHEM), which provides better solutions in target detection, particularly in sample level mismatch. However, due to additional memory and pace expenditure, this method leaves the training phase bloated.

While significant progress has been made, it is still a challenging task because of the cluttered backgrounds, occlusion, and large appearance variations of objects. Moreover, in the above-mentioned work, the researchers either considered positive samples or negative samples. There is still substantial potential to increase the accuracy, the distribution in feature space of positive vs hard negative, and their comparative similarity distances have yet to be researched to improve the efficiency of classification in the field of object detection. Our contributions can be summarized as:

In this paper, we proposed a triplet embedding to get more powerful features, with deep CNN Resnet101 and InceptionResnet-V2, by taking into account both positive and negative samples simultaneously. In this approach, the pre75 trained models are fine-tuned by using layer-wise techniques instead of block-wise, implemented in an end-to-end manner to enhance the accuracy and strengthen the classification of positive vs negative in various object classes. Additionally, the proposed method is well generalized, and therefore it can be adopted in many other tasks through transfer learning: such as medical image analysis, image classification, action detection, object tracking, etc. By comparing with other methods, the proposed method tackles the problem elegantly with a lower computational cost.

The rest of the paper is arranged as follows. The related work is discussed in Sect. 2. Section 3 describes the methodology. The experimental setup is presented in Sect. 4. Section 5 discusses the results, while the conclusion is drawn in Sect. 6.

2   Related Work

Object detection aims and attempt to find "what and where" each object instance is when given an image. In the early days, handcrafted engineering techniques were used for extracting features from images, such as HOG [18], SIFT [19], Selective Search [11], and Edge Box [10]. For a long time, the dominant methods among standard object detectors were the Deformable Parts Model (DPM) [20], and its variants. With the accelerated development of deep convolutional neural networks, impressive performance was achieved. These deep CNN-based object detectors are typically divided into two sections of the network layout. The first one is called the backbone network, and the second one is the detection head.

The object detection backbone networks are usually borrowed from the ImageNet [21]. ImageNet has been considered the most prominent dataset in recent years to test the potential of deep convolution neural networks. To develop a very deep network VGGNet was proposed [1], the majority of the succeeding studies adopt VGG as a structure and design a better component at each point. A new initiation block to include more diverse features is proposed by GoogleNet [22], another work, ResNet [23], adopts a "bottleneck" architecture with residual sum operation at each point, which has been demonstrated to be a simple and efficient way to create a deeper neural network. To substitute traditional convolution, ResNext [23], and Xception [24], use the grouping convolution layer, which helps in parameter reduction while increasing the accuracy concurrently. While DenseNet [25], densely concretes many layers, which further decreases parameters while preserving comparative precision.

The detection head is typically connected to the backbone, and trained on the ImageNet for classification. Two distinct design logic exist for detecting objects. One and two stage method, the two-stage detector like Faster R-CNN [26], will predict several suggestions first, based on the backbone, after this an additional classifier is used for classification of proposals and regression. Faster R-CNN uses Region Proposal Network (RPN) which generates proposals directly from the backbone network. R-FCN [27], use the output of the backbone to generate a feature map. On the other side, the one-stage detector uses the backbone directly for the prediction of object instances, these detectors have been modified for speed but their accuracy slopes that of two-stage detectors. In a related study, an Improved Grey-Scale (IGS) method was used for color-image quantization to enhance image classification accuracy in content-based image retrieval systems, demonstrating the importance of optimized feature extraction across tasks [40].

To overcome the accuracy problem RetinaNet [28] proposes a focal loss function on a basic feature extractor backbone for addressing the foreground (positive) and background (negative) issues. The prime sample attention (PISA) [29], approach shows that improvement can be gained through a positive sample alone. A more comprehensive methodology is proposed in OHEM [17], which considers loss values of positive and negative samples. OHEM, however, requires extra memory which reduces the speed of training. To achieve optimum training and completely leverage the capacity of model architectures, it is important to mitigate intra-class and inter-class variations in the training phase of a classifier for object detection. A large number of object categories, on the order of 104–105, needs considerable discrimination capacity from the backbone classifier to differentiate between slightly distinct inter-class variants, in addition to intra-class variations.

3   Methodology

This section provides the technical details of the proposed framework. We proposed Resnet101 and InceptionReset-V2 with triplet-loss function. We first present triplet embedding as well as the hard triplet unit's selection strategy, to select only those triplets which violate the triplet constraint. In the proposed method, the networks are first fine-tuned to obtain f (k) embedding of an image k into d-dimensional Euclidean space Rd, then using the corresponding d-dimensional embedding, to calculate the distances between all input images using L-2, while the L-2 distance remains independent of each factor regarding the input images, such as physical assortment, scaling, shade, and arrangement. That triplet loss imposes the margin in each class and differentiates them in images from other classes. In this way, it improves the classification of negative vs positive, about various object classes. The framework of the proposed method is illustrated in Fig. 1.

3.1   Network Architecture

Convolutional neural networks act as a backbone network to classify images and extract features for the object detection task. These deep CNN networks can be trained effectively for many tasks through transfer learning. Most pre-trained models are selected by the researcher doing fine-tuning through backpropagation instead of using randomly initialized parameters. We implement our methods based on ResNet101 and InceptionResNet-V2 network pre-trained on ImageNet, using the models released by [27,30]. Resnet101 having a total of 5 convolutional blocks (conv1-5), is constructed by using 4 residual blocks. RPN features are extracted from conv-2x to conv4-x, while the last one is used for predicting region proposals, and at the conv5-x, the box classifier features are extracted. InceptionResNet-v2 are networks in the Inception-style that use residual connections rather than concatenating filters, one small technical difference between residual and non-residual inception variants is the use of batch-normalization on the top of traditional layers. For the models trained with the proposed triplet loss, we changed and fine-tuned ResNet101 and InceptionResNet-V2 for feature extraction on top of this any detection branch can be used for detection, we chose SSD and changed the VVG16 backbone used in the original paper with ResNet101 or InceptionResNet-V2. By removing the last layer, we optimized both networks, taking one fully connected layer, a dropout layer with a 0.3 rate, and an L2 regularization layer to learn d-dimensional features as an identity descriptor. Besides, it helps in reducing the problem of vanishing gradient.

3.2   Triplet Loss

It is crucial to design a proper loss function during the training phase of the proposed network so that the extracted features have sufficient discriminatory potential, which is essential for the object detection task. The triplet loss is particularly effective in learning a good embedding, $f(k)$, of an image k into a d-dimensional Euclidean space $\mathbb{R}^d$, i.e., $f(k) \in \mathbb{R}^d$. The main objective is to ensure that an anchor image pixel k_a is closer to all other positive pixels k_c^p with the same label, compared to any negative pixel k_c^n with different labels.

The objective can be defined as:

$$\|k_c^a - k_c^n\|_2^2 + \alpha_t < \|k_c^p - k_c^n\|_2^2 \tag{1}$$

$\forall k_c^a, k_c^p, k_c^n \in \tau$, where τ represents the set of all possible triplets in training samples, while N is the cardinality. Where $f(k_c^a)$, $f(k_c^p)$, and $f(k_c^n)$ are the embedding of a triplet $(k_c^a; k_c^p; k_c^n)$, while α_t is a predefined margin imposed between positive and negative classes. Triplet loss is back-propagated if any constraint is violated, so when the loss is minimized, it can be defined as:

$$L = \sum_{i=1}^{N} \max\left(\|f(k_c^a) - f(k_c^p)\|_2^2 + \alpha - \|f(k_c^a) - f(k_c^n)\|_2^2, 0\right) \tag{2}$$

During training all possible triplets would be generated, which is not desirable, as it does not make any contribution to the training, causing slow convergence. So, it's important to select the hard triplets during training to achieve improvement in accuracy. In the following section, the hard triplet embedding selection approach is discussed which we had adopted during training.

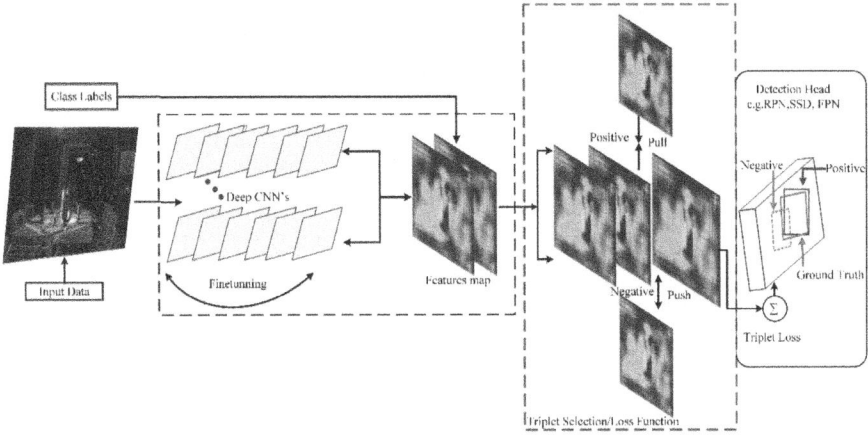

Fig. 1. Proposed method framework illustration, triplet embedding decrease the distance between the positive, and increase the distance between negative through similarity learning, strengthening optimization, and enhancing classification and detection accuracy

3.3   Hard Triplet Units Selection

In an image, there are around 2000 possible proposals produced by edge-box [10], or selective search [11], where the number of possible triplets can go up to 2000^3. So, it's important to select those triplets which violate the triplet constraint, to make sure of fast convergence. As the similarity constraint is not violated by a large number of triplet units, to perform efficient and effective training, it is necessary to select hard triplet units.

To avoid this problem, we directly minimize the bias. By selecting hard triplet's units within ground-truth, $k_c^p \| f(k_c^a) - f(k_c^p) \|_2^2$, and $\arg \min k_c^n \| f(k_c^a) - f(k_c^n) \|_2^2$, values are calculated for making equal contribution and an unbiased situation for possible triplets, while $k_c^a, k_c^p, k_c^n \in G_C$ (ground-truth). Mathematically, it can be expressed as follows:

$$\max \arg \left(k_c^p \| f(k_c^a) - f(k_c^p) \|_2^2 \right) < \min \arg \left(k_c^n \| f(k_c^a) - f(k_c^n) \|_2^2 \right) \tag{3}$$

where $k_c^a, k_c^p, k_c^n \in \tau$.

4   Experiments

4.1   Datasets

For training and evaluating the proposed model, we used PASCAL VOC 2007 and PASCAL VOC 2012 [13], datasets. The PASCAL VOC 2007 consists of 9963 images, while PASCAL VOC 2012 contains 22,531 images. These datasets are divided into training, testing, and validation subsets, with 20 object classes.

4.2   Implementation Details

For training and testing, the TensorFlow framework is used following strategies provided by the Detection repository [32]. The model is end-to-end trained on an NVIDIA GTX 1080 GPU. If not specifically stated otherwise, the pre-trained model, as discussed in Sect. 3, is adapted for object detection tasks, similar to the SSD [33] strategy. The backbone structure is modified by removing a fully connected layer and optimized through synchronized stochastic gradient descent (SGD) [34], with an L2 regularization layer, a momentum decay of 0.9, and a weight decay of 0.0001. The total number of iterations was set to 110k. During the first 60k iterations, we set the learning rate to 10^{-3}, and then continued with 30k and 20k iterations using learning rates of 10^{-4} and 10^{-5}, respectively. The proposed method's performance is recorded and evaluated based on several aspects, such as parameter values, accuracy, false positives, training error, etc.

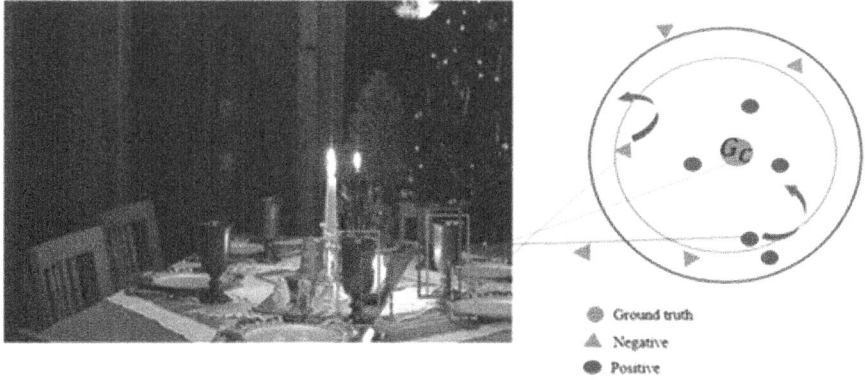

Fig. 2. Triplet illustration, the green colors denote ground truth, red is positive class and blue is negative, the approach aims to improve accuracy by dealing with positive and negative class features via similarity distance learning. (Color figure online)

4.3   Evaluation Methods

The proposed approach is evaluated by the Oracle method using True Positive (TP), True Negative (TN), False Positive (FP), and False Negative (FN). TP means that true samples are detected as positive, TN means true samples are detected as negative, and FP means negative samples are detected as positive. FN means that positive samples are detected as negative samples.

Mathematically, recall and precision are computed as:

$$\text{Recall} = \frac{TP}{TP + FP} \tag{4}$$

$$\text{Precision} = \frac{TP}{TP + FN} \tag{5}$$

In this way, precision and recall curves are achieved and computed as the mean average precision (mAP).

5   Results and Discussion

Tables 1 and 2 show the results on the PASCAL VOC [31] benchmark datasets. We performed experiments on both pre-trained models incorporating the triplet loss function, which show an improvement of 82.8% mAP and 84.2% mAP respectively on VOC 2007. This outperforms the best variants such as PISA and OHEM from online hard example mining methods. From the results, one can see that the proposed method successfully classifies and detects the majority of objects with high confidence, having less localization error and less confusion for similar object categories.

The training loss and accuracy curve against the number of iterations is plotted as shown in Fig. 3. To check the efficiency, we performed a deeper error analysis using the method proposed in [39]. For this, challenging categories of object classes were selected from PASCAL VOC 2007. Due to space and time limitations, we selected five classes in this analysis: Chair, TV, Aero, Table, and Boat.

Table 1. The results of the PASCAL VOC 2007 test dataset

Method	Dataset	Map	Aero	Bike	Bird	Boat	Bottle	Bus	Car	Cat	Chair	Cow	Table	Dog	Horse	Bike	Person	Plant	Sheep	Sofa	Train	Tv
VGG16 [35]	07	73.2	76.5	79	70.9	65.5	52.1	83.1	84.7	86.4	52.0	81.9	65.7	84.8	84.6	77.5	76.7	38.8	73.6	73.9	83.0	72.6
OHEM [17]	07	75.1	77.7	81.9	76	64.9	55.8	86.3	86.3	86.8	53.2	82.9	70.3	85	86.3	78.7	78.0	46.8	76.1	72.7	80.9	75.5
MR-CNN [36]	07	78.2	80.3	84.1	78.5	70.8	68.5	88.0	85.9	87.8	60.3	85.2	73.1	87.2	86.5	85.1	76.4	48.5	76.3	75.5	85.0	81.0
PISA [29]	07	79.1	-	-	-	-	-	-	-	-	-	-	-	-	-	-	-	-	-	-	-	-
Residual-101 [37]	07	81.5	86.6	86.2	82.6	74.9	62.5	89.0	88.7	88.8	65.2	87.0	78.7	88.2	89.0	87.5	83.7	51.1	86.3	81.6	85.7	83.7
AC-CNN [13]	07	72.0	79.3	79.4	72.5	61.0	43.5	80.1	81.5	87.0	48.5	81.9	70.7	83.5	85.6	78.4	71.6	34.9	72.0	71.4	84.3	73.5
Yuting et al. [38]	07	68.5	74.1	83.2	67.2	50.8	51.6	76.2	81.4	77.2	48.1	78.9	65.6	77.3	78.4	75.1	70.1	41.4	69.6	60.8	70.2	73.7
Proposed (Resnet101+Triplet)	07	82.8	86.6	87.3	86.4	79.9	63.2	92.1	90.2	87.2	68.7	89.2	79.3	89.3	91.0	86.7	85.1	59.1	84.1	81.3	89.9	87.2
Proposed (InceptionresnetV2+Triplet)	07	84.2	89.1	88.2	87.7	81.1	69.6	93.9	92.1	90.9	71.1	90.2	83.5	92.1	93.3	90.1	87.6	60.2	87.7	79.9	92.3	91.1

It is visualized through a pie chart in Fig. 3, which shows the percentage of correct (Cor) predictions made as well as the false-positive ratio, confusion

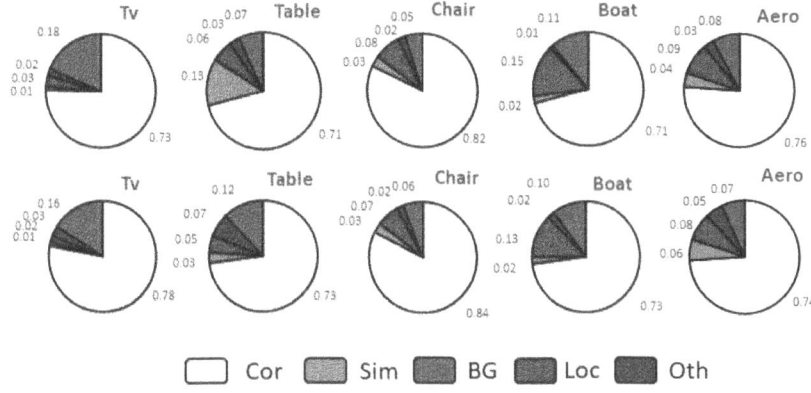

Fig. 3. Deep analysis of proposed method on selected classes from PASCAL VOC 2007 test set, top column shows the accuracy of the network (Resnet101+Triplet, InceptionRestnet-V2+Triplet). The percentage of correct (Cor) prediction made as well as false-positive ratio, confusion with a background (Bg), confusion with similar (Sim) objects, or confusion with other objects (Oth). It is noticeable that the proposed method has achieved desirable accuracy.

Fig. 4. Qualitative detection results on the PASCAL VOC 2007 dataset

with the background (Bg), confusion with similar (Sim) objects, or confusion with other objects (Oth). Notably, the proposed method has achieved desirable accuracy, and this is attributed to the use of a triplet loss function with deep CNNs, which enhances the discriminative prowess of the backbone for decreasing the class imbalance problem and having less confusion with other and similar categories.

Fig. 5. Qualitative detection results on the PASCAL VOC 2012 dataset

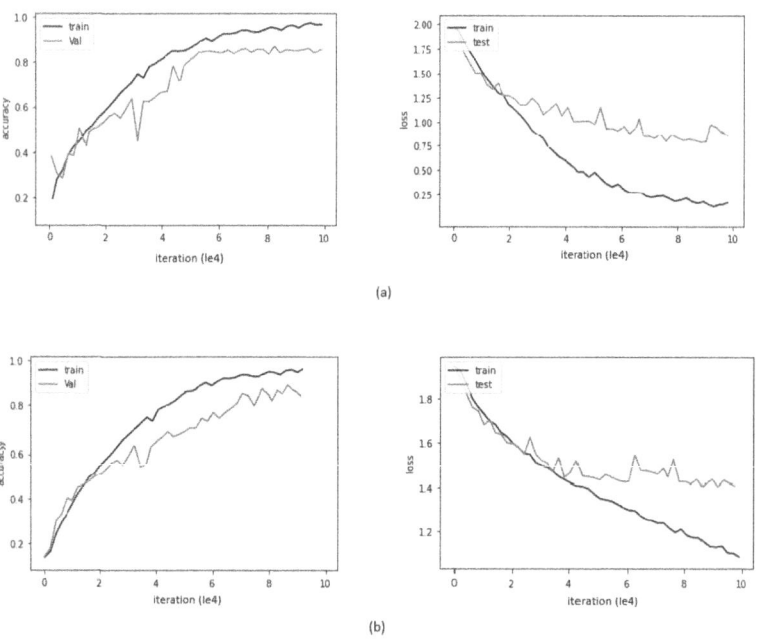

Fig. 6. Shows the accuracy and loss of proposed methods (a). for Resnet101 and (b). for InceptionResnet-V2, incorporating triplet loss.

Taking advantage of this strategy helps in obtaining more positive samples during the training phase and aids in performing a better detection task. For further evaluation of the proposed method, the PASCAL VOC 2012 test set is used, which consists of more challenging categories of object classes, such as dense objects, serious deformation, and occlusion scenarios. Results are presented in Table 2.

To examine the effects of parameters for balancing the training and validation loss measures on the classification convergence rate, the networks are tested on different α_t values. Our findings from testing with different parameters show that classification accuracy yielded optimal results at a threshold value of 0.4, but started dropping when the threshold was adjusted further. Therefore, we conclude that the best performance is achieved at a threshold value of 0.4.

Moreover, we present qualitative results on PASCAL VOC 2007 in Fig. 4 and PASCAL VOC 2012 in Fig. 5, where we selected hard examples from both datasets. Detection results with a score of over 0.6 are included. We observe that the proposed method classifies and detects every single class with high confidence. Results are best viewed in color and with zoom.

Table 2. Table captions should be placed above the tables.

Method	Train Dataset	Test Dataset	mAP
VGG16 [35]	07+12	12	70.4
OHEM [17]	07+12	12	72.9
MR-CNN [36]	07+12	12	73.9
Residual 101 [37]	07+12	12	80.0
AC-CNN [13]	07+12	12	70.6
Yuting et al. [38]	07+12	12	66.4
Proposed	07+12	12	81.2
Proposed	07+12	12	83.1

6   Conclusion

In this paper, we proposed the triplet loss function incorporated with deep CNNs, which efficiently enforces the similarity distance constraints between negative, positive, and ground truth samples. This results in more accurate classification scores for both positive and negative samples. Extensive experiments on the benchmark PASCAL VOC datasets demonstrate the efficiency and effectiveness of the proposed approach. Moreover, this approach is well generalized with various backbones for both single-stage and two-stage detectors.

Future work will concentrate on advancing this approach by using unsupervised or semi-supervised methods to further enhance intra-class and inter-class separability.

References

1. Simonyan, K., Zisserman, A.: Very Deep convolutional networks for large-scale image recognition. arXiv preprint arXiv:1409.1556 (2015)
2. Mamatkulovich, B.B.: A design of small scale deep CNN model for facial expression recognition using the low-resolution image datasets. Models Methods Increasing Effi. Innov. Res. **2**(19), 284–288 (2023)
3. Gao, Y., Mu, S., Xu, S.: Toward unified end-to-end license plate detection and recognition for variable resolution requirements. IEEE Trans. Intell. Transp. Syst. **25**(9), 10689–10701 (2024)
4. Khan, S.U., et al.: Visual appearance and soft biometrics fusion for person re-identification using deep learning. IEEE J. Sel. Top. Sig. Process. **17**(3), 575–586 (2023)
5. Veluchamy, S., Muthukrishnan, R., Karthi, S.: HY-LSTM: a new time series deep learning architecture for estimation of pedestrian time to cross in advanced driver assistance systems. J. Vis. Commun. Image Represent. **97**, 103982 (2023)
6. Sadeghian, A., Alahi, A., Savarese, S.: Tracking the untrackable: learning to track multiple cues with long-term dependencies. In: Proceedings of the IEEE International Conference on Computer Vision, pp. 300–311 (2017)
7. Ristani, E., Solera, F., Zou, R., Cucchiara, R., Tomasi, C.: performance measures and a data set for multi-target, multi-camera tracking. In: European Conference on Computer Vision, pp. 17–35. Springer (2016)
8. Kumar, K.K., et al.: Criminal face identification system using deep learning algorithm multi-task cascade neural network (MTCNN). Mater. Today Proc. **80**, 2406–2410 (2023)
9. Sharada, K., et al.: Deep learning techniques for image recognition and object detection. EDP Sci. **399**, 04032 (2023)
10. Zhou, C., et al.: Multi-scale pseudo labeling for unsupervised deep edge detection. Knowl.-Based Syst. **280**, 111057 (2023)
11. Railkar, Y., et al.: Object detection and recognition system using deep learning method. In: 2023 IEEE 8th International Conference for Convergence in Technology (I2CT), pp. 1–6. IEEE (2023)
12. Ren, S., He, K., Girshick, R., Sun, J.: Faster R-CNN: towards real-time object detection with region proposal networks. arXiv preprint arXiv:1506.01497 (2015)
13. Li, J., et al.: Attentive contexts for object detection. IEEE Trans. Multimedia **19**(5), 944–954 (2016)
14. Li, J., et al.: Scale-aware fast R-CNN for pedestrian detection. IEEE Trans. Multimedia **20**(4), 985–996 (2017)
15. Bosquet, B., et al.: A full data augmentation pipeline for small object detection based on generative adversarial networks. Pattern Recogn. **133**, 108998 (2023)
16. Dewi, C., et al.: Robust detection method for improving small traffic sign recognition based on spatial pyramid pooling. J. Ambient Intell. Humaniz. Comput. **14**(7), 8135–8152 (2023)
17. Shrivastava, A., Gupta, A., Girshick, R.: Training region-based object detectors with online hard example mining. In: Proceedings of the IEEE Conference on Computer Vision and Pattern Recognition, pp. 761–769 (2016)
18. Bhattarai, B., et al.: Histogram of oriented gradients meet deep learning: a novel multi-task deep network for 2D surgical image semantic segmentation. Med. Image Anal. **85**, 102747 (2023)

19. Lowe, D.G.: Distinctive image features from scale-invariant keypoints. Int. J. Comput. Vis. **60**(2), 91–110 (2004)
20. Girshick, R.B., Felzenszwalb, P.F., McAllester, D.: discriminatively trained deformable part models release version 5 (2012)
21. Russakovsky, O., et al.: ImageNet large-scale visual recognition challenge. Int. J. Comput. Vis. **115**(3), 211–252 (2015)
22. Szegedy, C., et al.: Going deeper with convolutions. In: Proceedings of the IEEE Conference on Computer Vision and Pattern Recognition, pp. 1–9 (2015)
23. Xie, S., et al.: Aggregated residual transformations for deep neural networks. In: Proceedings of the IEEE Conference on Computer Vision and Pattern Recognition, pp. 1492–1500 (2017)
24. Xia, Y., Chen, S.: Dual aggregated federated learning with depthwise separable convolution for smart healthcare. In: ICC 2023—IEEE International Conference on Communications. IEEE (2023)
25. Huang, G., et al.: Densely connected convolutional networks. In: Proceedings of the IEEE Conference on Computer Vision and Pattern Recognition, pp. 4700–4708 (2017)
26. Dai, J., Li, Y., He, K., Sun, J.: R-FCN: object detection via region-based fully convolutional networks. arXiv preprint arXiv:1605.06409 (2016)
27. Szegedy, C., Ioffe, S., Vanhoucke, V., Alemi, A.: Inception-v4, Inception-ResNet, and the impact of residual connections on learning. In: Proceedings of the AAAI Conference on Artificial Intelligence, vol. 31 (2017)
28. Lin, T.-Y., et al.: Focal loss for dense object detection. In: Proceedings of the IEEE International Conference on Computer Vision, pp. 2980–2988 (2017)
29. Cao, Y., Chen, K., Loy, C.C., Lin, D.: Prime sample attention in object detection. In: Proceedings of the IEEE/CVF Conference on Computer Vision and Pattern Recognition, pp. 11583–11591 (2020)
30. He, K., Zhang, X., Ren, S., Sun, J.: Deep residual learning for image recognition. In: Proceedings of the IEEE Conference on Computer Vision and Pattern Recognition, pp. 770–778 (2016)
31. Kaur, R., Singh, S.: A comprehensive review of object detection with deep learning. Digital Sig. Process. **132**, 103812 (2023)
32. Wu, Y., et al.: Detectron2 (2019). https://github.com/facebookresearch/detectron2
33. Syed, S., Malathi, K.: Single shot multi-box detector algorithm over fast R-CNN: an ingenious technique for increasing object detection classification accuracy. J. Surv. Fish. Sci. **10**(1S), 2193–2203 (2023)
34. Even, M.: Stochastic gradient descent under Markovian sampling schemes. In: International Conference on Machine Learning, pp. 9412–9439 (2023)
35. Ren, S., He, K., Girshick, R., Sun, J.: Faster R-CNN: towards real-time object detection with region proposal networks. IEEE Trans. Pattern Anal. Mach. Intell. **39**(6), 1137–1149 (2016)
36. Gidaris, S., Komodakis, N.: Object detection via a multi-region and semantic segmentation-aware CNN model. In: Proceedings of the IEEE International Conference on Computer Vision, pp. 1134–1142 (2015)
37. Fu, C.-Y., et al.: DSSD: deconvolutional single shot detector. arXiv preprint arXiv:1701.06659 (2017)
38. Zhang, Y., Sohn, K., Villegas, R., Pan, G., Lee, H.: Improving object detection with deep convolutional networks via bayesian optimization and structured prediction. In: Proceedings of the IEEE Conference on Computer Vision and Pattern Recognition, pp. 249–258 (2015)

39. Hoiem, D., Chodpathumwan, Y., Dai, Q.: Diagnosing errors in object detectors. In: European Conference on Computer Vision, pp. 340–353. Springer (2012)
40. Artemi, M., Liu, H.: Image optimization using improved gray-scale quantization for content-based image retrieval. In: Proceedings of the 2020 IEEE 6th International Conference on Optimization and Applications (ICOA), pp. 1–6 (2020)

**Emerging Applications /The
Cloud-Edging Integration Applications**

An LLM-Based Agent Framework for Dynamic and Semantic Data Fusion, Integration and Engineering for Data Analysis

Hong Qing Yu$^{(\boxtimes)}$ and Kasun C. Siriwardhana

University of Derby, Derby DE22 1GB, UK
`h.yu@derby.ac.uk`

Abstract. Large Language Models (LLMs) have revolutionized numerous domains but face challenges in effectively harnessing enterprise data while safeguarding privacy. This study presents a novel framework combining LangChain technology with OpenAI's GPT-3.5 model, bridging the gap between enterprise data and LLM capabilities. By ensuring robust privacy safeguards through Explainable AI, LangChain facilitates secure data utilization without compromising sensitive information. The proposed framework accommodates major data source types and offers scalability to incorporate additional data types and sources. It features an LLM-powered data ingestion system, enabling automation and enhancing business intelligence applications. Leveraging advanced NLP capabilities, the system excels in language-driven data ingestion, showcasing the potential of LLMs. The efficacy of framework is evaluated against existing data ingestion methods, highlighting its dynamic nature empowered by a Python framework. Through a comprehensive analysis encompassing accuracy, response quality, usability, and profitability, LangChain demonstrates its superiority. The major advantage of this framework is the transparency, which is prioritized through a human-readable insights approach, providing users visibility into AI-generated content. Rigorous testing methodology, employing a diverse set of questions, showcases framework's satisfactory accuracy rate, with 12 out of 15 responses meeting expectations.

Keywords: Machine Learning · Large Language Model · LangChain · Enterprise Data Integration · Data Engineering · Context-Aware LLM Frameworks · Secure LLM Applications · AI Solutions · Explainable AI

1 Introduction

In the rapidly evolving landscape of technology, the ascent of Artificial Intelligence (AI), particularly with the remarkable advancements in Large Language Models (LLMs), has heralded a transformative era in intelligent framework development. This progress is propelled by the cognitive prowess exhibited by LLMs, enabling tasks such as multi-step reasoning, natural language comprehension, and innovative artifact design (Collins et al. 2021).

© ICST Institute for Computer Sciences, Social Informatics and Telecommunications Engineering 2026
Published by Springer Nature Switzerland AG 2026. All Rights Reserved
X. Feng et al. (Eds.): CloudComp 2024, LNICST 617, pp. 159–171, 2026.
https://doi.org/10.1007/978-3-031-92517-7_12

This study delves into the intricate relationship between LLMs and data engineering, aiming to devise a pioneering framework that seamlessly integrates data into LLM solutions securely, dynamically, and semantically. While the spotlight often shines on ChatGPT for its exceptional text generation capabilities, it's essential to acknowledge the emergence of even more potent models like GPT-4, capable of handling vast amounts of text with robust reasoning capabilities (OpenAI 2024).

This breakthrough has paved the way for frameworks like LangChain, which enhance application development powered by language models by offering tools and abstractions aimed at customization, accuracy, and data relevance (AWS 2024). Through an extensive literature review, this research aims to illuminate the state-of-the-art in LLM architectures, data-indexed GPT-based frameworks, data integration and ingestion techniques, and prompt engineering methodologies.

By critically analyzing existing studies, we aim to identify limitations in current data integration approaches and propose a framework to address these shortcomings. Empowering LLMs, particularly ChatGPT, to dynamically and semantically integrate data sources fosters robust and versatile solutions, contributing to AI advancement across various domains and enhancing businesses' ability to maximize data usage.

The journey begins with an exploration of LLM architectures and their significance in leveraging external data and AI capabilities. We delve into generative AI and augmented Natural Language Processing (NLP), highlighting their impact on content creation and identifying research opportunities.

Further examination focuses on embeddings and In-Context Learning within LLMs, elucidating their role in enhancing semantic understanding and contextual relevance. The LangChain ecosystem's potential in seamlessly integrating AI through an innovative Agent concept is explored, along with its transformative impact on resource utilization and use cases across domains.

Synthesizing these domains underscores the transformative potential of combining data fusion, integration, and engineering with LLMs, paving the way for innovative AI applications and technology advancements.

2   Related Work

2.1   Generative AI

The objective of generative AI is to instill machines with creativity by training them on vast datasets to recognize underlying patterns. Leveraging these patterns, models can generate entirely novel data points, contributing to enhanced understanding and reasoning.

A prominent architecture in generative AI is the Generative Adversarial Network (GAN), introduced by (Ian J. Goodfellow, Jean Pouget-Abadie, Mehdi Mirza, Bing Xu, David Warde-Farley, Sherjil Ozair, Aaron Courville, Yoshua Bengio 2014). GANs orchestrate a contest between two models: a generator, tasked with producing realistic data, and a discriminator, responsible for identifying falsified data. This adversarial setup drives both models to refine their abilities, resulting in progressively more authentic generated content.

Generative AI finds applications across diverse domains:

- Image and Video Creation: Tools like OpenAI Sora (OpenAI 2024) and Midjourney (2024) employ generative AI to produce videos and images based on user prompts, respectively.
- Code Generation: Systems such as Copilot utilize generative AI to aid programmers by suggesting or even generating code snippets.
- Large Language Models (LLMs): LLMs like OpenAI GPT-4 and Google Gemini exhibit powerful capabilities in understanding and generating various forms of creative text, language translation, and informative responses to questions.
- Audio Generation: Tools like Meta AudioCraft (Meta 2024) leverage generative AI to create professional music and voice composing experience.

This enumeration underscores the versatility of generative AI and its profound impact across creative and technical domains.

2.2   Augmented NLP

Augmented Natural Language Processing (NLP) revolutionizes traditional NLP models by integrating external knowledge sources, enabling them to comprehend language in a richer context. This augmentation enhances accuracy, reasoning capabilities, and reduces bias, extending NLP's applicability to diverse real-world scenarios. For instance, incorporating knowledge graphs or domain-specific ontologies empowers NLP models to provide more accurate sentiment analysis, insightful information extraction, and contextually relevant question answering. In practical applications like customer service chatbots, medical diagnosis support systems, and legal document analysis, augmented NLP facilitates more comprehensive and accurate outcomes. As the field progresses, advancements in techniques such as data fusion, integration, and engineering will play a crucial role in further enhancing NLP models' capabilities (Ziyang Luo 2023). By streamlining these processes, augmented NLP continues to unlock new possibilities in different domains, as evidenced by studies in fields such as legal services (Kishan Kanhaiya 2023) and medicine (Panagoulias et al. 2023). This concept underscores the importance of carefully exposing data to LLMs, opening new research avenues, and highlighting the criticality of data handling procedures.

2.3   Embeddings and In-Context Learning with LLMs

In the context of Large Language Models (LLMs), an embedding refers to a dense vector representation of words or tokens in a continuous vector space. These embeddings encode semantic meaning and contextual relationships between words based on their usage in large text corpora. Essentially, embeddings map words to vectors in such a way that similar words are represented by vectors that are close together in the vector space (T. Mikolov et al. 2013). Moreover, embeddings serve as the primary input for LLMs like ChatGPT, as depicted in Fig. 1.

Embeddings play a crucial role in empowering Large Language Models (LLMs) with semantic understanding, bridging the gap between words and their meaning in natural language processing (NLP) tasks. Traditional encoding methods like one-hot encoding lack the ability to capture semantic richness, whereas embeddings provide

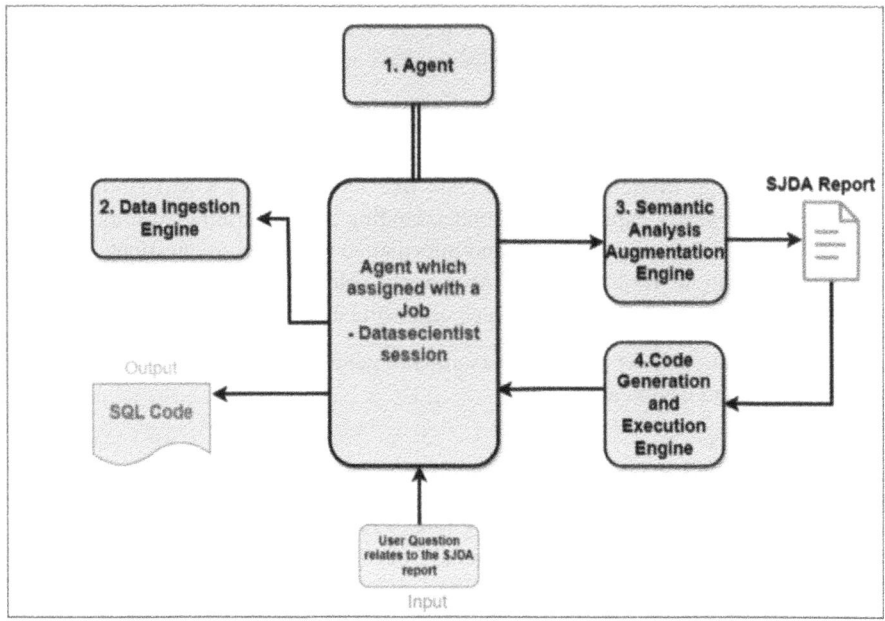

Fig. 1 Architectural framework proposal

dense vector representations that encode semantic meaning and context based on word co-occurrence patterns. Techniques and studies such as Word2Vec (T. Mikolov et al. 2013), GloVe (J. Pennington et al. 2014), FastText, BERT (J. Devlin et al. 2019), and GPT have revolutionized how LLMs understand and process language by providing them with nuanced representations of word semantics (S. Remus et al. 2018).

The benefits of embeddings for LLMs are immense. They enable LLMs to move beyond simple word lookup and understand the deeper relationships within text, facilitating tasks such as semantic search, document clustering (W. Mu et al. 2022), and topic modelling (H.U.M Belmonte et al. 2021). Embeddings also enhance transfer learning (Aman Yadav et al. 2023) by providing pre-trained representations of linguistic knowledge, accelerating the training process for specific downstream tasks, and improving performance.

Custom embeddings play a pivotal role in enhancing LLM performance by capturing domain-specific expertise and vocabulary. Additionally, they help mitigate biases inherited from pre-trained embeddings, ensuring more accurate, equitable, and fair outcomes in language models, as highlighted in studies such as (Peters 2018). Through training on domain-specific data, LLMs develop embeddings fine-tuned to the nuances of a particular field, leading to improved accuracy and relevance in domain-specific tasks.

In-context learning (ICL), which demonstrates more generalization capability, offers an alternative approach to tailoring a Large Language Model (LLM) while maintaining its broad applicability, even if its performance might be suboptimal without specific task training (H. Yang et al. 2024).This technique relies on prompt engineering, as discussed in (Chen 2023), for the development of proposing framework as well.

Overall, embeddings serve as a cornerstone technology for LLMs, unlocking their full potential and fostering deeper human-machine interaction through language. By leveraging both pre-trained and custom embeddings, LLMs can perform a wider range of tasks with greater accuracy and contextual understanding, paving the way for advanced NLP applications across diverse domains.

2.4   RAG-LLM Agent

Retrieval-Augmented Generation (RAG) models or agents represent a significant advancement in integrating retrieval mechanisms with large language models (LLMs). These agents leverage LLMs to generate responses while dynamically retrieving relevant information from external data sources, thereby enhancing the accuracy and relevance of the generated content (Google 2024).

The typical architecture consists of two main components: a retriever and a generator. The retriever component searches for relevant documents or snippets from a predefined knowledge base or external data source, which are then fed into the generator component (an LLM) to produce a coherent and contextually enriched response.

This architecture usually involves several stages (LangChain 2024):

- Indexing: This involves ingesting data from a source and indexing it. Data is loaded using document loaders, split into smaller chunks with text splitters, and then stored in a VectorStore with embedding's for efficient retrieval.
- Retrieval and Generation: At runtime, the user's query is processed to retrieve relevant data from the indexed storage. This data is then incorporated into the prompt for the LLM to generate a precise and contextually appropriate response.

The hybrid nature of RAG-LLM agents enables them to address several limitations of standalone LLMs, such as hallucinations and the inability to access updated information. By incorporating retrieved data, these agents can provide more accurate, up-to-date, and contextually relevant outputs. This makes them highly suitable for applications in customer support, healthcare, legal advisory, and more. The key advantages include:

- Enhanced Accuracy: By augmenting the LLM with specific, relevant data retrieved in real-time, RAG models produce more accurate and relevant responses.
- Updated Information: They can include the most current information from live data sources, overcoming the limitation of the LLM's training cut-off date.
- Contextual Relevance: Retrieved data ensures that the responses are contextually appropriate, addressing the exact query posed by the user.

Recent research has focused on improving the efficiency, scalability, and integration capabilities of RAG-LLM agents. Key advancements include optimizing retrieval mechanisms, enhancing coherence between retrieved documents and generated responses, and developing fine-tuning techniques to better align with specific application domains. The key Developments in RAG-LLM Agents:

Optimized Retrieval Mechanisms: Techniques such as Passage Search (O. Khttab et al. 2020) and Passage Retrieval (DPR) (V. Karpukhin el al. 2020) have improved the efficiency of retrieving relevant documents from large datasets.

Enhanced Coherence (Brecque 2024): Research has focused on ensuring that the retrieved documents and generated responses are highly coherent, providing seamless and natural answers.

Fine-Tuning Techniques (K. Guu et al. 2020, G. Izacard et al. 2021, P. Lewis et al. 2020): Fine-tuning LLMs with domain-specific data enhances their performance for particular applications, such as legal or medical or open domain question answering.

3   Research Methodology and Implementation

This research proposes a novel framework built on the LangChain ecosystem to create a virtual semantic warehouse that fuses, engineers, and integrates data utilizing ChatGPT. This methodology employs a systematic and iterative approach, combining software development practices with architectural design and framework integration. Here, we delve into the key steps and methodologies used to implement the core components, including empirical testing and human-in-the-loop evaluation, with a focus on linguistic fidelity.

3.1   Research Strategy

The research strategy used to build and evaluate the data fusion, integration, and engineering framework, which combines Large Language Models (LLMs) and the LangChain ecosystem, followed a comprehensive and cyclical approach. This method combined established software development practices, basic architectural design principles, and a mix of theoretical testing and practical evaluation. This overview outlines the main research strategies employed at each stage of the study, emphasizing the combination of theories, iterative design and development, and the important role of Human-in-the-Loop evaluation in improving the system's effectiveness, context awareness, and linguistic accuracy. By strategically applying these methods, the study aimed to address the challenges of integrating LLMs into enterprise data warehousing systems, ensuring smooth, secure, and efficient data management.

3.1.1   Problem Understanding and Analysis

The problem understanding and analysis phase involved exploring the transformative impact of artificial intelligence (AI), large language models (LLMs), and the LangChain framework on user interactions, content generation, and data integration. This included examining the evolution of LLMs, their capabilities in understanding and generating complex text, and the integration of external knowledge sources through augmented natural language processing (NLP) and human-in-the-loop AI integration. The primary aim was to establish a robust groundwork for the research endeavor, discerning existing frameworks, methodologies, and potential gaps in the field.

3.1.2   Requirement Specification and Design

Clear requirements were meticulously outlined for each component of the proposed system. This entailed defining the functionalities, inputs, and outputs, along with the implementation of human-in-the-loop integration, a dynamic data integration system, a code-generating system, and a LangChain-based LLM system. Architectural design decisions were thoughtfully made, with careful consideration given to factors such as modularity, scalability, and seamless integration with external frameworks.

3.1.3   Implementation and Development

Agent

The Agent class is crafted to emulate human job roles and facilitate interactive abilities, empowering seamless integration of new modules on demand. This enhances its functionality, enabling a versatile approach to various tasks. The *data_scientist.py* module, developed as a subclass of the Agent framework, specifically empowers Data Scientists in data analysis tasks. It offers vital functionalities for data ingestion, semantic analysis, and code generation, thereby streamlining data processing and analysis tasks efficiently. The design allows the Agent to adapt to new requirements, ensuring it can evolve as needed to meet emerging challenges in data analysis and integration.

Data Ingestion Engine

As a crucial system ability of the Data Scientist, this module facilitates seamless ingestion and analysis of structured data files and databases. It offers versatile file reading capabilities, including support for CSV and Excel formats, and currently extracts detailed schema information from SQLite databases. However, the module is designed to be extensible for other data sources, ensuring adaptability and scalability in data processing workflows.

Semantic Analysis and Augmentation Engine

The *semantic_analysis_augmentation.py* module enhances Data Scientist capabilities by fusing essential information from file-based and database-based data sources using the OpenAI ChatGPT 3.5 model. Functions analyze data sources and generate comprehensive reports, facilitating deeper data and metadata understanding. The module's flexibility allows for potential extensions to other data sources, ensuring adaptability and scalability. Additionally, reports can be saved in PDF format for documentation and sharing. Overall, this layer empowers Data Scientists with actionable insights from diverse data sources.

Code Generation Execution Engine

The code_generation_execution_engine.py script empowers the Agent module with the ability to generate code in multiple languages based on user queries and the Semantic Job Data Awareness (SJDA) report. Leveraging advanced AI models and document processing techniques, the module preprocesses the SJDA report, contextualizes user questions, and generates code tailored to the provided language. By integrating with the Agent's chat history and state management, it ensures seamless interaction and personalized responses. Overall, this engine enhances the Agent's functionality by automating code generation tasks with contextual awareness.

3.1.4   Evaluation and Testing

Functional Testing
Each module in the framework was tested, specifically the *semantic analysis and augmentation engine* and the *code generation execution engine*, as these modules directly rely on large language model (LLM). The intermediate output generating by semantic_analysis_augmentation.py module as Semantic Job Data Awareness (SJDA) report also tested for accuracy and all functions in the module code_generation_execution_engine.py underwent meticulous functional testing to ensure compliance with predefined requirements. The *code generation engine's* critical steps, including context contextualization, prompts, and code generation, were rigorously tested to validate their accuracy and reliability. Specifically, the robustness of the contextualization mechanism in understanding and processing user queries was evaluated. Additionally, the code generation functionality was assessed to ensure the generation of clear and relevant outputs. Furthermore, consistency of the generated code in the given programming language were thoroughly examined to guarantee adherence to coding standards and logical coherence.

Integration Testing
Integration testing was conducted to assess the seamless interaction between different components of the code_generation_execution_engine.py module and its integration with the different modules to facilitate the framework. The interoperability of the code generation engine with other modules, such as the *data_ingestion_engine* and *semantic_analysis_augmentation_engine*, was evaluated to ensure consistent data flow and functionality across the system. Integration tests verified the compatibility of the code generation engine with different data sources and configurations, including SQL, CSV, and Excel. Furthermore, as the framework was developed in object-oriented approach, studies were carried out to understand how this can be utilized in real-world scenarios. In such cases, using API, Wrappers, and SDKs, Agent's abilities can be improved, and studies were performed to validate the module's compatibility with external frameworks and libraries commonly used data storing and analysis.

Performance Testing
Performance testing focused on evaluating the speed, scalability, and resource utilization of the framework. The response time for generating code snippets across different data sources was considered under varying workloads to assess the module's efficiency. Additionally, resource utilization metrics, such as CPU and memory usage, were monitored to identify any performance bottlenecks and optimize resource allocation.

Accuracy Testing
Accuracy testing was carried out to validate the correctness and precision of the generated code and the semantic job data awareness report. Test cases covering a wide range of input queries and scenarios were designed to evaluate the module's ability to produce accurate and reliable code outputs. The generated code was compared against expected outputs based on predefined criteria, including syntactic correctness, adherence to coding standards, and logical consistency. Any discrepancies or deviations from the expected behavior were identified and addressed to enhance the module's accuracy and reliability.

Iterative Refinement

In an iterative refinement process, feedback from testing sessions played a pivotal role in enhancing the system's capabilities. Iterative modifications were made to refine and improve various aspects, including design, modularization, output, and intermediate results. The focus was on optimizing data ingestion, enhancing context awareness, and fine-tuning language-driven decision-making through prompt engineering and optimizations. This iterative approach aimed to address any identified shortcomings and align the system with expectations, ensuring continuous improvement and evolution in line with academic standards.

4   Outcomes of the Analysis/Testing and Evaluation

The successful implementation of the proposed framework, enhanced with generative AI capabilities, requires meticulous analysis, rigorous testing, and thorough evaluation. This section outlines the systematic approach used to assess the developed system's performance in data integration, prompt-engineered analysis, and code generation. Emphasis is placed on evaluating the Language Model (LLM)-based system, focusing on its language-oriented AI capabilities and context-sensitive content generation.

4.1   Test Setup: Agent Ecosystem

The approach began with a theoretical foundation, followed by practical evaluation. This involved a deep understanding of the problem through a literature review, clearly defined requirements, solution implementation, and ongoing refinements based on testing feedback. This iterative cycle led to continuous improvements in design, usability, and functionality.

To guarantee the reliability and accuracy of the LLM-based system, a two-pronged testing approach was employed. Unit testing focused on isolating and testing individual system components, verifying their proper functioning against design specifications. Integration testing then assessed seamless interaction and data flow between different modules, ensuring effective communication across the entire system. For the test datasets, the framework worked excellently, providing the expected intermediate outputs.

4.2   Initial LLM System Evaluation

Investigation uncovered three key findings regarding the model's performance:

- Processing Time: The model exhibited a reasonable processing time, taking approximately 1.5–3 min to generate results and produce SJDA (Structured Job Data Analysis) reports on datasets varying from 1 to 6.
- Consistency: The model demonstrated an inability to generate consistent outputs initially. However, it tended to provide more reliable and accurate outputs with increased testing.
- Prompt Sensitivity: The model showed significant variation depending on prompt template and query adjustments. Intensive recursive testing was necessary to identify the optimal prompt, which should strike a balance between being neither too simple nor too complex.

4.3 JSON-Based Evaluation Technique

To systematically evaluate the framework, a set of JSON-based questions was used, categorized by difficulty: simple, medium, and hard. Each category contained five questions, totaling fifteen test cases. The following figure shows an example (Fig. 2).

```json
{
  "difficulty": "simple",
  "question": "Retrieve the names and counts of individuals from the NationalNames table
  "expected_sql": "SELECT Name, Count FROM NationalNames WHERE Gender = 'F';",
  "received_answer": ""
}
```

Fig. 2 JSON based question format used for evaluation

4.3.1 Overall Results

The framework was tested against 15 cases, with the system generating correct outputs 12 out of 15 times. The distribution of correct answers by difficulty level was as follows:

Simple: 5/5

Medium: 4/5

Hard: 3/5

The testing revealed that the framework generally performed well, although manual verification was necessary in some cases due to the code generator providing alternative solutions. This iterative testing process helped in identifying and refining the prompts to enhance consistency and accuracy.

Accuracy & Precision

Accuracy: The framework's accuracy was high, as it correctly generated outputs for 73.33% (22/30) of the test cases (12/15). Accuracy measures the overall correctness of the system in producing the expected results.

Precision: Precision was also notable, particularly in simple and medium difficulty cases. Precision is the ratio of correctly generated outputs to the total number of outputs generated. For the simple and medium difficulty levels, the precision was close to 100%, but slightly lower for hard cases due to some incorrect outputs.

In individual test cases minor deviations are noted. Overall, the framework demonstrated strong performance, particularly in generating accurate and precise outputs for simpler queries. The insights gained from manual verification and iterative testing were crucial in refining the system to improve its recall and precision, especially for more complex queries.

In this setup, the framework, supported by the SJDA report, was evaluated using a range of simple to complex queries against the datasets. The provided response example aligns with user expectations, yielding promising results and indicating fruitful areas for further research to enhance consistency. The current goal is to streamline the transition from Online Transaction Processing (OLTP) to Online Analytical Processing (OLAP) systems by leveraging metadata from data sources and augmenting the perspectives of data experts with systems capable of context-aware tasks based on provided data sources.

5   Synthesis and Future Directions

5.1   Limitations and Challenges

The agent framework designed to generate Semantic Job Data Awareness (SJDA) and SQL queries is highly dependent on the accuracy and completeness of the data sources and the prompt engineering mechanisms used. While the framework can effectively retrieve metadata, execute SQL code, and draft responses from data sources, several limitations have been identified:

Data Complexity and Result Accuracy

The performance of the framework declines with larger datasets, primarily due to token limitations and inconsistent outputs. The current token limit of approximately 4,000 tokens in OpenAI's ChatGPT restricts the framework's ability to process extensive metadata, leading to incomplete SJDA reports. Additionally, the framework's outputs are sensitive to the prompt templates and questions, often resulting in variable and sometimes invalid responses.

Handling Novel Frameworks

The integration of rapidly evolving data warehousing technologies requires rigorous fine-tuning to ensure reliability in business-critical environments. This process is time-consuming but necessary to leverage AI capabilities effectively. There is also a risk of bias in AI-generated outputs, which must be managed carefully. Although the introduction of Explainable AI with SJDA has mitigated this to some extent, further improvements are still needed.

5.2   Recommendations for Improvement

To enhance the framework's efficacy and reliability, several recommendations have been proposed:

Enhanced Stability and Performance

Continuous refinement and optimization are necessary to improve the framework's stability and performance. This includes identifying and addressing potential bottlenecks and inefficiencies and developing optimal prompts that balance token size and result accuracy. A mechanism must be implemented to manage metadata from large datasets that exceed the token limit.

Scalability

To handle growing data volumes and increasing complexity, the framework must be scalable. Optimizing algorithms, infrastructure, and resources is crucial to accommodate larger datasets and more complex analytical tasks. Establishing live connections with multiple data sources is also critical for efficient querying and data processing. However, this approach could affect the accuracy of query outcomes, as the framework retrieves results from the original data source, relying on the currency and accuracy of the data.

User-Friendly Interface

Improving the user interface and experience will enhance the framework's usability and adoption. This involves developing intuitive dashboards, providing comprehensive documentation, and offering user training and support.

Integration with External Systems

Enhancing interoperability by integrating the framework with external systems, tools, and platforms will broaden its utility. Developing APIs, connectors, or plugins can facilitate seamless data exchange and integration with existing workflows. Additionally, leveraging capabilities from other models like Google Gemini (S. Pichai, Demis Hassabis 2023), Perplexity (2024), Bing AI (Microsoft 2024), and Amazon CodeWhisperer (Amazon 2024) can complement each other's strengths and enhance the framework's overall power.

Security and Compliance

Implementing robust security measures and ensuring compliance with data privacy regulations is essential. This includes encryption, access controls, audit trails, and adherence to industry standards such as GDPR and the EU AI Act.

6 Conclusion

The proposed framework for dynamic and semantic data fusion, integration, and engineering for LLM-based solutions offers significant potential for business-critical applications. By streamlining data engineering and enhancing AI intelligence with contextual understanding, the framework can drive substantial improvements in decision-making and innovation.

Addressing the identified challenges and implementing the recommended improvements will be crucial to realizing the full benefits. Enhanced stability, scalability, user-friendliness, integration capabilities, security, and continuous improvement will make the framework robust and reliable. Systematically evaluating and measuring LLM performance in real-world scenarios will ensure their effectiveness and reliability. By following these guidelines, organizations can unlock new insights from their data resources and harness the full potential of AI-driven solutions.

References

Mikolov, T., et al.: distributed representations of words and phrases and their compositionality (2013)

Aman, Y., et al.: Natural language processing through transfer learning: a case study on sentiment analysis (2023)

Amazon, Amazon CodeWhisperer (2024). https://aws.amazon.com/codewhisperer/

AWS. What Is Langchain? (2024). https://aws.amazon.com/what-is/langchain/

Brecque, C.: What is Retrieval-Augmented Generation? (RAG) (2024). https://teams.live.com/_?utm_source=OfficeWeb#/modern-calling/

Chen, B.: Unleashing the potential of prompt engineering in Large Language Models: a comprehensive review (2023)

Collins et al.: Artificial intelligence in information systems research: a systematic literature review and research agenda. Int. J. Inform. Manage. 18 (2021)

Izacard, G., et al.: Distilling knowledge from reader to retriever for question answering. In: International Conference on Learning Representations (ICLR) (2021)

Google. What is Retrieval-Augmented Generation (RAG)? (2024). https://cloud.google.com/use-cases/retrieval-augmented-generation

Yang, H., et al.: Unveiling the generalization power of fine-tuned large language models (2024)

Belmonte, H.U.M., et al.: Word embeddings for topic modeling: an application to the estimation of the economic policy uncertainty index (2021)

Goodfellow, I.J., et al. Generative Adversarial Nets (2014)

Devlin, J., et al.: BERT: pre-training of deep bidirectional transformers for language understanding (2019)

Pennington, J., et al.: GloVe: global vectors for word representation. In: 4 Conference on Empirical Methods in Natural Language Processing (2014)

Guu, K., et al.: REALM: retrieval-augmented language model pre-training. In: International Conference on Machine Learning (ICML) (2020)

Kanhaiya, K.: AI enabled- information retrival engine (AI-IRE) in legal services: an expert-annotated NLP for legal judgements. In: International Conference on Augmented Intelligence and Sustainable Systems (2023)

LangChain. Build a Retrieval Augmented Generation (RAG) App (2024). https://python.langchain.com/v0.2/docs/tutorials/rag/

Microsoft. Copilot and Bing's AI features (2024). https://www.microsoft.com/en-us/bing/do-more-with-ai/bing-ai-features?form=MA13KP

Khttab, O., et al.: ColBERT: E€icient and E€ective passage search via contextualized late interaction over BERT. In: International ACM SIGIR Conference on Research and Development in Information Retrieval (2020)

OpenAI. Transforming work and creativity with AI (2024). https://openai.com/product. Accessed 13 March 2024

Lewis, P., et al.: Retrieval-augmented generation for knowledge-intensive NLP tasks. Advances in Neural Information Processing Systems (2020)

Panagoulias et al.: Rule-augmented artificial intelligence-empowered systems for medical diagnosis using large language models. International Conference on Tools with Artificial Intelligence (2023)

Perplexity, T.: Perplexity launches Enterprise Pro (2024). https://www.perplexity.ai/hub/blog/perplexity-launches-enterprise-pro

Peters, M.E.: Deep contextualized word representations. NAACL-HLT (2018)

Pichai, S., Hassabis, D.: Introducing Gemini: our largest and most capable AI model (2023). https://blog.google/technology/ai/google-gemini-ai/

Remus, S., et al.: More like this: semantic retrieval with linguistic information. In: Conference on Natural Language Processing (2018)

Karpukhin, V., et al.: Dense passage retrieval for open-domain question answering (2020)

Mu, W., et al.: A clustering-based topic model using word networks and word embeddings. J. Big Data (2022)

Luo, Z.: Augmented large language models with parametric knowledge guiding (2023)

AI for Law and AI Under Law in China

Junke Xu and Jian Wang[✉]

China Foreign Affairs University, Beijing 100037, China
wangjian@cfau.edu.cn

Abstract. This article briefly examines the impact of Artificial Intelligence (AI) on Chinese Legislation and the legal sector. It highlights the emerging issues that have come to the forefront due to the rapid advancement of AI. Furthermore, it will assess how the Chinese regulatory regime addresses these problems and how AI technology transforms the legal industry.

Keywords: Generative AI · Risk Mitigation · Regulatory Philosophy · Data Classification

1 Introduction

At the end of 2022, the release of the ChatGPT developed by OpenAI swiftly triggered an extensive global interest in the field of generative AI. Generative AI is applied in a broader range of scenarios while efficiently contributing to the development of the economy and society. The revolutionary results have prompted a new phase. However, generative AI has brought technological impact to legislation multi-faceted challenges.

2 Issues Arising from Generative AI

2.1 Data Security

Generative AI refers to models and related technologies that can autonomously generate content such as text, images, audio, video, and so forth. Unlike traditional simple content generation based on orders or templates, generative AI relies on the results of training on big data by language models, which mainly carry out unsupervised learning on a large amount of unlabelled data and extracting the rules and patterns in the data. Large Language Models (LLMs) may unintentionally release information from training data, including private or sensitive data or material covered by copyright protection. These LLMs may store this kind of information and leak it under the inducement of deliberate questions. This concern also occurred in reality. On 23 March 2023, Open AI's CEO Sam Altman publicly admitted that an error in the open-source repository led to some users' names, email addresses, last four digital numbers of the credit card and chat history with ChatGPT leaked [1]. After Samsung allowed the use of ChatGPT, the company exposed to data breaches that led to the leakage of sensitive and confidential information in internal meetings [2].

X. Feng et al. (Eds.): CloudComp 2024, LNICST 617, pp. 172–182, 2026.
https://doi.org/10.1007/978-3-031-92517-7_13

Data scraping is an accepted practice in the digital realm, operating within the boundaries of what is considered lawful. Nonetheless, the delineation of these boundaries can sometimes be obscured, particularly when it comes to the data removal. For instance, the OpenAI terms of services do not clearly outline the data removal process or the means to execute it, presenting a loophole that may challenge the established constraints of legitimate data management [3]. Moreover, this could lead to the retention of information for large model training, potentially violating an individual's rights to consent and erasure. Accordingly, the Italian Data Protection Authority (DPA) banned the use of ChatGPT starting from March 31, 2023, due to suspicions of OpenAI's illegal scraping of a large amount of personal information data of Italian users [4].

2.2 Risk of Generating Incorrect or Misleading Information

In the areas of specialization that require high levels of information accuracy, particularly in the legal industry, relying solely on information generated by large models without verifying it could result in considerable damage. Two lawyers in the US state of New York cited six cases collected by ChatGPT in legal papers submitted to the court. However, the court eventually fined the lawyers and their firm $5,000 respectively after they found that ChatGPT fabricated the cases [5]. Moreover, owing to the excellent text-generation capabilities and human-like interaction features, generative AI is at risk of being exploited for malicious purposes, which could produce large quantities of **realistic and misleading disinformation**, making the generation of disinformation more intricate to recognize. For instance, Deepfake can duplicate the facial, voice, and even behavioral patterns of one person to another, creating fictional content that appears to be authentic. It is worth noted that advancements in deepfake technology have transcended previous limitations. The collection of biometric information has become pervasive across diverse settings. In the past, a simple waving hand gesture before the face was sufficient to reduce facial clarity if the face was fake. However, this approach is now obsolete considering involved Deepfake capabilities, which can bypass such basic testing method.

As a result, information security and public trust are being challenged as never before [6]. When the public progressively receives information that is not trustworthy, the credibility of society as a whole is undermined over time.

2.3 Attribution and Integrity

Generative AI LLMs built on the results of pre-existing human artistic creations have led creators to worry about the repercussions of copyright ownership of their works. The latest video release from Open AI's Sora is 60 s long, with more complex scenes and delicate images. It makes the standard of creativity less stringent, and everyone can be an amateur director and editor. The Hollywood Screenwriters' Strike comes as screenwriters fear that the rise of generative AI will adversely impact their visionary work [7]. They made several demands to protect their copyright and ensure that AI does not replace their work, including not treating AI-generated literary material as if it had been written by humans and banning the fruits of screenwriters' labor to train AI. On 27 December 2023, the New York Times sued Open AI and Microsoft, accusing the two companies of using millions of its articles to train artificial intelligence models [8].

Given that the case has not yet reached a verdict, there are two pivotal legal questions that need to be addressed by the court. Firstly, the court should determine whether the utilization of copyrighted material for the training of AI models constitutes a violation. Secondly, the court should assess the allegations regarding the infringement of writers' rights by the generative AI content.

2.4 Ethical Challenges

Applying the notion of human neurons to AI algorithms boosts ML (Machine Learning) capability and intelligence level by emulating the most intricate information processing system in nature—the human brain.

AI algorithms now reflect a more sophisticated mimicry of human cognitive functions. Scientists are concerned that AI technology might become uncontrollable and develop its personality in the foreseeable future, such as emotions and intentions. However, given the current algorism capacity, AI remains within a manageable range for the time being. Nevertheless, the darker facets of AI have already started to threaten human moral and ethical norms.

Subtle Influence

It is acknowledged that LLMs should be trained under a political correctness framework, which implies that the content outputs consistent with mainstream values regarding matters like affirmative action, gender issues, equal pay and so on. However, as long as the model's comprehension of the world is shaped by its underlying algorithms and the choices of its creators, the language model is hardly free from bias.

AI recruitment seems to mitigate the interference of subjective biases, aligning candidate capabilities more accurately with job requirements. However, this technological advancement also harbors the potential for subtler forms of discrimination to be implanted within decision-making systems. From a larger picture, entities that develop generative AI could train these models with data skewed toward specific political aims or interests, crafting responses that draw a particular ideological line and manipulate users' thoughts and preferences in a direction that may serve their agendas. Consequently, the risk of bias in generative AI poses significant latent security threats.

Information Cocoon

Websites employ algorithms that recommend content based on user preferences, geographical region, browsing history, and search queries. Similar opinions and perspectives are continuously repeated and reinforced in a closed social environment, so users may assume that the viewpoints they have are the ones shared by the majority. For example, when social media algorithms detect a user's interest in climate change, they may fill the user's front page with environmental protection content. The horizon of users' viewpoints was once confined to a limited expanse, it may narrow users' tolerance for diverse viewpoints. Thus, society is increasingly segmented into distinct factions, with individuals being categorized and labeled according to their affiliations.

3   The Current Chinese Legal Regime on Generative Artificial Intelligence

3.1   Classified Data Protection

The increasing prominence of Generative AI has captured legislators' attention, prompting legal frameworks in this field. The table below lists a compilation of laws and regulations in recent years (Table 1).

Table 1. Laws and Regulations about AI in China

Authority Level	Document Name	Effective Date
Regulatory Documents of the State Council	Notice of the State Council on Issuing the Development Plan on the New Generation of Artificial Intelligence	07-08-2017
Judicial Interpretation Nature	Opinions of the Supreme People's Court on Regulating and Strengthening the Applications of Artificial Intelligence in the Judicial Fields	12-08-2022
Departmental Rules	Interim Measures for the Administration of Generative Artificial Intelligence Services	08-15-2023
Laws	Cybersecurity Law of the People's Republic of China	06-01-2017
Laws	Data Security Law of the People's Republic of China	09-01-2021
Laws	Personal Information Protection Law of the People's Republic of China	11-01-2021
Laws	Law of the People's Republic of China on Scientific and Technological Progress (2021 Revision)	01-01-2022

The Cybersecurity Law of the People's Republic of China states that network operators shall adopt practices like the systematic classification of data. *The Data Security Law of the People's Republic of China* regulates that the state shall establish a categorized and hierarchical data protection system to mitigate data risk. Moreover, data are classified into core data, important data, and the rest data on the basis of security risk. Depending on the category of data, different levels of protection are available. In addition, as the first generative AI regulatory rule, *the Interim Measures for the Administration of Generative Artificial Intelligence Services* implement classified supervision of generative AI services and take into account the data specificity of different groups for that it stipulates effective measures to prevent over-reliance or indulgence in generative AI services by users who are minors.

3.2 Trustworthy AI Regulatory Models

Transparency and interpretability are the requirements for the design of AI systems. The decision-making process must be transparent so that users and regulators can understand the rationale of the training models and the basis for decisions. To better accomplish this objective, the trustworthy human-centered model seems to be a more compatible way of AI regulation.

Nowadays, machine learning is the underlying structure of AI, while the algorithm functions as the black box. In the best-case scenario, the design of AI foundational framework systems should be comprehensible and the decision-making process should be transparent so that users and regulators can understand how it works. To regulate the algorithm, it is necessary to open that black box. From a legal point of view, algorithms naturally create information asymmetry, and this unbalanced information structure between providers and users gives rise to the right, also referred to as social right by Foucault. This generative social right does not have a subjective character and creates a one-way transparency in this norm. In brief, one party knows clearly what the other party knows, while the other party lacks awareness. The core of algorithm regulation is to enable transparency and thus having a mutual apprehension of the rights and obligations of both parties. In addition, regulators need to know what the algorithms are about and how they are in the design of control, and it is critical to understand the latter.

Nevertheless, algorithmic transparency is a false choice to some extent, for algorithms are inherently unenforceable for technical reasons. Therefore, trustworthy AI or human-centered AI is more appropriate for AI regarding regulation. On one hand, algorithmic transparency is difficult to achieve because algorithms are in black boxes, and humans do not know what is happening inside them. On the other hand, algorithms are technical confidentiality, and allowing companies to disclose them undoubtedly adds to their compliance costs. Especially in the early stage of the development of artificial intelligence, detailed regulatory requirements on algorithmic transparency hinder the innovation of the enterprises. In essence, it has transformed from the previous methodology of people to technology to the adjustment of the relationship between people and people.

3.3 Provider Obligation

Artificial intelligence is always driven by human beings, and the operation of AI requires human participation and control. When evaluating the regulatory scheme of AI, the value-orientated approach seems more rational than the technology-orientated one. From this perspective, it is better to regulate the providers who are empowered with the ability to carry out pre-training and optimized training. Provisions on *the Administration of Deep Synthesis of Internet-Based Information Services* and *the Interim Measures for the Administration of Generative Artificial Intelligence Services* both enforce the obligations of the service providers.

Indeed, providers are on the cutting edge of training-data processing activities. As the binding party of the contract, it shall obtain consent from the individual at the first step, and then with the collective data, it shall bear the responsibility of not infringing on the personal rights enjoyed by users. Personal information of particular communities, for example, minors or identifiable personal health data in the field of medical artificial intelligence, once improperly analyzed and exploited, can lead to adverse outcomes in a variety of ways, including economically, socially, or psychologically.

Moreover, due to the black-box nature of the algorithms, there is a lag in the occurrence of infringement or the discovery of the results of infringement damages. Providers shall bear the obligation to receive feedback from users and discover illegal content, in which case the provider is liable to take timely disposal measures such as putting a pause on generation, transmission, and any other applicable method that can eliminate the subsequent impact. Furthermore, providers shall have the obligation to take measures such as ML (Machine Learning)/DL (Deep Learning) and model optimization and training for rectification and to report to the relevant competent authorities.

4 The Transformation of AI Technology in the Legal Industry

4.1 Law Enforcement

Facial Recognition Systems
By comparing images captured by surveillance cameras with facial information in the database, AI-driven facial recognition systems can quickly target individuals and identify suspects or missing persons, thus boosting case detection rates. When dealing with a large volume of video data, in addition to significantly reducing search time, it also improves the accuracy of identification. Facial recognition systems facilitate where there are higher security needs, such as verifying travelers' identities and protection against terrorist threats. Moreover, they are used in public safety to maintain order and respond quickly to emergencies, such as assisting in the search for missing children.

Telecommunication Fraud Detection
In December 2019, the Criminal Investigation Bureau of China's Ministry of Public Security, in cooperation with Alibaba, launched the Money Shield Anti-Fraud Robot to identify fraud calls and improve the answer rate. When the system detects potential telecommunications network fraud, the anti-fraud robot automatically calls the victim and sends SMS warnings. In 2021, the government developed the National Anti-Fraud App as a mobile application that can prevent scams, monitor real-time malware to block nuisance calls and texts, and report scam content, thus enabling citizens to identify promptly and react accurately.

Data Transportation
In 2019, the first video intelligent resolution platform was released to monitor traffic accidents, send early warnings, automatically determine the type of accident, and spontaneously alert the police within 30 s after the accident's occurrence. Moreover, it verifies the discretion of law enforcement in that the application of artificial intelligence to fix evidence has become the method of investigation.

4.2 Administration of Justice

The principle of *Supporting Adjudication listed in Opinions of the Supreme People's Court on Regulating and Strengthening the Applications of Artificial Intelligence in the Judicial Fields* indicates the three most essential regulatory implementations in the AI administration of Justice. Firstly, artificial intelligence shall not replace judges when making legal decisions in any case, disregarding technological progress. Secondly, the judicial decision is always made by the judge. The generative AI assistance result can only be used as a reference for trial work, supervision and management. The trial organization shall exercise the decision-making authority, and the judge shall take the ultimate judicial responsibility. Thirdly, all users have the right to choose whether to use judicial AI assistance or terminate their interface with AI products and services.

The application scope of AI in the Chinese Judicial Court falls into the case-handling process. Specifically, AI supports the guidance and review of evidence, legal regulations push, similar case recommendations, judges' essential work assistance, and legal document generation. In other words, AI reduces the inundated workload of judicial personnel by streamlining the administrative tasks of the court and increasing the efficiency of the court routine.

Artificial intelligence provides visual analyses for case trials, taking case information recorded in text and other forms of structured information and presenting it in graphical or pictorial formats. For example, in criminal proceedings, the complete construction of the facts of the crime and thoroughly explaining the alleged crime's internal components demand abundant work. The current technical level of artificial intelligence has been capable of applying evidence to prove the facts of the crime and the reasoning logic of intelligent visual displays. Moreover, with the help of physical identification technology, LLMs can identify and extract the evidence analysis part of the review report and automatically generate the corresponding presentation way, such as a mind map or timeline, and so on. With the premise of structuring the information, the above visualized presentation form can be converted arbitrarily according to the needs.

Despite playing such a prominent part in trial activity, AI technology cannot replace the intelligence of human judges. It is mainly reflected in the following two aspects. Firstly, human judges will use value judgment when they hear cases. In criminal law cases that account for the complexity of human nature, the process of weighing and grasping human nature plays a crucial role in the trial. Whether or not generative AI will form human emotional thinking patterns in the future is still debatable and unclear. The current AI cannot accurately capture the adjudication process of emotional value orientation. Secondly, AI technology faces moral and ethical obstacles. The hidden logic of the algorithmic black box is contradictory to the open procedural principle of the judicial process. The predictive or suggestive adjudication provided by generative AI in the application manifests a simple conclusion rather than providing rational proof with an argumentative process.

How are the algorithms used in the argumentation process? How does its arithmetic logic unfold? Is there any algorithmic discrimination in it? The answers to these questions are confidential intellectual property belonging to the technology company that is only possible for insiders with in-depth understanding to detect. It is worth mentioning that even if AI dramatically improves the efficiency of the administration and reduces the workload of judges, AI can only serve as the car but cannot be the driver holding the steering wheel.

4.3 Law Firm

Legal technology has evolved rapidly with the introduction of numerous intelligent search engines designed to assist lawyers in performing intensive reading and analysis work. The following legal search platforms are the most used in practice (Table 2).

Table 2. Various applications of AI search platforms.

Platform Name	Functions	Features
FaXin	- Classified case search - Same case-wise pushing - Keyword search	- Guided Case Filtering - Assists in case analysis and dispute focus
Westlaw China	- Precise search - Case analysis	- Comprehensive resource collection - Diverse search criteria
Wolters Kluwer	- Legal literature and cases recommendation - Provides legal document templates	- Personalized recommendations - Highly customizable document templates - Online editing and collaboration
Mecheck	- Contract review - Litigation risk advice - Suggestion for revision	- Contract risk management
Pecoepic	- Intellectual property infringement investigation - Evidence collection	- Expertise in IP litigation - Optimizes evidence chain algorithm
Fagougou	- Risk level assignment	- Risk assessment
Xiaobaogong	- Criminal case analysis	- Anticipatory penalty projections
Metalaw	- Generative AI search - Automatic summary	- Simple operation - Low Legal Expertise Requirement

Faxin

FaXin [9] is the platform that combines big data and machine learning technologies as well as professional legal knowledge mapping to provide functions such as searching for classified cases and same case-wise pushing. Lawyers can use FaXin to search by inputting keywords or actively scrutinize for relevant disputed cases, offenses, and administrative acts according to different legal sections, such as civil, criminal and administrative enforcement. FaXin can be a great help in analyzing the cause of the case, the characteristics of the case, the focus of the dispute, and filters out the guiding cases of the Supreme People's Court and the Supreme People's Procuratorate, the typical cases as well as the reference cases issued by the provincial high people's courts according to the source of the validity of the cases. It enables lawyers to shortlist legal instruments of reference value among numerous cases.

Westlaw

Westlaw China [10] is a pioneer in developing the application of artificial intelligence search technology in lawyers' services. Westlaw China has established a legal intelligence database that has gathered substantial resources, including laws, regulations, cases and academic articles. Based on the platform, lawyers conduct precise searches by examining assorted conditions such as case type, court level, ruling date, and other frequently used keywords. It empowers lawyers and legal professionals with efficient legal research and case analysis.

Wolters Kluwer

Thanks to big data analysis and machine learning technology, Wolters Kluwer [11] is equipped with the ability to recommend relevant legal literature and cases based on lawyers' search preferences and history, helping lawyers to thoroughly grasp the gist of the legal issues of a case, predict the trend of decisions and analyze the logic of court rulings. In addition, it provides legal document templates, which cover contracts, litigation papers, legal advice, and other types of legal documents. The templates are highly tailored to the requirements of the users and can be adapted and edited according to the users' individual needs. Moreover, online editing and collaboration features enable lawyers and team members to collaborate on the same document.

Mecheck

Mecheck [12] reviews the contract, advising on potential litigation risks and offering suggestions for revisions. Moreover, by providing comprehensive support that includes risk assessment, digital tracking of review feedback, and identifying differences between versions, it streamlines the process and guarantees a more refined and effective interaction between the users and the platform.

Pecoepic

Pecoepic [13] provides intellectual property lawyers with infringement investigations, especially evidence collection services in trademark, patent and copyright infringement cases. It helps lawyers optimize the algorithm for sorting and screening to form the chain of evidence.

Fagougou

Regarding criminal cases, Fagougou [14] displays the analysis outcomes by categorizing them, intelligently assigns risk levels as high, medium, or low, and swiftly identifies the crucial issues.

Xiaobaogong

Xiaobaogong [15] employs the principles of legal empirical analysis to help users efficiently handle and analyze extensive legal datasets. For instance, it analyzes correlations among various elements and helps users grasp the underlying logical connections within the data. Moreover, it adds functionalities to estimate the fine amount based on the prediction of the sentence.

Metalaw

The search engines mentioned above all require users to have specialized legal knowledge to some extent, but new generative AI alters the present situation. Thus, the traditional relationship between lawyers and their clients is challenging. There has always been a considerable knowledge gap between lawyers and their clients, but the dynamics have changed. For instance, the application's search mode of a Generative AI search engine like Metalaw [16] is more straightforward. Entering the case dispute, it will automatically compile a summary of pertinent rulings and referenced legislation without requiring the user to have professional legal skills.

Generative AI has displayed a breathtaking ability to handle digital information and help people face the "digital debt" overwhelmingly created by digital work. However, people's concerns about being replaced by artificial intelligence are, more precisely, concerns about being replaced by those who effectively possess and utilize AI technology. This concern is especially prominent in industries involving extensive paperwork, such as the legal sector. As a result, some law firms are anxious about their services being overtaken by AI. To make headway in light of AI times, law firms are integrating artificial intelligence technology platforms into their legal services to offer expedited, productive, and customized services, especially for the cloud- computing cases.

5   Conclusion

Generative AI technology has facilitated the digital transformation of burdensome paperwork in legislative, judicial, and law enforcement activities, but technological advances have created challenges at the same time. Considering the widespread use of generative AI, legislators, scholars and the legal industry still have a long way to go in risk mitigation for the evolving technology. The trustworthy AI regulatory philosophy is worth further perception or insight by those in the field of legislation. Furthermore, the service providers shall take corporate social responsibility. They ought to protect the users' privacy rather than focusing mainly on liability avoidance, particularly at digital forensics on the cloud-edging computing cases. For instance, they shall set up a "systematic pre-application ethical tendency test" before generative AI applications. Moreover, given the cross-border nature of generative AI technology, we look forward to collaborative efforts among the international community for the well-being of humankind.

References

1. Derico, B.: ChatGPT bug leaked users' conversation histories, BBC News. https://www.bbc.com/news/technology-65047304. Accessed 1 March 2024
2. Gurman, M.: Samsung Bans Staff's AI Use After Spotting ChatGPT Data Leak (2), Bloomberg law. https://news.bloomberglaw.com/tech-and-telecom-law/samsung-bans-staffs-ai-use-after-spotting-chatgpt-data-leak-2. Accessed 1 March 2024

3. Yang, Y.: Canada Begins Investigating OpenAI: Personal Information Collected and Used Without Consent, Becoming the Second Country Globally to Do So, Thepaper. https://www.thepaper.cn/newsDetail_forward_22589116. Accessed 1 March 2024
4. Doherty, L., Braithwaite, S.: Italy blocks ChatGPT over privacy concerns, CNN. https://edition.cnn.com/2023/03/31/tech/chatgpt-blocked-italy/index.html. Accessed 1 March 2024
5. Merken, S.: New York lawyers sanctioned for using fake ChatGPT cases in legal brief, Reuters. https://www.reuters.com/legal/new-york-lawyers-sanctioned-using-fake-chatgpt-cases-legal-brief-2023-06-22. Accessed 1 March 2024
6. Somers, M.: Deepfakes, explained," MIT Sloan. https://mitsloan.mit.edu/ideas-made-to-matter/deepfakes-explained. Accessed 1 March 2024
7. Kelly, S.M.: TV and film writers are fighting to save their jobs from AI. They won't be the last, CNN. https://edition.cnn.com/2023/05/04/tech/writers-strike-ai/index.html. Accessed 10 March 2024
8. Goldman David, C.D.: The New York Times sues OpenAI and Microsoft for copyright infringement, CNN. https://edition.cnn.com/2023/12/27/tech/new-york-times-sues-openai-microsoft/index.html. Accessed 5 March 2024
9. FaXin is a legal information platform co-founded by the Supreme People's Court of the People's Republic of China and the People's Court Press. FaXin. https://www.faxin.cn/html/about/about.aspx. Accessed 5 March 2024
10. Westlaw China is a legal platform offered by Thomson Reuters Legal Information designed specifically for Chinese legal professionals. Westlaw China. https://www.thomsonreuters.cn/zh/products-services/legal/westlaw.html. Accessed 5 March 2024
11. Wolters Kluwer, one of the early international professional information publishers and service providers, entered the Chinese mainland market in 1985. Wolters Kluwer. https://www.wolterskluwer.cn/about-us. Accessed 1 March 2024
12. Mecheck is a legal search platform launched by a start-up AI company named Beijing Power-Law Intelligence Technology Limited Liability Company (PowerLaw Intelligence, PowerLaw AI), which provides intelligent contract reviews. Mecheck. https://mecheck.net.cn/home/homepage. Accessed 10 March 2024
13. Pecoepic is the leading search engine for Intellectual Property practitioners. Pecoepic. http://home.zy-hq.com/#about. Accessed 12 March 2024
14. Fagougou was established in 2016 and serves as the search engine for sentence prediction for criminal cases. Fagougou. https://fagougou.com/about/?t=AboutIntro. Accessed 12 March 2024
15. Xiaobaogong offers empirical legal research in criminal law on its platform. Xiaobaogong. https://www.xiaobaogong.com/fanwen/lawdata.html. Accessed 14 March 2024
16. Metalaw, an AI-powered legal tool, offers efficient case retrieval and analysis of litigation ideas. Metalaw. https://meta.law/. Accessed 14 March 2024

Enhancing Biometric Security: Advancements in Environment-Independent Channel State Information Analysis

Lukasz Migacz[✉]

University Of Bedfordshire, Vicarage Street, Luton 1 3JU, UK
Lukasz.migacz@study.beds.ac.uk

Abstract. This study explores the use of Channel State Information for biometric authentication, focusing on addressing the challenges posed by environmental variations. To achieve this, experiments were conducted using off-the-shelf ESP32 devices to collect CSI data across different environments, including urban, suburban, and rural settings. The primary objective was to analyze the influence of external environmental factors on the accuracy of CSI-based biometric systems and to develop methods to mitigate these effects. The significant subcarrier selection method was combined with a weighted Random Forest classifier to improve the system's performance.

The results demonstrated that certain subcarriers are more sensitive to environmental changes, and by assigning different weights to these subcarriers the authentication accuracy improved to 93.33%. These findings highlight the potential of CSI-based biometrics to offer reliable and environment-independent authentication, making them suitable for real-world applications in dynamic settings, such as smart homes and vehicular systems. This research lays the groundwork for further studies aimed at developing more resilient biometric systems capable of operating effectively across diverse environments.

Keywords: Wi-Fi Sensing · Channel State Information · ESP32 · Radio Biometrics · Environment-Independent · Random Forest Classifier

1 Introduction to CSI Biometrics

1.1 Channel State Information

In recent years, the exploration of radio biometrics, particularly through Channel State Information (CSI) analysis, has gained increasing attention within the area of user authentication systems. CSI authentication uses the unique characteristics of wireless signals, offering a promising method for improving security and convenience in various applications, including access control in smart environments and vehicular authentication systems. CSI is a measurement employed in Orthogonal Frequency-Division Multiplexing (OFDM) to represent fluctuations of amplitude and phase shifts during the transmission

© ICST Institute for Computer Sciences, Social Informatics and Telecommunications Engineering 2026
Published by Springer Nature Switzerland AG 2026. All Rights Reserved
X. Feng et al. (Eds.): CloudComp 2024, LNICST 617, pp. 183–200, 2026.
https://doi.org/10.1007/978-3-031-92517-7_14

of wireless signals across different subcarrier frequencies between the transmitter and receiver in wireless networks, such as IEEE 802.11n. OFDM serves as a modulation scheme to encode data streams across multiple subcarriers. A product of CSI estimation is a CSI matrix, which is a "complex matrix containing a complex value for each subcarrier representing the Channel Frequency Response (CFR)" [1]. That complex value consists of real and imaginary parts which can be used to calculate amplitude and phase values for a given subcarrier. The detailed definition of CSI and description of methods to retrieve amplitude and phase values from the matrix can be found in reference [1]. The example of CSI frame has been depicted in the Fig. 1. This frame has been captured using EPS32 device using 802.11n, 20 MHz. It contains 64 subcarriers in total, where 48 are used for actual data transmission. The CSI frames contains other information besides CSI matrix, such as timestamp, MAC address, RSS and more [2].

```
CSI_DATA,AP,24:DC:C3:9F:DB:60,-56,11,1,6,1,1,1,1,0,0,0,-96,1,6,1,12488270,0,84,0,0,
12.6782,384,[84 -64 4 0 0 0 0 0 0 0 0 0 15 3 15 3 15 2 15 3 15 4 15 6 15 7 15 8 15 8
14 7 14 9 15 10 14 9 14 9 14 9 13 11 13 11 12 11 13 10 13 10 12 10 12 10 12 11 12 10
12 10 12 10 0 0 12 10 12 9 12 8 12 9 12 8 12 7 12 7 12 7 13 8 13 7 13 7 12 5 13 5 13
5 13 6 14 5 14 4 15 4 15 4 15 3 15 4 15 3 15 3 16 2 16 3 16 2 0 0 0 0 0 0 0 0 0 0 ]
```

Fig. 1. Example of CSI frame

1.2 Radio Biometrics

Pattern recognition using CSI data, referred to as Wi-Fi sensing, has emerged as technology which bridges fields of both computer networking and data science. This technique enables recognition of biometric traits, object movements and object detection among others. Wi-Fi has evolved from providing network communication to sensing physical environments based on the interaction of Wi-Fi signals with objects and human bodies, leading to applications in intrusion detection, smart homes, healthcare, and more [3]. Wi-Fi Sensing finds application in a diverse array of tasks, including but not limited to occupancy detection, activity recognition, fall detection, gesture recognition, people counting, pose estimation [4] and even calories expenditure estimation [5]. Advantages of Wi-Fi sensing include high coverage, pervasiveness, low cost, robustness, and lightweight in terms of computation and device size [6]. RF-based sensing has unique advantages over vision-based sensing like effectiveness under adverse light and texture scenarios [6].

2 Related Studies

The change in CSI caused by the presence human body can be used to uniquely identify the person as shown in multiple studies and is referred to as Radio Biometrics (RB). RB using CSI have found applications in diverse fields. In one investigation [7], researchers utilized RB to authenticate users sitting at the desk, achieving high accuracy (98%) in identity recognition, while maintaining low training requirements and minimal cost.

The researchers in study [3] utilized CSI for gait and respiration biometrics. The proposed framework breaks down noisy CSI measurements into intrinsic mode functions (IMF) via empirical mode decomposition. It then extracts robust and distinctive multidomain intrinsic features from the IMF components which helps to handle environmental changes. The use of such technique enables this system to improve accuracy by 18.9%.

In another study researchers [8] applied Wi-Fi sensing technology for driver authentication in a car. The impact of the human body on multipath CSI is limited, affecting only a few paths, and the energy associated with these paths is relatively low due to the body's low reflectivity and permittivity compared to static objects like walls and furniture. Consequently, the radio biometrics of an individual, captured through radio shots, become submerged amidst other components in the CSI. In simpler terms, the CSI obtained from a radio shot of a person exhibits a high correlation with the surrounding environment. In reality, the in-car environment undergoes constant changes over time. Therefore, alterations in the in-car environment lead to corresponding changes in the CSI containing the driver's radio biometrics [8]. The car's interior resembles a metal enclosure, causing most multipath signals to remain confined within, given the limited penetration capability of radio waves through metal (see Fig. 2). Secondly, the car's movement has minimal impact on signal propagation within, as crucial components such as the transmission, engine, and wheels are positioned external to the primary cargo space, shielded by metal. Additionally, experimental validation indicates that changes in the external environment do not significantly alter the multipath conditions inside the car. Consequently, the interior of a car can be perceived as an indoor setting with abundant multipath propagation, and its dynamic state has limited influence on RF sensing [8].

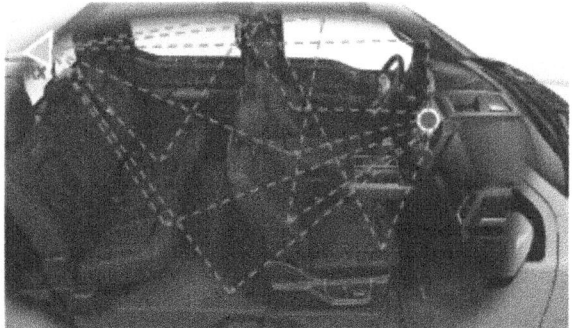

Fig. 2. Multipath Propagation within in-car environment [8].

The metal exterior of a car creates a rich multipath environment, enhancing the reliability of wireless sensing [8]. Despite this, some noise and interference reach the car's interior, affecting the system's performance. Proposed system achieves around 89% accuracy using NN with a two-driver scenario. In the same paper, researchers suggested the system relying on the grouping technique to enhance accuracy by combining decisions from multiple radio shots taken during each session. During each data collection session, four radio shots are recorded with the test subject sitting in the driver's seat.

Between each radio shot, the CSI of the empty car is recorded to serve as a baseline. Each radio shot taken with the driver present is then compared to the corresponding baseline measurement. The method used to utilize the empty car CSI shots its called grouping. By feeding that data to Neural Network (NN) and analyzing the differences between the two sets of CSI data, unique biometric features of the driver were extracted. This comparative analysis identifies patterns specific to each individual driver, enhancing the system's ability to distinguish between different drivers. This process increases the system's accuracy to 95% [8].

In a preceding study [9] the researchers analyzed the influence of external environment on the in-car CSI and concluded that "the effect of the external environment is insignificant". However that study considered only the scenario where there were other cars parked nearby, without taking into account the interference caused by the presence nearby Wi-Fi networks and other factors like temperature or movement of objects. That claim was also repeated in [8] stating that "because most of the multipaths are restricted inside the car, outside activities can hardly introduce false alarms." Also study [9] collected data using devices operating 5.2-GHz band over four channels with 114 usable subcarriers, which provides high quality data. Despite the advent of higher frequency bands like 5 GHz and 6 GHz, which provide faster data transmission, the 2.4 GHz band continues to be the most commonly used, particularly in scenarios where range and backward compatibility with older devices are vital. Additionally, a large number of Internet of Things (IoT) devices favor the 2.4 GHz band due to its consistent reliability and more efficient energy use compared to higher frequencies [10]. Off-the shelf CSI collection devices like ESP32, operating on the 2.4 GHz band may be prone to the changes caused by the presence of large number of other devices operating ion the same band. Also devices operating on 5 GHz band usually require NIC and are difficult to hide [1], which may not be the best in term of car security.

There are numerous existing studies and surveys that provide a broad range of insights into Wi-Fi sensing and related topics [4, 6, 11–15]. However, few works address environmental changes and cross-environment adaptability. One such attempt is the study in [16], which employs a Federated Learning Strategy. This system integrates a federated learning approach, allowing the model to be trained across multiple environments without the need to share raw data between them. Instead, each environment processes its data locally and shares only the processed results with a central server. This preserves privacy and ensures that the system can generalize effectively across different environments. The system achieves independence from environmental variations through several sophisticated techniques. It employs adversarial learning to distinguish between environment-specific features and those related to activities, ensuring that the model concentrates on identifying activities without being affected by changes in the environment. To help the model generalize effectively across diverse environments, the Johnson–Lindenstrauss transform is used to reduce data dimensionality while retaining key features. Additionally, the system enhances its effectiveness by transferring activity-related knowledge from one environment to another. By incorporating an environment classifier along with adversarial loss, the system is trained to disregard environment-specific details, allowing it to adapt to new environments without the need for retraining.

The paper [17] tackles the problem of environmental changes by employing advanced techniques such as transfer learning, cross-domain sensing, and a triplet loss function. Transfer learning is utilized to adapt WiFi sensing models to new environments with minimal labeled data, reducing the need for extensive retraining when the deployment environment differs significantly from the initial training environment. Furthermore, the system reframes the WiFi sensing task as an image classification problem, using pre-trained convolutional neural networks (CNNs) to extract features that are naturally more resistant to environmental variations. The inclusion of a triplet loss function further strengthens the system's robustness by minimizing intra-class variations across different environments and maximizing the separation between different classes, thereby maintaining consistent performance despite environmental changes.

2.1 Environmental Noise and Data Quality

When there is no person present within a WiFi link, the signal's multipath or scattering effect remains relatively stable. Any variations in the signal are mainly due to observational error, thermal noise, or signal interference [18]. Consequently, the amplitudes of CSI across all subcarriers tend to be relatively stable [18]. Wi-Fi CSI continually monitors the frequency response of OFDM subcarriers, capturing different environmental changes like:

- Variations in signal reflections: frequency-selective fading, shadowing, multipath effects [15],
- Interference: constructive and destructive interference [15],
- Movement of objects:such as shifts in furniture position [7],
- Whether conditions: temperature, humidity fluctuations [7].

Data quality is also influenced by device and hardware limitations, such as: thermal noise and packet loss [19], phase errors [20], and noise from internal circuits of sender and receiver network interface cards [21].

Denoising is a critical step in processing CSI data to ensure high-quality and accurate measurements. Denoising also improves the reliability of CSI measurements by addressing temporal bias and interference in CSI data, thus enhancing data quality for user authentication [22]. For accurate user identification and activity recognition, signal preprocessing techniques such as Butterworth filters, PCA, and DWT are commonly used [15].

2.2 Data Collection Setup

In study [7], the investigators use network operating in the 2.4 GHz band with a channel bandwidth of 20 MHz, encompassing 64 subcarriers. Conventional Access Points (APs), like the one employed in this study, emit approximately 10 beacon frames per second, corresponding to a sampling frequency (f) of 10Hz. A time window (w) of 1 s is considered. The count of captured beacons within this time frame typically ranges between 9 and 11. To mitigate such variations, only the initial 9 beacon frames received within a window are taken into account, while subsequent arrivals are disregarded. Consequently, within a time window of $w = 1s$, consistently sized segments comprising 9×64 CSI samples are obtained.

During the experiments, the researchers in [22] collected a total of 400 packets at each location. For each packet, both CSI and Received Signal Strength (RSS) values were recorded. A commercial wireless access point, namely Linksys E2500, transmitted packets that were captured by the monitoring laptops. The simulation involved using the ping command on the two laptops to generate continuous authentication packets transmitted over the network. The packet rate was set at 10 packets per second. For each packet, CSI data was extracted for 30 subcarrier groups, evenly distributed among the 56 subcarriers of a 20 MHz channel.

In the study [4], data was collected within an in-car environment using a 5 GHz Wi-Fi frequency with 40 MHz bandwidth and a 30 Hz sounding rate, yielding satisfactory results for driver recognition. However, in another related study focused on in-car environments [21], the Linux 802.11n CSI Tool was used on an Intel Wi-Fi Wireless Link 5300 802.11n MIMO radio at a rate of 100 packets per second, achieving an accuracy of around 92% to 97% in driver recognition. Another study [22], investigated the in-car environment using an ESP32 to collect data at 2.4 GHz with 128 subcarriers, continuously collecting data for 20 min, though the specific number of frames collected was not mentioned.

The choice of data collection toolkit and setup is crucial and depends on the specific use case and requirements of the study. The selection of tools, data rates, and sample sizes has a direct impact on the system's performance. Large, high-quality datasets generally result in more accurate and reliable Wi-Fi sensing outcomes [1].

3   Motivation and Method Selection

Despite significant progress, challenges remain in achieving environment-independent RB with high performance in changing conditions. Existing Wi-Fi-based sensing systems are limited in scale and require data collection and model training in the same environment [17]. Models trained in one environment do not generalize well to new environments or new users [17]. Addressing these challenges is critical for the widespread adoption of Wi-Fi sensing technologies in real-world applications such as smart homes, healthcare monitoring, and security systems.

The objectives of this study are:

1. To study the influence of the external environmental changes on the CSI data collected inside the car by data collection in a real world environment using off-the shelf devices.
2. Mitigate of the influence of external environment on the performance of CSI biometric authentication system using significant subcarrier selection method.
3. To outline future research task and challenges aiming towards enhancement in environment in depended radio biometrics.

This pilot study lays the groundwork for the development of environment-independent radio biometrics, offering the essential components needed for further research in this field. The ultimate aim of this and subsequent studies is to create a radio biometric system capable of achieving high performance irrespective of environmental variations and changes. Additionally, the system is designed to be resilient against adversarial attacks, ensuring a seamless and efficient authentication service.

3.1 Method

Based on the analysis of relevant studies, the following methodology consists of several key steps: data collection, data preprocessing, feature extraction, data analysis, significant subcarrier selection process, weight adjustment and evaluation with Random Decision Forest. A diverse range of parking locations, including urban, suburban, and rural environments, was selected to capture the full spectrum of potential interference scenarios. At each location, factors such as temperature, weather conditions, and the number of available Wi-Fi networks were recorded to account for environmental changes that might affect CSI data quality. Data collection was conducted at different times of the day and under comparable weather conditions to account for temporal and environmental variations. Data was collected with ESP32- CSI-Tool [23]. The ESP32 devices have been selected to study the influence of the external environment on the-in car environment due to their:

– accessibility – low price < £10
– availability – CSI collection tools repositories are freely available
– portability – small size and can be powered via USB.

To determine the most optimal data collection configuration, a pilot data collection was conducted across 10 different locations. Initially, data was gathered from a stationary car with the engine and infotainment devices turned off, and the car was unoccupied, to capture the purest possible state of the in-car environment. The key lessons learned from this pilot data collection were as follows:

3.1.1 Attachment of Tx/Rx Devices

It is crucial to securely attach the devices to prevent any movement, as this directly impacts multipath propagation and, consequently, the quality of the data. Movement of the devices during data collection can cause significant inconsistencies between consecutive CSI samples, leading to high variability and reduced data reliability. The devices must be fixed in place and located inside the car to minimize variability, ensuring that any observed differences in the data could be attributed to external factors rather than changes in the experimental setup.

3.1.2 Sampling Rate, Baud Rate and Frame Count

After conducting several data collection activities, it was determined that the optimal number of CSI frames per shot is between 1,000 and 2,000, with a packet rate of 500 Hz and one shot per location. At each location, 10,000 frames were collected, and a set of 1,000 consecutive frames was used for further analysis. The CSI data collection tool allows for different baud rate settings. To identify the most optimal rate, various combinations of low and high baud rates were tested against high and low packet rates.

Based on these experiments (as shown in Table 1), the combination of a 150,000 baud rate with a 500 Hz packet rate was selected. This configuration offers a good balance between data collection frequency and consistency, providing sufficient detail to detect potential interference without introducing extreme variability that could obscure the identification of specific issues.

Table 1. Results of baud rate and packet rate analysis

Baud rate/packet rate	Average Interval	Standard Deviation
150000/500 Hz	0.00625	0.00507
150000/100 Hz	0.01055	0.00472
926100/100 Hz	0.00994	0.00258
926100/500 Hz	0.00830	0.00610

A high packet rate of 500 packets per second was selected as the baseline to capture detailed signal variations, striking an effective balance between data granularity and manageability in processing. Additionally, a substantial number of CSI frames (10,000 per shot) were collected at each location to ensure statistical significance and minimize the impact of outliers or transient noise, particularly on channel 6.

3.1.3   Data Collection Locations

The study addressed environmental changes, noise, and data quality issues through several strategies. The use of diverse locations allowed for the examination of how varying levels of Wi-Fi network density and environmental clutter influenced the CSI data, thereby enabling the generalization of findings across multiple real-world scenarios. Noise was mitigated by applying wavelet denoising during data preprocessing, which effectively removed irrelevant noise and emphasized signal variations caused by external factors. Consistent device placement and regular calibration further ensured data quality by reducing variability and enabling accurate comparisons across different environments.

4   Experiment Setup

4.1   CSI Data Collection

Data collection toolkit consisted of:

- MacBook Air 2017 8GB RAM 125 SSD with 2x3m USBA to USBC cables
- 2 x ESP32 boards attached as on the Fig. 3.
- 2021 Toyota CH-R as car environment

The second data collection was performed on 10 parking locations (see Table 2), selected by type where x is a number of networks:

- Urban Car Parks: High density of WiFi networks (x > 10),

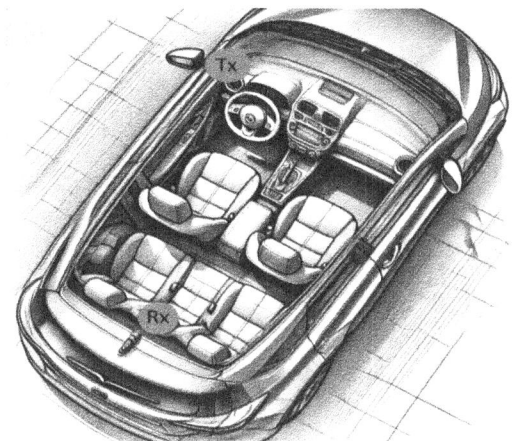

Fig. 3. Placement of transceiver (Tx) and received (Rx) devices.

- Suburban Car Parks: Moderate density of WiFi networks (x < 10),
- Rural Car Parks: Low or no WiFi networks(x = 0).

Data collection was conducted on the same day during both peak and off-peak hours to account for potential variations in environmental factors. The temperature, monitored using the car's onboard thermometer, remained consistent between 20 and 21 degrees Celsius. The weather was cloudy and stable, with minimal fluctuations in humidity, making these variations negligible. The Rx/Tx devices were securely fixed to prevent any movement, and their locations were kept constant throughout the data collection process.

Table 2. Specification of data collection locations

Location	Type	Wi-Fi networks	Temperature (C)
1	Urban	22	20
2	Suburban	12	20
3	Suburban	8	21
4	Suburban	6	21
5	Rural	0	21
6	Rural	0	20
7	Urban	21	21
8	Urban	29	21
9	Suburban	9	21
10	Urban	22	21

Table 3. Specification of data collection participants

Participant	Weight (kg)	Height (cm)
1	94	172
2	75	186
3	87	188

The number of available Wi-Fi networks was assessed using the MacBook network connection tool. The car was parked in various locations, with the engine and infotainment systems turned off to minimize internal interference and noise. All mobile phones and the MacBook's Wi-Fi were set to airplane mode during data collection to eliminate additional sources of interference. Participants were seated in the driver's seat and instructed to remain still during the radio shots to maintain consistent conditions.

Although the data collection took place in a real-world scenario, efforts were made to minimize significant movement around the car to ensure that any environmental changes captured were primarily due to external factors. The number of participants in the data collection was limited to three, as the study primarily focused on changes in the empty car environment across locations. However, the participants were selected based on their distinct body types to introduce some variability in the data while maintaining the study's focus (Table 3).

4.2   Data Analysis

4.2.1   Data Preprocessing

The collected data was preprocessed by extracting CSI matrices from CSI frames. The CSI matrices were used to extract amplitude values. The amplitude $A_{i,j}$ for subcarrier j at time i is given by:

$$A_{i,j} = \sqrt{(\text{Real}_{i,j})^2 + (\text{Imaginary}_{i,j})^2} \tag{1}$$

where Real i,j and Imaginary i,j represent the real and imaginary parts of the CSI signal, respectively.

The unusable subcarriers: 1, 2, 3, 4, 5, 6, 33, 60, 61, 62, 63, 64 were removed as they are not used for actual data transmission. The null values were removed and replaced with "0".

At this stage the data collected contained the noise, which can be visible on the Fig. 4. The two distinct groups present regular signal as well as signal altered by noise and environmental factors.

4.2.2   Wavelet Denoising

The wavelet-based denoising using the Daubechies 4 (db4) wavelet level 3 was used to remove noise. This technique effectively reduces noise while preserving the signal

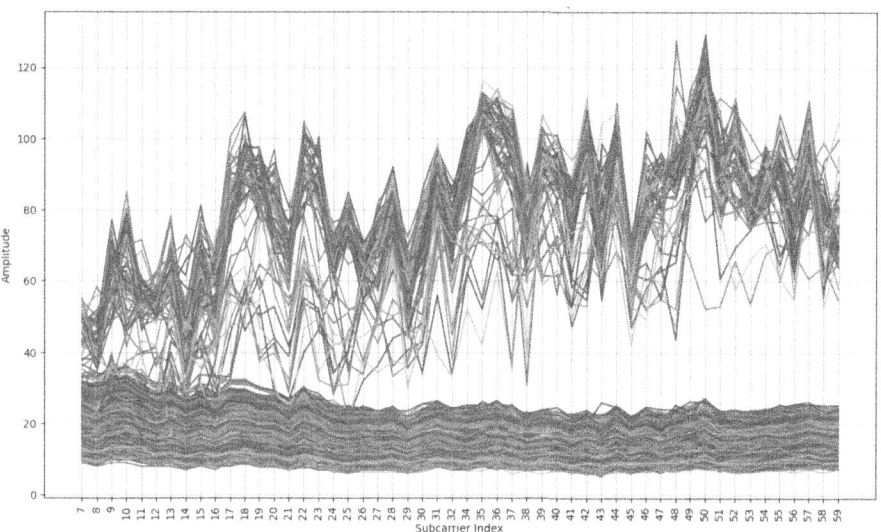

Fig. 4. Raw CSI amplitudes across 1000 frames

characteristics critical for user authentication. The wavelet denoising process can be mathematically described as:

$$\text{Denoised Signal} = \sum_k \text{Wavelet Coefficients}_k \cdot \psi_k(t) \tag{2}$$

Where $\psi_k(t)$ represents the wavelet basis functions and k denotes the level of decomposition.

4.2.3 Feature Extraction

A comprehensive set of statistical and spectral features from the denoised amplitude data. The extracted features were selected based on their ability to capture both the central tendency and the variability of the signal, as well as its frequency-domain characteristics:

Mean (μ):

$$\mu_j = \frac{1}{N} \sum_{i=1}^{N} A_{i,j} \tag{3}$$

where N is the number of samples.

Variance (σ^2):

$$\sigma_j^2 = \frac{1}{N} \sum_{i=1}^{N} (A_{i,j} - \mu_j)^2 \tag{4}$$

Skewness:

$$\text{Skewness}_j = \frac{\frac{1}{N} \sum_{i=1}^{N} (A_{i,j} - \mu_j)^3}{\sigma_j^3} \tag{5}$$

Kurtosis:

$$\text{Kurtosis}_j = \frac{\frac{1}{N}\sum_{i=1}^{N}(A_{i,j} - \mu_j)^4}{\sigma_j^4} - 3 \tag{6}$$

Standard Deviation (σ):

$$\sigma_j = \sqrt{\sigma_j^2} \tag{7}$$

Root Mean Square (RMS):

$$\text{RMS}_j = \sqrt{\frac{1}{N}\sum_{i=1}^{N} A_{i,j}^2} \tag{8}$$

Spectral Centroid:

$$\text{Spectral Centroid}_j = \frac{\sum_k f_k \cdot S(f_k)}{\sum_k S(f_k)} \tag{9}$$

where f_k is the frequency and $S(f_k)$ the magnitude of the Fourier Transform at frequency f_k

Spectral Bandwidth:

$$\text{Spectral Bandwidth}_j = \sqrt{\frac{\sum_k (f_k - \text{Spectral Centroid}_j)^2 \cdot S(f_k)}{\sum_k S(f_k)}} \tag{10}$$

Spectral Contrast:

$$\text{Spectral Contrast}_j = \frac{\text{Max}(S(f_k)) - \text{Min}(S(f_k))}{\text{Max}(S(f_k)) + \text{Min}(S(f_k))} \tag{11}$$

Spectral Flatness:

$$\text{Spectral Flatness}_j = \frac{\text{Geometric Mean}(S(f_k))}{\text{Arithmetic Mean}(S(f_k))} \tag{12}$$

These features were computed for each subcarrier, resulting in a rich set of descriptors for the CSI data.

4.2.4 Subcarrier Significance Analysis

To identify the most significant subcarriers, a comprehensive analysis has been conducted by testing each subcarrier's ability to differentiate between users and environments. This was done by comparing the extracted features across different scenarios and calculating their statistical significance. Subcarriers that consistently showed high variability and significance across users and environments were flagged as important.

4.2.5 Model Testing with Random Forest

A Random Forest classifier was employed to authenticate users based on the extracted features. The model was tested under several conditions to evaluate its performance:

Initial Testing On Denoised Amplitudes

The model was first tested using the denoised amplitude values without any feature extraction to provide a baseline understanding of how well the raw, preprocessed data could distinguish between users.

Testing With Extracted Features

The model was then trained using the full set of extracted statistical and spectral features to allow to assessing the added value of these features in improving user authentication accuracy.

Weighted Subcarrier Testing

Finally, different weights were assigned to the subcarriers based on their significance. Subcarriers identified as more important were given higher weights, enhancing their influence in the model. The weighted Random Forest model was expected to improve performance, particularly for users whose significant subcarriers were heavily weighted.

Each test was conducted on subsets of 1,000 frames from the original 10,000-frame (per location) dataset. This division into smaller sets allowed for a more granular analysis and helped in preventing overfitting by ensuring that the model was tested on diverse samples.

5 Results

The expanded analysis confirms the critical role of certain subcarriers in different environments. Subcarriers like 9, 10, 13, 28, 50, and 53 consistently appear as significant across various settings, indicating their importance in maintaining communication quality and reliability. The significance of different subcarriers across different environments has been displayed in Fig. 5.

Urban Environments: Subcarriers 9, 10, and 13 show the highest significance, indicating their strong relevance in urban settings, reflecting their sensitivity to the conditions found in these settings.

Rural Environments: Subcarriers 18, 38, 43, and 47 show increased significance in rural environments, reflecting their sensitivity to user presence.

Suburban Environments: The significance is generally lower in suburban environments, with a more balanced distribution across various subcarriers.

5.1 Test 1 - Testing Without Feature Extraction

The model was first tested using the denoised amplitude values without any feature extraction. This provided a baseline understanding of how well the raw, preprocessed data could distinguish between users. The accuracy of this test was equal to: 74.17% Fig. 6 presents the confusion matrix. It shows high accuracy for User 2 and User 3, however low score for identifying empty car case.

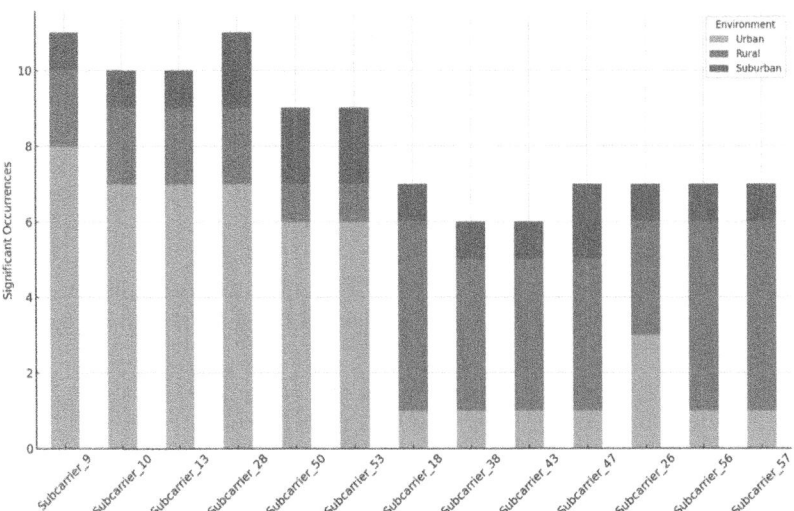

Fig. 5. Significance of subcarriers across environments

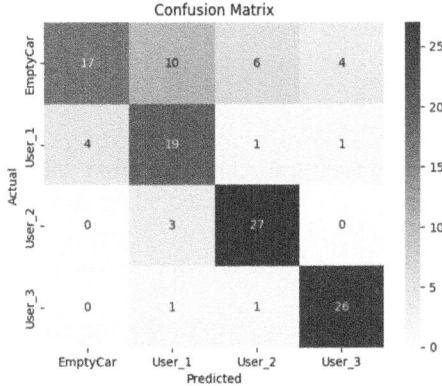

Fig. 6. Test 1 confusion matrix.

5.2 Test 2 - Testing with Extracted Features.

The model was then trained using the full set of extracted statistical and spectral features. This allowed to assess the added value of these features in improving user authentication accuracy to 90.83%.

5.3 Test 3 - Weighted Subcarrier Testing.

Finally, different weights were assigned to the subcarriers based on their significance. Subcarriers identified as more important were given higher weights, improving their influence in the model. The weighted Random Forest model was expected to improve

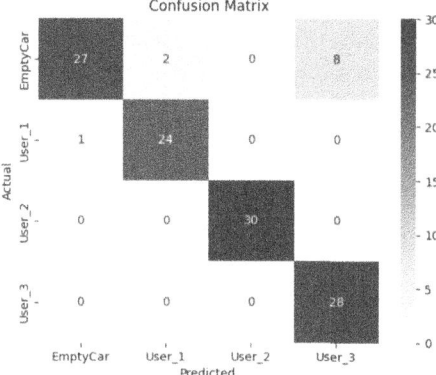

Fig. 7. Test 2 confusion matrix.

performance, particularly for users whose significant subcarriers were heavily weighted. This method achieved test accuracy of 93.33%

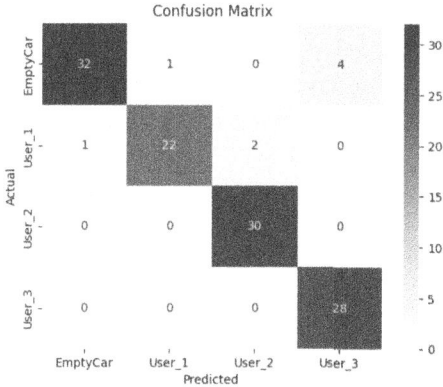

Fig. 8. Test 3 confusion matrix

As depicted in Figs. 7 and 8, adjusting weights for each environmental setting helps to reduce misclassification for each user, improve overall accuracy and model confidence.

6   Discussion

The findings highlight the critical role of environmental factors in CSI-based biometric systems. While the use of subcarrier significance analysis has shown promise in improving accuracy, challenges remain in developing models that are fully environment-independent. The study's results suggest that further refinement in data preprocessing, such as advanced denoising techniques and the integration of additional environmental sensors, could improve the robustness of these systems. Future research should also consider the scalability of such models and their performance in real-time applications. Additionally, exploring different environments and incorporating a broader range of data collection scenarios will be crucial in advancing the field.

7 Future Work

The following future work tasks were identified:

7.1 Lack of End-to-End Wi-Fi Sensing Tutorial

At present, there is no comprehensive tutorial available on end-to-end radio biometric authentication. Future work will focus on developing both a paper and a video course that will showcase the entire radio biometrics process from data collection, through data preparation and processing, to the implementation of ML techniques for data analysis.

7.2 Development of the Subtraction Model

Currently, environmental changes are primarily addressed through data preprocessing and denoising techniques. A future objective of this research is to develop a subtraction model capable of detecting interference and environmental changes using external sensors and applying ML/DL techniques to remove this information from the collected data. This approach would isolate the relevant biometric data, enhancing the decision-making process by leaving only the pertinent information. Possibly using PCA or ICA for feature extraction and identifying features related to environmental changes.

7.3 Investigation of Data Collection Within Interference-Free Environment

Previous studies [9] and [8] have shown promising results using a grouping technique to address environmental changes. By placing the car in an interference-free environment, such as a Faraday cage, it would be possible to capture the purest state of the in-car environment. This data could then be used as a baseline for calibration and grouping techniques, potentially further improving the system's performance.

7.4 Exploring Mesh Networks for More Consistent Data Collection

Future research may also explore the use of mesh networks to achieve more consistent data collection. ESP32 Mesh networks could provide a more reliable and stable data collection environment, helping to mitigate the impact of environmental fluctuations and ensuring higher data quality throughout the Wi-Fi sensing process.

8 Conclusion

This paper contributes to the growing field of Wi-Fi sensing and CSI-based biometrics by proposing a novel approach to handling environmental variations in biometric data. The proposed methodology, which includes significant subcarrier selection and weighted Random Forest models, demonstrates improved accuracy in user authentication across different environments. The research sets the stage for future studies aimed at developing more robust, environment-independent biometric systems that can be deployed in diverse real-world scenarios.

The research conducted in this paper addresses this challenge by exploring how environmental changes, such as varying Wi-Fi network densities and physical obstructions, impact the performance of CSI-based biometric systems. Using off-the-shelf ESP32 devices, CSI data was collected across diverse environments, including urban, suburban, and rural locations. This comprehensive data collection allowed for the examination of how external factors influence CSI data quality and, subsequently, the accuracy of biometric authentication.

A novel methodology was developed, involving the selection of significant subcarriers and the application of a weighted Random Forest classifier. This approach was designed to improve the system's ability to distinguish between different users despite environmental variations. The study found that certain subcarriers are more affected by environmental changes, and by assigning greater importance to these subcarriers in the analysis, the system's accuracy was significantly improved, reaching up to 93.33%.

The implications of these findings are substantial. By demonstrating that CSI-based biometrics can be made more robust against environmental changes, this research paves the way for the deployment of these systems in real-world scenarios where environmental conditions are not static. The results suggest that with further refinement, such as the integration of advanced denoising techniques and the development of environment-specific models, CSI-based biometrics could become a reliable and widely used technology for secure authentication.

References

1. Hernandez, S.M.: WiFi sensing at the edge towards scalable on-device wireless sensing systems. Doctoral dissertation, Virginia Commonwealth University (2023)
2. ESP-IDF Programming Guide: Wi-Fi (ESP-IDF v4.4). https://docs.espressif.com/projects/esp-idf/en/stable/esp32/api-guides/wifi.html. Accessed 15 July 2024
3. Wang, J., Zhao, Y., Fan, X., Gao, Q., Ma, X., Wang, H.: Device-free identification using intrinsic CSI features. IEEE Trans. Veh. Technol. **67**(9), 8571–8581 (2018)
4. Yang, J., et al.: SenseFi: a library and benchmark on deep-learning-empowered WiFi human sensing. Patterns **4**, 100703 (2023)
5. Rahaman, H., Dyo, V.: Counting calories without wearables: device-free Human Energy Expenditure Estimation. In: 2020 16th International Conference on Wireless and Mobile Computing, Networking and Communications (WiMob), IEEE (2020)
6. Yang, Z., Zhang, Y., Chi, G., Zhang, G.: Hands-on wireless sensing with Wi-Fi: a tutorial. arXiv preprint arXiv:2206.09532 (2022)

7. Turetta, C., DeRose, F., Kindt, P.H., Masrur, A., Pravadelli, G.: Practical identity recognition using WiFi's channel state information. In: Design, Automation and Test in Europe Conference (2022)

8. Xu, Q., Wang, B., Zhang, F., Regani, D.S., Wang, F., Liu, K.J.R.: Wireless AI in smart car: how smart a car can be? IEEE Access **8**, 55091–55110 (2020)

9. Regani, S.D., Xu, Q., Wang, B., Wu, M., Liu, K.J.R.: Driver authentication for smart car using wireless sensing. IEEE Internet Things J. **7**(3), 2235–2246 (2020)

10. Martínez, V.M.G., Ribeiro, M.R.N., Mota, V.F.S.: Wi-Fi faces the new wireless ecosystem: a critical review. Ann. Telecommun. **79**, 397–413 (2024)

11. Khalili, A.M., Soliman, A.-H., Asaduzzaman, M., Griffiths, A.: Wi-Fi sensing: applications and challenges. Staffordshire University, United Kingdom (2019)

12. Li, W., Bocus, M.J., Tang, C., Vishwakarma, S., Piechocki, R.J., Woodbridge, K., Chetty, K.: A Taxonomy of WiFi Sensing: CSI vs Passive WiFi Radar. Department of Security and Crime Science, University College London, UK; Department of Electrical and Electronic Engineering, University of Bristol, UK; Department of Electronic and Electrical Engineering, University College London, UK (2020)

13. Tan, S., Ren, Y., Yang, J., Chen, Y.: Commodity WiFi sensing in 10 years: status, challenges, and opportunities. IEEE Internet Things J. (2024)

14. Ma, Y., Zhou, G., Wang, S.: WiFi sensing with channel state information: a survey. ACM Comput. Surv. **52**(3), Article 46 (2019)

15. Wang, Z., et al.: A survey of user authentication based on channel state information. Wireless Commun. Mobile Comput. (2021)

16. Zhang, L., Cui, W., Li, B., Chen, Z., Wu, M., Gee, T.S.: Privacy-preserving cross-environment human activity recognition. IEEE Trans. Cybern. **53**(3), 1765–1775 (2023)

17. Bu, Q., Ming, X., Hu, J., Zhang, T., Feng, J., Zhang, J.: TransferSense: towards environment independent and one-shot wifi sensing. Pers. Ubiquit. Comput. **26**, 555–573 (2022)

18. Choi, H., Fujimoto, M., Matsui, T., Misaki, S., Yasumoto, K.: Wi-CaL: WiFi sensing and machine learning based device-free crowd counting and localization. IEEE Access **10**, 24395–24408 (2022)

19. Chowdhury, T.Z.: Using Wi-Fi Channel State Information (CSI) for human activity recognition and fall detection. Master's Thesis, The University of British Columbia, Vancouver (2018)

20. Yousefi, S., Narui, H., Dayal, S., Ermon, S., Valaee, S.: A survey on behavior recognition using WiFi channel state information. IEEE Commun. Mag. **55**(10), 98–104 (2017)

21. Yang, Y.-J., Chao, C.-M., Yeh, C.-C., Lin, C.-Y.: WFID: driver identity recognition based on Wi-Fi signals. IEEE Trans. Veh. Technol. **72**(1), 679–688 (2023)

22. Liu, H., Wang, Y., Liu, J., Yang, J., Chen, Y.: Practical user authentication leveraging Channel State Information (CSI). In: Proceedings of the 2014 ACM Asia Conference on Computer and Communications Security (ASIA CCS '14), pp. 389–400. ACM, New York (2014)

23. ESP32-CSI-Tool. https://github.com/StevenMHernandez/ESP32-CSI-Tool. Accessed 15 July 2024

Monitoring Patient Apps Security Vulnerabilities

Khalid Hussein[✉]

School of Computer Science and Technology, University of Bedfordshire, University Square,
Luton 1 3JU, UK
Khalid.Hussein@study.beds.ac.uk

Abstract. The rapid growth of self-monitoring patient apps has revolutionized the healthcare industry, enabling individuals to track their health metrics and engage more actively in their own care. However, this technological advancement has also introduced significant security and privacy concerns. This article examines the security vulnerabilities inherent in self-monitoring patient apps, highlighting the risks to patient data and the potential consequences of these vulnerabilities. It explores the common security flaws found in these apps, such as weak authentication mechanisms, inadequate data encryption, and the lack of secure data transmission protocols. The article also discusses the regulatory landscape and the need for comprehensive security standards to protect patient privacy and ensure the integrity of health data. Additionally, it delves into emerging technologies and their impact on app security, as well as the role of user education in maintaining app security. Finally, it provides recommendations for app developers, healthcare providers, and policymakers to address these vulnerabilities and enhance the security of self-monitoring patient apps.

Keywords: Self-monitoring patient apps · security vulnerabilities · data encryption · authentication · data privacy · healthcare security · mobile health applications

1 Introduction

The proliferation of self-monitoring patient apps has transformed the healthcare landscape, empowering individuals to take a more active role in managing their health. These apps, which enable users to track various health metrics, such as physical activity, heart rate, blood pressure, and glucose levels, have become increasingly popular among patients and healthcare providers alike. The ability to access real-time health data and share it with healthcare professionals has the potential to improve disease management, early detection, and overall patient outcomes [1].

However, the widespread adoption of self-monitoring patient apps has also led to a growing concern about the security and privacy of sensitive health data. These apps often contain a wealth of personal and medical information, making them a prime target for cyber threats. Vulnerabilities in the design, development, and implementation of

© ICST Institute for Computer Sciences, Social Informatics and Telecommunications Engineering 2026
Published by Springer Nature Switzerland AG 2026. All Rights Reserved
X. Feng et al. (Eds.): CloudComp 2024, LNICST 617, pp. 201–210, 2026.
https://doi.org/10.1007/978-3-031-92517-7_15

these apps can expose patients to a range of security risks, including data breaches, unauthorized access, and the manipulation of health data [2].

This article delves into the security vulnerabilities inherent in self-monitoring patient apps, exploring the common security flaws and their potential consequences. It also examines the regulatory landscape and the need for comprehensive security standards to protect patient privacy and ensure the integrity of health data. Furthermore, it investigates the impact of emerging technologies on app security and discusses the importance of user education in maintaining app security. Finally, it provides recommendations for app developers, healthcare providers, and policymakers to address these vulnerabilities and enhance the security of self-monitoring patient apps.

2   Security Vulnerabilities in Self-monitoring Patient Apps

Self-monitoring patient apps are susceptible to a variety of security vulnerabilities that can compromise the confidentiality, integrity, and availability of sensitive health data. These vulnerabilities can arise from various aspects of the app's design, development, and implementation, including:

- Weak Authentication Mechanisms: Many self-monitoring patient apps rely on weak or outdated authentication methods, such as simple passwords or lack of multifactor authentication. This makes it easier for unauthorized individuals to gain access to patient data [3].
- Inadequate Data Encryption: Improper encryption of data, both at rest and in transit, can allow cyber attackers to intercept and read sensitive health information, such as personal details, diagnoses, and treatment plans [4].
- Unsecure Data Transmission Protocols: Self-monitoring patient apps often transmit data over unsecured channels, such as unencrypted HTTP connections, making it vulnerable to man-in-the-middle attacks and data interception [5].
- Lack of Secure Software Development Practices: Poor coding practices, such as the use of outdated libraries, improper input validation, and the presence of known vulnerabilities, can create exploitable entry points for attackers [6].
- Insufficient Access Controls: Inadequate control over user permissions and the lack of granular access management can lead to unauthorized access to sensitive patient data [7].
- Poorly Configured Cloud Storage: Many self-monitoring patient apps utilize cloud-based storage for patient data, and improper configuration of cloud security settings can result in data breaches and unauthorized access [8].
- Insufficient Logging and Monitoring: Lack of comprehensive logging and monitoring mechanisms can hinder the detection and investigation of security incidents, making it difficult to identify the source and extent of the breach [9].
- Third-Party Integration Risks: Many apps integrate with third-party services or APIs, which can introduce additional vulnerabilities if not properly vetted and secured [10].
- Insecure Data Storage on Mobile Devices: Improper storage of sensitive data on mobile devices can lead to unauthorized access if the device is lost, stolen, or compromised [2].

These vulnerabilities can have serious consequences for patient privacy and the integrity of health data. Cyber attackers can exploit these flaws to gain unauthorized access to patient records, steal sensitive information, manipulate health data, or even hold data for ransom. The consequences can include financial losses, reputational damage, and, most importantly, the potential for negative impacts on patient health and well-being [11].

3   Regulatory Landscape and Security Standards

The security and privacy of patient data in self-monitoring apps are subject to various regulatory frameworks and industry standards. In many countries, healthcare data is governed by specific laws and regulations, such as the Health Insurance Portability and Accountability Act (HIPAA) in the United States, the General Data Protection Regulation (GDPR) in the European Union, and the Personal Information Protection and Electronic Documents Act (PIPEDA) in Canada [12–14].

These regulations mandate the implementation of robust security measures to protect patient data, including the use of encryption, access controls, and data breach notification protocols. However, the enforcement and compliance with these regulations can be inconsistent, and the rapid pace of technological change often outpaces the development of updated security standards [15].

To address this, industry organizations and standards bodies, such as the National Institute of Standards and Technology (NIST) and the International Organization for Standardization (ISO), have developed guidelines and frameworks for securing mobile health applications. These standards provide a comprehensive set of security controls and best practices that can be adopted by app developers and healthcare providers to enhance the security of self-monitoring patient apps [16, 17].

3.1   Challenges in Regulatory Compliance

Despite the existence of regulations and standards, several challenges persist in ensuring compliance:

– Jurisdictional Differences: The global nature of app distribution means developers must navigate varying regulatory requirements across different countries and regions [18].
– Rapid Technological Advancements: The fast-paced evolution of technology often outpaces regulatory updates, creating gaps in coverage for new security threats [19].
– Small Developer Constraints: Smaller app developers may lack the resources and expertise to fully implement comprehensive security measures and comply with complex regulations [20].

3.2 Emerging Regulatory Trends

As the landscape of patient apps evolves, so do the regulatory approaches:

– Risk-Based Frameworks: Regulators are increasingly adopting risk-based approaches to security, focusing on the potential impact of data breaches rather than prescriptive measures [21].
– International Harmonization Efforts: There are growing initiatives to harmonize security standards across borders, facilitating compliance for global app distribution [22].
– Emphasis on Privacy by Design: Regulators are pushing for the integration of privacy and security considerations from the earliest stages of app development [23].

4 Recommendations for Securing Self-monitoring Patient Apps

To mitigate the security vulnerabilities in self-monitoring patient apps and protect patient privacy, a multi-stakeholder approach is necessary. The following recommendations can be considered:

– Implement Robust Authentication and Access Control Mechanisms: Employ strong authentication methods, such as multi-factor authentication, biometric authentication, and role-based access controls, to ensure that only authorized users can access patient data [24].
– Enhance Data Encryption and Secure Data Transmission: Implement end-to-end encryption for data at rest and in transit, using up-to-date encryption algorithms and secure communication protocols, such as HTTPS and TLS [25].
– Adhere to Secure Software Development Practices: Adopt secure coding practices, including regular security audits, vulnerability assessments, and the use of secure coding libraries and frameworks [26].
– Implement Comprehensive Logging and Monitoring: Establish robust logging and monitoring mechanisms to detect and respond to security incidents, ensuring the traceability and accountability of user actions [27].
– Strengthen Cloud Security: Properly configure cloud storage and cloud-based services used by self-monitoring patient apps, ensuring the implementation of appropriate security controls, access management, and data backup and recovery procedures [28].
– Establish Comprehensive Security Policies and Training: Develop and implement comprehensive security policies and provide regular training to app developers, healthcare providers, and end-users to raise awareness and promote a security-conscious culture [29].
– Engage in Regular Security Assessments and Penetration Testing: Conduct periodic security assessments and penetration testing to identify and address vulnerabilities in self-monitoring patient apps, ensuring continuous improvement in security posture [30].
– Advocate for Stricter Regulatory Standards and Enforcement: Collaborate with policymakers, regulatory bodies, and industry organizations to advocate for the development and enforcement of stricter security standards for self-monitoring patient apps, ensuring the protection of patient privacy and the integrity of health data [31].

– Implement Secure Third-Party Integration Practices: Carefully vet and monitor third-party integrations, implementing strict security controls and data access limitations for external services [32].
– Develop Incident Response and Data Breach Notification Protocols: Create and maintain comprehensive incident response plans, including clear procedures for notifying affected users and relevant authorities in the event of a data breach [33].

By implementing these recommendations, app developers, healthcare providers, and policymakers can work together to enhance the security of self-monitoring patient apps, safeguarding patient data and building trust in these essential healthcare technologies.

5 Emerging Technologies and Their Impact on App Security

The landscape of self-monitoring patient apps is continually evolving with the introduction of new technologies. This section explores how emerging technologies are shaping the security landscape of these apps.

5.1 Artificial Intelligence and Machine Learning

AI and ML are increasingly being used to enhance app security [30, 44]:

– Anomaly detection: Identifying unusual patterns in data access or user behavior.
– Predictive analysis: Forecasting potential security threats based on historical data.
– Automated patch management: Using AI to prioritize and apply security updates.

5.2 Blockchain Technology

Blockchain offers potential solutions for enhancing data integrity and traceability [4, 41, 49]:

– Immutable audit trails: Recording all data access and modifications.
– Decentralized data storage: Reducing the risk of centralized data breaches.
– Smart contracts: Automating and securing data sharing agreements.

5.3 Edge Computing

The shift towards edge computing presents new security challenges and opportunities [8, 39]:

– Reduced data transmission: Processing data locally to minimize exposure during transfer.
– Enhanced privacy: Keeping sensitive data closer to the source.
– Distributed security model: Implementing security measures across multiple edge devices.

5.4 5G Networks

The rollout of 5G networks will impact app security [35, 40]:

– Increased connectivity: More devices and data points to secure
– Network slicing: Potential for improved isolation of sensitive health data
– Enhanced monitoring capabilities: Real-time threat detection and response

5.5 Internet of Medical Things (IoMT)

The integration of IoMT devices with patient apps introduces new security considerations.

- Device authentication: Ensuring only authorized devices can connect and share data
- Data integrity: Maintaining the accuracy and consistency of data from multiple sources
- Scalable security: Implementing security measures that can adapt to a growing number of connected devices

These emerging technologies present both new security challenges and potential solutions for self-monitoring patient apps. Developers and healthcare providers must stay informed about these advancements to effectively integrate them into their security strategies.

6 The Role of User Education in App Security

While robust technical measures are crucial for app security, user education plays a vital role in maintaining the overall security of self-monitoring patient apps. This section explores the importance of user awareness and best practices for promoting security-conscious behavior among app users.

6.1 Importance of User Awareness

- First Line of Defense: Informed users can act as the first line of defense against many security threats, such as phishing attempts or social engineering attacks [34].
- Proper App Usage: Educating users on the correct use of app features and security settings can significantly reduce the risk of accidental data exposure [35].
- Incident Reporting: Users who are aware of potential security issues are more likely to report suspicious activities or potential breaches promptly [36].

6.2 Key Areas for User Education

- Password Hygiene: Teaching users the importance of strong, unique passwords and the benefits of using password managers [37].
- Data Sharing Practices: Educating users on the implications of sharing health data and how to control app permissions [38].
- Device Security: Instructing users on maintaining the security of their mobile devices, including regular updates and avoiding unsecured networks [39].
- Phishing Awareness: Training users to recognize and avoid phishing attempts targeting their health data [40].
- Privacy Settings: Guiding users through app privacy settings and explaining the implications of different options [41].

6.3 Strategies for Effective User Education

- In-App Tutorials: Implementing interactive tutorials within the app to guide users through security features and best practices [42].
- Regular Communication: Sending periodic security tips and updates to users via app notifications or email newsletters [43].
- Clear Privacy Policies: Providing easily understandable privacy policies and terms of service that highlight key security and privacy information [44].
- Community Forums: Creating user communities where individuals can share experiences and learn from each other about app security [45].
- Gamification: Incorporating gamification elements to incentivize users to learn about and implement security best practices [46].

By prioritizing user education alongside technical security measures, app developers and healthcare providers can create a more comprehensive and effective security ecosystem for self-monitoring patient apps.

7 Conclusion

The proliferation of self-monitoring patient apps has revolutionized the healthcare industry, empowering individuals to take a more active role in their own care. However, the security vulnerabilities inherent in these apps pose significant risks to patient privacy and the integrity of health data. By addressing the common security flaws, such as weak authentication mechanisms, inadequate data encryption, and unsecure data transmission protocols, app developers and healthcare providers can enhance the security of self-monitoring patient apps and build trust in these essential healthcare technologies [47].

Regulatory bodies and industry organizations must also play a crucial role in developing and enforcing comprehensive security standards to protect patient data. A multistakeholder approach, involving app developers, healthcare providers, and policymakers, is essential to mitigate security vulnerabilities and ensure the safe and responsible use of self-monitoring patient apps [48].

As the healthcare industry continues to embrace technological advancements, the security and privacy of patient data must remain a top priority. The integration of emerging technologies such as AI, blockchain, and edge computing offers new opportunities to enhance app security, but also introduces new challenges that must be carefully addressed. Furthermore, the role of user education in maintaining app security cannot be overstated, as informed and vigilant users form a crucial component of the overall security ecosystem.

By addressing the security vulnerabilities in self-monitoring patient apps through a combination of robust technical measures, regulatory compliance, emerging technologies, and user education, the healthcare community can unlock the full potential of these technologies. This comprehensive approach will empower patients and improve health outcomes while safeguarding the confidentiality and integrity of sensitive health data [49].

As we move forward, continuous research, collaboration, and innovation in the field of app security will be essential to stay ahead of evolving threats and ensure that self-monitoring patient apps remain a trusted and valuable tool in modern healthcare.

References

1. Huckvale, K., Prieto, J., Tilney, M., Benghozi, P., Car, J.: Unaddressed privacy risks in accredited health and wellness apps: a cross-sectional systematic assessment. BMC Med. **13**(1), 214 (2015)
2. Dehling, A., Gao, F., Schneider, S., Sunyaev, A.: Exploring the far side of mobile health: information security and privacy of mobile health apps on iOS and Android. JMIR Mhealth Uhealth **3**(1), e8 (2015)
3. Heurix, J., Zimmermann, P., Neubauer, T., Fenz, S.: A taxonomy for privacy enhancing technologies. Comput. Secur. **53**, 1–17 (2015)
4. Esposito, C., De Santis, A., Tortora, G., Chang, H., Choo, K.K.: Blockchain: a panacea for healthcare cloud-based data security and privacy? IEEE Cloud Comput. **5**(1), 31–37 (2018)
5. Dorri, A., Kanhere, S.S., Jurdak, R., Gauravaram, P.: Blockchain for IoT security and privacy: the case study of a smart home. In: 2017 IEEE International Conference on Pervasive Computing and Communications Workshops (PerCom Workshops), pp. 618–623 (2017)
6. Rushanan, M., Rubin, A.D., Kune, D.F., Swanson, C.M.: SoK: Security and privacy in implantable medical devices and body area networks. In: 2014 IEEE Symposium on Security and Privacy, pp. 524–539 (2014)
7. Camara, C., Peris-Lopez, P., Tapiador, J.E.: Security and privacy issues in implantable medical devices: a comprehensive survey. J. Biomed. Inform. **55**, 272–289 (2015)
8. Stergiou, C., Psannis, K.E., Kim, B.G., Gupta, B.: Secure integration of IoT and cloud computing. Futur. Gener. Comput. Syst. **78**, 964–975 (2018)
9. Gentry, A., Anderson, J.P., Houlding, P.F.: Logging and monitoring requirements for healthcare IT security and compliance. In: 2011 1st IEEE Workshop on Enabling Technologies for Smartphone and Internet of Things (ETSIoT), pp. 39–44 (2011)
10. Grundy, Q., Chiu, K., Held, F., Continella, A., Bero, L., Holz, R.: Data sharing practices of medicines related apps and the mobile ecosystem: traffic, content, and network analysis. BMJ **364**, 1920 (2019)
11. Shostack, A.: Threat modeling: designing for security. Wiley (2014)
12. Health Insurance Portability and Accountability Act of 1996 (HIPAA), Pub. L. No. 104-191, 110 Stat. 1936 (1996)
13. Regulation (EU) 2016/679 of the European Parliament and of the Council of 27 April 2016 on the protection of natural persons with regard to the processing of personal data and on the free movement of such data (General Data Protection Regulation) (2016)
14. Personal Information Protection and Electronic Documents Act (PIPEDA), S.C. 2000, c. 5 (2000)
15. Wachter, S.: Normative challenges of identification in the Internet of Things: privacy, profiling, discrimination, and the GDPR. Comput. Law Secur. Rev. **34**(3), 436–449 (2018)
16. NIST Special Publication 800-66 Revision 1, An Introductory Resource Guide for Implementing the Health Insurance Portability and Accountability Act (HIPAA) Security Rule (2008)
17. ISO/IEC 27001:2013. Information technology – Security techniques – Information security management systems – Requirements (2013)
18. Torous, J., Nicholas, J., Larsen, M.E., Firth, J., Christensen, H.: Clinical review of user engagement with mental health smartphone apps: evidence, theory and improvements. Evid. Based Ment. Health **21**(3), 116–119 (2018)

19. Parker, L., Karliychuk, T., Gillies, D., Mintzes, B., Raven, M., Grundy, Q.: A health app developer's guide to law and policy: a multi-sector policy analysis. BMC Med. Inform. Decis. Mak. **17**(1), 141 (2017)
20. Howard, M., Lipner, S.: The security development lifecycle. Microsoft Press, Redmond, WA (2006)
21. Vatsalan, D., Sehili, Z., Christen, P., Rahm, E.: Privacy-preserving record linkage for big data: current approaches and research challenges," in Handbook of Big Data Technologies, pp. 851–895 (2017)
22. Patsakis, C., Bouroche, M., Aguiar, A.: Towards a holistic privacy and security solution for mHealth. In: IEEE 16th International Conference on e-Health Networking, Applications and Services, pp. 226–230 (2014)
23. Rindfleisch, P.: Privacy, information technology, and health care. Commun. ACM **40**(8), 92–100 (1997)
24. Berdichevsky, D., Neuenschwander, E.: Toward an ethics of persuasive technology. Commun. ACM **42**(5), 51–58 (1999)
25. Breitinger, M., Froehlich, J., Windisch, A.: Security and privacy of cloud-based health data. In: IEEE 16th International Conference on e-Health Networking, Applications and Services, pp. 221–225 (2014)
26. Mitnick, K., Simon, W.: The art of deception: controlling the human element of security. Wiley, Indianapolis, IN (2002)
27. McGraw, G.: Software security: building security in. Addison-Wesley, Upper Saddle River, NJ (2006)
28. Sweeney, L.: Simple demographics often identify people uniquely. Health (San Francisco) **671**, 1–34 (2000)
29. Spiekermann, S., Cranor, L.F.: Engineering privacy. IEEE Trans. Software Eng. **35**(1), 67–82 (2009)
30. Manyika, J., et al.: Big data: the next frontier for innovation, competition, and productivity. McKinsey Global Institute (2011)
31. Zhou, L., Bao, J., Parmanto, B.: Systematic review protocol to assess the effectiveness of usability questionnaires in mHealth app studies. JMIR Res. Protocols **6**(8), e151 (2017)
32. Wang, L., Yang, Y., Ren, J.: Building security framework in healthcare mobile apps. Procedia Comput. Sci. **37**, 321–328 (2014)
33. Singh, A., Chatterjee, K.: Cloud security issues and challenges: a survey. J. Netw. Comput. Appl. **79**, 88–115 (2017)
34. Zhang, R., Liu, L.: Security models and requirements for healthcare application clouds. In: IEEE 3rd International Conference on Cloud Computing, pp. 268–275 (2010)
35. Kumar, P., Lee, H.J.: Security issues in healthcare applications using wireless medical sensor networks: a survey. Sensors **12**(1), 55–91 (2012)
36. Dhillon, G., Backhouse, J.: Current directions in IS security research: towards socio-organizational perspectives. Inf. Syst. J. **11**(2), 127–153 (2001)
37. Coventry, L., Branley, D.: Cybersecurity in healthcare: a narrative review of trends, threats and ways forward. Maturitas **113**, 48–52 (2018)
38. Pussewalage, H.S.G., Oleshchuk, V.A.: Privacy preserving mechanisms for enforcing security and privacy requirements in E-health solutions. Int. J. Inf. Manage. **36**, 1161–1173 (2016)
39. Sun, W., Cai, Z., Li, Y., Liu, F., Fang, S., Wang, G.: Security and privacy in the medical Internet of Things. Secur. Commun. Networks **2018**, 1–9 (2018)
40. He, D., Zeadally, S., Wu, L.: Certificateless public auditing scheme for cloud-assisted wireless body area networks. IEEE Syst. J. **12**(1), 64–73 (2018)
41. Azaria, A., Ekblaw, A., Vieira, T., Lippman, A.: MedRec: using blockchain for medical data access and permission management. In: International Conference on Open and Big Data, pp. 25–30 (2016)

42. Fernández-Alemán, J.L., Señor, I.C., Lozoya, P.Á.O., Toval, A.: Security and privacy in electronic health records: a systematic literature review. J. Biomed. Inform. **46**(3), 541–562 (2013)

43. Li, M., Yu, S., Zheng, Y., Ren, K., Lou, W.: Scalable and secure sharing of personal health records in cloud computing using attribute-based encryption. IEEE Trans. Parallel Distrib. Syst. **24**(1), 131–143 (2013)

44. Zhang, Y., Qiu, M., Tsai, C.W., Hassan, M.M., Alamri, A.: Health-CPS: healthcare cyber-physical system assisted by cloud and big data. IEEE Syst. J. **11**(1), 88–95 (2017)

45. Sahi, M.A., et al.: Privacy preservation in e-healthcare environments: state of the art and future directions. IEEE Access **6**, 464–478 (2018)

46. Kotz, D., Gunter, C.A., Kumar, S., Weiner, J.P.: Privacy and security in mobile health: a research agenda. Computer **49**(6), 22–30 (2016)

47. Yang, Y., Liu, X., Zheng, Y., Ai, C., Cai, Z.: A novel privacy-preserving framework for healthcare data sharing. IEEE Access **7**, 7299–7311 (2019)

48. Abouelmehdi, K., Beni-Hssane, A., Khaloufi, H., Saadi, M.: Big healthcare data: preserving security and privacy. J. Big Data **5**(1), 1–18 (2018)

49. Chen, Y., Ding, S., Xu, Z., Zheng, H., Yang, S.: Blockchain-based medical records secure storage and medical service framework. J. Med. Syst. **43**(1), 1–9 (2019)

Leveraging Artificial Intelligence Integration in Regional Sports Education to Foster Equitable and Sustainable Development

Shuyi Li[1]([⊠]) [ID] and Zhongxin Zhang[2]

[1] College of Sports, Dalian Maritime University, Dalian, China
`lishuyi@dlmu.edu.cn`
[2] Department of Basics, Naval Dalian Naval College, Dalian, China

Abstract. Objective: Regional disparities in sports education have become a critical issue in the education sector. Variances in sports education resources, educational levels, and participation exist among different regions, leading to disparities in students' physical fitness, health conditions, and developmental opportunities.

Method: This paper aims to demonstrate the feasibility of using artificial intelligence to improve equity in regional sports education through literature review, expert interviews, and data analysis.

Conclusion: The causes of this phenomenon primarily involve various factors such as differences in economic development levels, urban-rural disparities, regional differences, and ethnic disparities. Measures to address this issue include raising public awareness and demand for artificial intelligence technology, developing suitable solutions, enhancing teacher training, and establishing demonstration points and cooperative schools. The application of artificial intelligence technology in regional sports education involves balancing benefits and risks, including risks related to data privacy and security, technological reliability and effectiveness, education and teaching quality, regional and cultural differences, as well as legal and ethical risks.

Recommendations: It is recommended to strengthen data privacy protection, improve technological reliability, emphasize teacher guidance and supervision, and establish clear legal and ethical guidelines when promoting the application of artificial intelligence technology in regional sports education. Additionally, diversification in development pathways should be established, encouraging participation and support from various sectors of society to collectively promote the reasonable application and development of artificial intelligence technology.

Keywords: Regional Disparities · Artificial Intelligence · Equity · Sports Education

1 Introduction

Education inequality has been one of the significant challenges globally (UNESCO 2020). This inequality stems from various factors, including unequal educational opportunities, differences in dropout rates, and variations in student academic performance,

X. Feng et al. (Eds.): CloudComp 2024, LNICST 617, pp. 211–220, 2026.
https://doi.org/10.1007/978-3-031-92517-7_16

each having diverse influences and potential consequences. This education inequality is closely related to the development levels of various countries or regions (Reimers et al. 2020). Necessitating effective interventions tailored to the characteristics and needs of different regions.

In China, the uneven distribution of educational resources has long been a key challenge in educational development (Hong et al. 2018). This imbalance is primarily manifested in the unequal allocation of educational resources between different regions, including disparities in educational resources within the same province, between different cities and counties, and even between urban and rural areas (Vittorio Daniele 2020). This regional imbalance has resulted in the waste and concentration of educational resources, making it difficult for students in impoverished areas to access quality educational resources. In the field of physical education, this issue similarly presents significant disparities involving educational resources, educational levels, and student participation. Recent studies indicate that although the physical fitness level of Chinese students has improved, issues such as visual problems and obesity rates continue to rise (Li, Chen, & Sun 2022). At the same time, China's physical education faces the problem of imbalanced teaching staff and facilities, particularly among different geographical regions (Li, Li, & Chu 2023). This inequality leads to a growing gap among students in terms of physical fitness, health status, and development opportunities, which is detrimental to the comprehensive development of young people.

To address the issue of regional inequality in sports education, it is necessary to explore new teaching models that adapt to the geographical environments and needs of different regions. The release of the "Outline of the National Medium- and Long-Term Education Reform and Development Plan (2010–2020)" by the State Council in 2010 marked a shift in China's educational reform policy from "priority development focused on efficiency" to "balanced development oriented towards fairness". Promoting the high-quality and balanced development of education has long been a key focus of the Chinese government and an area of concern for educational researchers. In recent years, with the rapid development of artificial intelligence technology, its role in various fields, including social development and industrial manufacturing innovation, has become increasingly prominent. Therefore, exploring the role of artificial intelligence in promoting balanced development in sports education and how it can support this development is of significant importance and merits further in-depth consideration and research.

2 Opportunities Brought by Artificial Intelligence to Physical Education

According to the indicators of education equity in China, current research emphasizes career resource allocation indicators and educational scale indicators, but this one-dimensional perspective cannot comprehensively reflect all elements of educational equity (Zhou et al. 2023). From the perspective of Swedish scholar Torsten Husén (1987), education equity is divided into "equitable starting points," "equitable processes," and "equitable outcomes," emphasizing the importance of equal distribution of rights for individuals in their academic careers and fair treatment in the learning process. Recent research on the practical application of artificial intelligence in other disciplinary fields

(Williams et al. 2022; Smith et al.2022; Adams et al. 2022) has pointed out that the progress of computer-assisted learning provides new evidence for addressing the high cost of personalized tutoring for students. AI-driven computer-based tutoring not only improves students' learning efficiency but also maintains the scale of learning gains (Baker et al. 2020). These research findings highlight the promotion of educational equity and personalized education through the application of artificial intelligence in education.

Recent research has conducted in-depth analysis of the application of artificial intelligence in education from the perspective of the "technology-society-education" ecosystem (Lu Yu et al. 2023), highlighting the effective release of learners' individual potential through the application of artificial intelligence technology in education, thereby promoting educational equity. The research also emphasizes that AI has changed the way knowledge is produced and disseminated (Lee 2023), breaking down regional barriers to resources and achieving the boundaryless nature of learning resources and the personalized customization of learning modes. This application trend has prompted the transformation of education to digitalization, fostering more versatile and innovative talents tailored to future demands.

Furthermore, research analyzing the application of artificial intelligence in the field of education (Kohnke et al. 2023) indicates that the emergence of AI has shifted the education model from distribution to generation and from singularity to diversity. AI is seen as an accessible "super teacher" capable of interactive dialogue with learners, promoting personalized teaching according to individual abilities (Khan; Moore, et al. 2023). At the same time, the application of artificial intelligence can enhance the quality of teaching outcomes, strategies, and methods, enhance the interactivity of human-computer cooperation, and improve the generative and personalized nature of teaching feedback and evaluation.

In the field of physical education, the application of artificial intelligence may also bring opportunities for educational equity. With the support of AI technology, personalized allocation of physical education resources can be achieved to bridge the resource gap between different regions. Moreover, AI can also help improve the effectiveness and quality of physical education, promoting balanced development in students' physical fitness and skills. By accurately analyzing the characteristics and needs of individual students, artificial intelligence can provide teachers with targeted teaching strategies and methods, thereby promoting the personalized development of physical education and achieving the goal of educational equity.

3   Method

In this study, we will employ an in-depth interview approach to comprehensively collect and analyze relevant data and information. The in-depth interview phase will involve the participation of experts and educators in the field of physical education to gain insights into their attitudes and perspectives on the application of artificial intelligence technology, as well as their understanding and recommendations regarding equitable regional sports education (see Fig. 1).

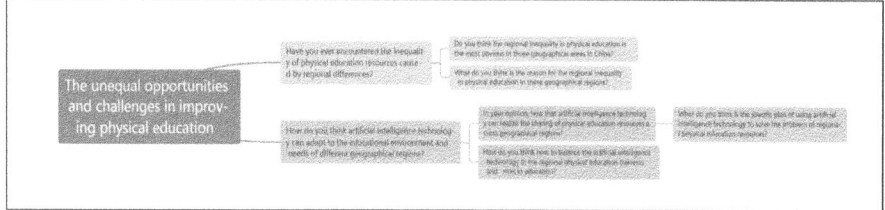

Fig. 1. Framework for Expert Interviews

Upon the completion of data collection and interview results, we will utilize Nvivo software to integrate the interview data with existing literature to conduct result comparisons and analyses, thereby deepening the breadth and depth of the research (see Fig. 2). We will perform data cleaning and processing, including data screening, filling in missing values, and handling outliers, to ensure data quality and reliability. In the initial investigation phase, we will combine questionnaire surveys and literature research to identify relevant issues concerning the application of artificial intelligence in the field of physical education, evaluating their importance, adaptability, and feasibility. Subsequently, we will formulate an expert consultation form and invite specialists from the fields of physical education, sociology of sports, and sports pedagogy to evaluate the listed relevant issues. To ensure the objectivity of the evaluations, expert opinions will be anonymously published, and horizontal communication between experts will be avoided to prevent the occurrence of convergence of opinions.

Fig. 2. Keyword Cloud from Expert Interviews

Ultimately, we will present a comprehensive analysis with constructive suggestions and recommendations based on the research questions. Through the integrated application of these methods, we expect to obtain more scientific, objective, and effective research results, providing valuable guidance and recommendations for the application of artificial intelligence in the field of physical education.

4   Research Findings

The expert interviews provide a multidimensional perspective and bring knowledge and experience from different fields of sports education reform, making this study possible.

4.1   Phenomenon and Causes of Regional Inequality in Sports Education

According to the results of in-depth interview research, the regional inequality in sports education has complex roots involving multiple factors. Disparities in economic development levels constitute a significant contributing factor. In relatively affluent regions, more funds are allocated for the construction of sports education resources and the training of teaching staff, aimed at providing comprehensive and high-quality sports education. In contrast, economically disadvantaged regions often face financial constraints and resource scarcity, making it challenging to offer sufficient sports education resources, thereby restricting students' access to sports training and development opportunities.

Disparities between urban and rural areas also play a crucial role in perpetuating regional inequalities in sports education. Urban areas typically boast more sports facilities and advanced sports infrastructure, providing students with diverse sports activities and training opportunities. In contrast, rural areas, due to inadequate infrastructure, often struggle to offer adequate sports fields and facilities, limiting students' access to sports activities and exercise opportunities. Furthermore, differences between eastern and western regions significantly impact the unequal distribution of sports education resources. The relatively higher levels of economic development and abundant educational resources in the eastern regions enable the provision of more sports education programs and high-quality teaching resources. Conversely, the lower economic levels and limited educational resources in the western regions restrict students' exposure to comprehensive sports education content and quality, impeding the holistic development of their sports proficiency. Additionally, disparities between ethnic regions also constitute a significant cause of regional inequality in sports education. Different ethnic regions exhibit cultural variances and diverse traditional practices, directly affecting the degree of emphasis and investment in sports education. Some ethnic minority regions, influenced by traditional practices, display a lower level of emphasis on sports education, leading to a scarcity of educational resources and inadequate sports education quality.

4.2   Customized Physical Education in Regional Disparities: Prospects of Artificial Intelligence Application

When discussing the applicability of artificial intelligence in the physical education environments and demands of different regions, AI demonstrates its flexibility by providing customized educational experiences for students in various areas through intelligent teaching methods and resource allocation. Data analysis and personalized guidance enable AI to tailor corresponding teaching programs and resource distribution to meet the learning needs of students in different regions more effectively. Moreover, artificial intelligence plays a significant role in teaching assistance, helping teachers and students adjust teaching content and learning progress in real time through intelligent physical education support systems and real-time monitoring tools, thus enhancing teaching efficiency and learning outcomes. At the same time, AI technology provides crucial data support and decision-making references for educators. Through in-depth analysis of students' learning processes and performance, educators can better understand students' learning characteristics and needs, thereby developing more accurate teaching plans and strategies. This personalized teaching approach can better stimulate students' learning interests and potential, promoting their comprehensive development. These aspects collectively reveal the positive role of artificial intelligence in regional physical education while also showcasing its potential in meeting the educational needs of different regions.

However, to achieve effective application of artificial intelligence in physical education across different regions, several key issues still need to be addressed. Firstly, it is essential to ensure the universality and adaptability of AI technology to meet the educational needs of various regions. Secondly, there is a need to strengthen teacher training and guidance on AI technology, enabling educators to better utilize AI technology for teaching and assistance. Additionally, attention should be paid to data privacy and security protection, with the establishment of relevant laws and guidelines to ensure the personal privacy and data security of students. Simultaneously, there should be enhanced supervision and management of AI technology to ensure the effectiveness and rationality of educational teaching. Through these measures, further promotion of the application of artificial intelligence in regional physical education can be achieved, thereby realizing the goals of educational equity and effective teaching.

4.3 Potential Risks of Artificial Intelligence Application in Regional Physical Education

Risks in the Utilization of Artificial Intelligence Application should not be overlooked when discussing the balance between the benefits and risks of AI technology, as it is an extremely critical issue. These risks include:

- Data Privacy and Security Risks: In physical education, artificial intelligence requires the collection and analysis of a large amount of student and teacher data, including sensitive information such as personal identity, exercise data, and health data. Without adequate protection measures, this data may be misused, leaked, or sold, causing adverse effects on individuals.
- Technical Reliability and Effectiveness Risks: Artificial intelligence technology requires a high level of accuracy and reliability. If there are malfunctions or errors in the technology, it may affect the normal conduct of physical education and the learning outcomes of students. In addition, if the effectiveness of AI technology is insufficient, it may have a negative impact on students' learning experiences and satisfaction.
- Risks to Education and Teaching Quality: Although AI technology can provide personalized teaching plans and learning experiences, the lack of sufficient teacher guidance and supervision may affect students' learning outcomes and performance. At the same time, excessive reliance on AI technology at the expense of traditional teaching methods and the role of teachers may affect the overall quality of education and teaching.

- Risks of Regional and Cultural Differences: The demands and characteristics of physical education in different regions and cultural backgrounds may differ. If the application of AI technology does not consider these differences, it may lead to a mismatch and even encounter resistance and opposition.
- Legal and Ethical Risks: In the process of applying artificial intelligence technology, the lack of clear legal provisions and ethical guidelines may lead to legal disputes and ethical issues, such as the infringement of the rights of learners and unfair treatment.

5 Suggestions and Strategy

5.1 Fostering Inclusive Regional Sports Education Initiatives

This necessity calls for the implementation of targeted interventions that are attuned to the unique characteristics and requirements of diverse regions. These interventions should encompass a multifaceted approach, incorporating comprehensive assessments of the specific challenges and opportunities present within each locality. A crucial aspect involves the development of region-specific educational policies that address the distinct socio-economic and cultural contexts. Furthermore, fostering collaborative partnerships among various stakeholders, including local communities, educational institutions, and governmental bodies, can facilitate the effective design and implementation of region-specific educational programs. Emphasizing the importance of context-sensitive strategies, such as the integration of culturally relevant teaching materials and the promotion of community engagement initiatives, is paramount for achieving sustainable and equitable educational development across regions. By recognizing the intricate interplay between regional disparities and the diverse educational landscapes, it becomes essential to formulate tailored interventions that foster inclusivity, encourage diversity, and promote equal access to quality education for all students.

5.2 Adaptability of Artificial Intelligence Technology and Equitable Resource Allocation Approach in Regional Sports Education

When discussing how to utilize artificial intelligence technology to promote equitable development in regional sports education, we have formulated the following comprehensive approaches:

- Raise awareness and demand: Increase public awareness and demand for artificial intelligence technology through education and promotion, enabling more people to understand its advantages and application prospects and generating the willingness and motivation to use it.
- Develop tailored solutions: Tailor artificial intelligence technology solutions to the characteristics and needs of regional sports education, including personalized teaching assistance systems, sports training management systems, and health monitoring and analysis tools, to meet the needs of different regions and schools. Strengthen teacher training: Enhance teachers' information literacy and technical abilities through training, enabling them to understand and use artificial intelligence technology more effectively in sports education.

- Establish demonstration sites and collaborative schools: Select some schools as demonstration sites and collaborate on projects to allow these schools to experiment with the use of artificial intelligence technology in sports teaching. Summarize experiences and lessons learned to provide references and guidance for other schools.
- Promote cross-regional cooperation and resource sharing: Facilitate balanced distribution and optimal allocation of regional sports education resources through cross-regional cooperation and resource sharing, promoting communication and collaboration among different regions to advance the application and development of artificial intelligence technology. Implement preferential policies: The government can introduce relevant preferential policies, such as financial support and tax incentives, to encourage enterprises and individuals to invest in the development and promotion of artificial intelligence technology in regional sports education.
- Establish a collaborative mechanism: Governments, businesses, schools, and social organizations can establish a collaborative mechanism to collectively promote the application of artificial intelligence technology in equitable regional sports education. They can provide comprehensive support and guarantees for its implementation.
- Establish a collaborative platform: Governments, businesses, schools, and social organizations can jointly establish a collaborative platform responsible for coordinating and promoting the application of artificial intelligence technology in equitable regional sports education. The platform can take various forms, such as official websites, WeChat public accounts, and apps, to facilitate communication and collaboration among all parties.
- Resource sharing and collaborative research and development: The platform can organize resource sharing and collaborative research and development among various stakeholders, pooling human, material, and financial resources to develop artificial intelligence technology solutions that are suitable for the characteristics of regional sports education.

Moreover, an open innovation approach can be adopted to attract more social forces to participate, enhancing the practicality and targeting of the technology solutions.

5.3 Addressing the Potential Risks of Artificial Intelligence Application in Regional Physical Education: Strategies and Solutions

The application of artificial intelligence (AI) technology in regional physical education does indeed bring about numerous potential risks, including data privacy and security risks, technological reliability and efficacy risks, risks associated with education and teaching quality, regional and cultural diversity risks, as well as legal and ethical risks. To address these issues, the following solutions can be considered:

- Data privacy and security risks: Strengthen data protection measures, including the establishment of strict data security management mechanisms, encryption and anonymization of sensitive information, and comprehensive data usage and sharing regulations.
- Technological reliability and efficacy risks: Establish strict technical detection and monitoring mechanisms, including ongoing technical evaluations and updates, fault

warning systems, and fault handling plans, to ensure the stability and reliability of AI technology.

- Risks associated with education and teaching quality: Strengthen teacher training and guidance, promote collaboration between teachers and AI technology, ensure that AI technology complements traditional teaching methods, and enhance education quality and student learning outcomes.
- Regional and cultural diversity risks: Develop diversified technological application solutions, considering the differences in various regions and cultural backgrounds, encourage localized and personalized AI applications to better meet the specific needs of different regions.
- Legal and ethical risks: Establish clear legal regulations and ethical guidelines, formulate strict regulations for the application of AI technology, safeguard the legal rights and privacy security of learners, and uphold educational fairness and social justice.

Adopting the aforementioned measures comprehensively can help mitigate the potential risks that AI technology may bring to regional physical education, promoting its safer, more stable, and sustainable application.

6 Conclusion

Although artificial intelligence holds immense potential in the field of physical education, offering innovative teaching tools and strategies to enhance learning outcomes, balancing educational equity and improving regional physical education efficiency remains a core issue. Future research should focus on evaluating physical education outcomes and integrating artificial intelligence with other teaching methods. The study found disparities in educational resources across different regions, leading to the gradual widening of gaps in students' physical fitness and developmental opportunities. While the application of artificial intelligence technology provides new avenues for resolution, risks related to data privacy and security, technological reliability and effectiveness, educational quality, regional cultural differences, as well as legal and ethical considerations, still demand attention. To address these risks, it is essential to establish stringent data protection mechanisms, strengthen monitoring and standard-setting, emphasize the role of teachers and local cultural characteristics, and promote educational equity and social harmony. These measures will contribute to promoting balanced development in regional physical education and fostering a constructive interaction between educational equity and social progress.

Statements and Declarations
The authors have no relevant financial or non-financial interests to disclose.

The authors have no competing interests to declare that are relevant to the content of this article.

All authors certify that they have no affiliations with or involvement in any organization or entity with any financial interest or non-financial interest in the subject matter or materials discussed in this manuscript.

The authors have no financial or proprietary interests in any material discussed in this article.

References

UNESCO. Global Monitoring Report on Education: Inclusion and Education for All*, p. 8. Paris (2020)

Reimers, F., Schleicher, A.: Schooling disrupted, schooling rethought: how the COVID-19 pandemic is changing education. OECD Publishing, Paris (2020)

Hong, C., Niu, X.: Research on the financial matching policy of social endowment of colleges and universities under the perspective of western higher education revitalization. Chongqing High. Educ. Res. **6**(04), 28–38 (2018)

Daniele, V.: Regional educational inequality and its impact on socioeconomic development: a case study of China. Educ. Res. Rev. **10**(2), 123–135 (2020)

Li, Y.-P., Chen, S.-Y., Sun, Q.-Z.: Research on the path of college students' physical fitness and health improvement under the perspective of healthy China. Sports Vision **2022**(11), 8–10 (2022)

Li, C., Li, Z., Chu, H.: Policy evolution and practice breakthrough of quality and balanced development of county compulsory education in the context of education power. Mod. Educ. Manage. **2023**(09), 10–21 (2023)

State Council. Outline of the National Medium- and Long-Term Education Reform and Development Plan (2010–2020). People's Daily, pp. 06–15 (2010)

Zhou, H., Li, Y.: ChatGPT's impact on education ecosystem and coping strategies. J. Xinjiang Normal Univ. (Philosophy Soc. Sci. Edn. **4**(1), 1–12 (2023)

Husén, T.: J. East China Normal Univ. (Educ. Sci.) **5**(3), 1–10 (1987)

Williams, R.K., Brown, M.T.: Closing the achievement gap: effective strategies for improving academic outcomes among disadvantaged youth. J. Educ. Res. **45**(3), 231–248 (2022)

Smith, A.B., Jones, C.D.: Implementing personalized learning strategies in algebra I classrooms. Educ. Assess **25**(2), 175–192 (2022)

Heller, S.B., Shah, A.K., Guryan, J., Ludwig, J., Mullainathan, S., Pollack, H.A.: Thinking, fast and slow? Some field experiments to reduce crime and dropout in Chicago. Q. J. Econ. **132**(1), 1–54 (2017)

Baker, R.S., Heffernan, N.T., Roll, I., Corbett, A., Koedinger, K.R.: Developing a generalizable detector of when students game the system. User Model User-Adap Inter. **30**(3), 243–289 (2020)

Lu, Y., Yu, J., Chen, P.: The educational application and outlook of generative AI: a case study with ChatGPT system. Chin. Distance Educ. (4), 1–11 (2023)

Lee, H.: The rise of ChatGPT: exploring its potential in medical education. Anatom. Sci. Educ. **14**(3), 1–6 (2023)

kohnke, l., et al.: chatgpt for language teaching and learning. RECL J. J. Lang. Teach. Res. **1**(1), 1–11 (2023)

Choi, J.-H., et al.: ChatGPT goes to law school. J. Legal Educ. (Forthcoming) **6**(1), 1–10 (2023)

Moore, S., et al.: Assessing the quality of student-generated short answer questions using GPT-3. In: European Conference on Technology Enhanced Learning, pp. 243–257 (2022)

Author Index

X. Feng et al. (Eds.): CloudComp 2024, LNICST 617, pp. 221–222, 2026.
https://doi.org/10.1007/978-3-031-92517-7

The manufacturer's authorised representative in the EU is Springer
Nature Customer Service Centre GmbH, Europaplatz 3, 69115 Heidelberg,
Germany. If you have any concerns regarding our products, please
contact ProductSafety@springernature.com

Printed and bound by CPI Group (UK) Ltd, Croydon, CR0 4YY
28/04/2026
02098521-0002